John Forster once wrote of Alexand(r)
that he "was a social man, had many
[and] was welcome everywhere for the
of his quiet talk, so full of varied k(n)
made doubly delightful by old-world
and courtesy." An obituary published
notes that "his intimate acquaintance with . . .
most of our living men of letters, must have
made him the depository of much of the literary
history of the present age."

The claims of the eminent biographer and the
admiring author of the eulogy were not excessive.
Dyce was extraordinarily gregarious, and it can
be said that he crossed paths with nearly everyone of consequence in England during the first
half of the nineteenth century. Any list of his
friends and acquaintances that consisted of only
the most famous among them would include
Wordsworth, Southey, Campbell, Leigh Hunt,
and the luminaries of the Rogers Circle, along
with many others.

Dyce wrote about all of them in his reminiscences, at which he was apparently still working
when he died in May of 1869, and which are
published here for the first time. He wrote, too,
of the great of the theater, which was the passion
of his life. He was the first modern editor of the
drama of George Peele, Robert Greene, Thomas
Middleton, and John Webster, and the first to
edit competently Christopher Marlowe and the
plays of Beaumont and Fletcher. His edition of
Shakespeare was one of the nineteenth century's
best, and he missed few of the major theatrical
events of his time.

His records of plays and performances, actors
and writers, scholars and critics, are all marked
by scrupulous attention to significant and telling
detail. Though he sometimes reports anecdotes
that have become familiar from other sources,
he focuses on his personal reactions to the persons he met, the spectacles he viewed, and the
parties he attended, thereby bringing to history
the immediacy of personal encounter.

Dyce's reminiscences are, then, a rich mine
of important information on his times and those
who lived them. They are, in addition — and no
less importantly — a thoroughly entertaining account of a fascinating age, rendered by a man of
humane wit, rare insight, and remarkable taste
and sensitivity.

Richard J. Schrader is assistant professor of
English at Princeton University.

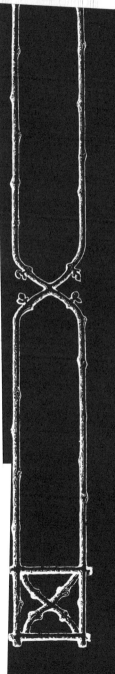

THE REMINISCENCES
OF ALEXANDER DYCE

ALEXANDER DYCE

THE
Reminiscences
OF
Alexander Dyce

EDITED, WITH A BIOGRAPHY

BY RICHARD J. SCHRADER

OHIO STATE UNIVERSITY PRESS

PR
29
.D9A3
1972

Library of Congress Catalog Card Number 75-157716
Standard Book Number 8142-0160-1
Manufactured in the United States of America

FOR MY PARENTS

CONTENTS

Illustrations

FRONTISPIECE: Portrait of Alexander Dyce from an
engraving by C. H. Jeens.

FACING PAGE 18: Folio 213ʳ in the Dyce manuscript.

FOREWORD

The Reverend Alexander Dyce's "Reminiscences" are contained in a generally unrevised manuscript in the Victoria and Albert Museum, South Kensington (pressmark D.26.E.9) ; they are here edited by permission of the Museum. Internal evidence suggests that Dyce wrote most of the essays between 1867 and his death in May 1869. A more specific description of the manuscript may be found in the section "Editorial Principles."

The "Reminiscences" (so styled on the covering leaf, not in Dyce's hand) were presented to the Museum in 1905 by Warwick Elwin, who found them among the papers of his father, the Reverend Whitwell Elwin, editor of the *Quarterly Review*. The manuscript probably came into the senior Elwin's possession through John Forster, who was one of Dyce's executors and who used a very small portion of the memoirs for a biographical "Sketch" of Dyce in 1875. From then until this book was in the last stages of preparation, no one seems to have taken advantage of the manuscript. Recently, however, Professor S. Schoenbaum has made reference to it in *Shakespeare's Lives* (Oxford, 1970) and has published some of its more striking passages in the *TLS*, 22 January 1971, pp. 101–2.

Regrettably, Dyce forebore discussing those of his contemporaries

still living in 1869. But these jottings of an eminent scholar nevertheless provide a close view of some of the most interesting literary and
theatrical figures in his lifetime. Occasionally he is content to rehearse
biographical data well known even then, but most often he focuses
upon his personal encounters with his subjects. Some anecdotes have
become known through other sources, but comparison will frequently
show that Dyce offers something original nonetheless, and his reputation for veracity and accuracy lends credence to many an otherwise
dubious tale. When he speaks from firsthand information, the result can
be remarkable, as in his description of Thomas Taylor's later years.
His broad survey of the stage reveals an expertise arising from considerable love for a field that also provided the chief occupation of his
scholarly life. The record of his fellow scholars is extremely entertaining, chiefly because so many of his subjects stand just this side of
lunacy. The last chapter deals primarily with literary artists and contains new material on authors ranging from Wordsworth to Mrs.
Barbauld.

Dyce has not been altogether forgotten in the last one hundred years.
Scholars still value many of his editions, and they have mined both his
Table-Talk of Samuel Rogers (especially for Taylor and Wordsworth)
and the manuscript notes scattered throughout his library, which remains intact at the Victoria and Albert. But no one has written an
adequate biography of him. I have had to settle for a patchwork account, drawn mostly from the printed records of his contemporaries.
The research for this biography involved as much hard labor as bibliographical ingenuity, for Dyce seems to have known everyone; and
though most of his acquaintances mention him, they seldom do so at
length. My labor has had the instructive result of showing the kinds
of sources one must consult in order to piece together the activities of
important ancillary figures like Dyce. But if he is ever to be included in
a comprehensive study of Victorian scholars, his many unprinted letters—to Egerton Brydges and William Carew Hazlitt, for instance—
and the possible allusions in the unpublished writings of Carlyle and
Crabb Robinson, all must be located and considered. The Museum has
eight volumes of Dyce's scrapbooks, which contain, in addition to
clippings and other scholarly memorabilia, numerous letters from his

legion of acquaintances. Most of the letters seem related to questions of editing and to other literary matters, and they would be useful chiefly to someone investigating in detail his scholarly life. Such was not my intention; as a result, I have let pass, among other things, the interesting problems connected with John Payne Collier and the Shakespeare forgeries. (On this subject one should consult the wealth of new material in Professor Schoenbaum's *Shakespeare's Lives.*) My biography, though the fullest to date, is not the last word.

I am very happy to acknowledge my great debt to the two men who have watched over this project from the beginning. The advice and example of Professor Richard D. Altick have not only sustained my work but have prevented the lapses that result from warbling one's footnotes wild. However, the flaws that remain must be set down solely to my own deficiencies. I am grateful to Mr. John P. Harthan, Keeper of the Library of the Victoria and Albert Museum, for calling my attention to the manuscript's existence, for securing the xerographic copy on which this edition is based, for numerous points of information, and for patience. The cooperation of the Library's staff, and notably of Mr. A. P. Burton, the Assistant Keeper, was splendid.

I have also to thank my colleagues, Professors Dudley Johnson, Alan Downer (now deceased), and Joseph Donohue, for reading and commenting on various sections of the book; the Ohio State University Libraries for permission to quote from Dyce's letter to Collier; my editor, Mr. Robert S. Demorest, for his care with the typescript; and Mr. D. R. MacDonald for criticism better than he knew.

R. J. S.

Princeton, N.J.
March 1971

THE REMINISCENCES
OF ALEXANDER DYCE

ALEXANDER ✦ DYCE

A RE WE TO HAVE no fuller biography of my old friend Dyce than the sketch which Mr. John Forster prefixed to the catalogue of his library, now in the South Kensington Museum?" So queried James Crossley in 1877,[1] two years after the sketch had appeared and eight years after his friend's death.[2] Crossley found that biographies by Forster, then recently deceased, failed in general to tell "the whole truth" about their subjects.[3] The charge was seconded shortly thereafter by another of Alexander Dyce's friends, John Bulloch.[4] Indeed, Forster has not given a full portrait in what remains the only substantial biography of Dyce. Even though he drew largely from the manuscript edited below, he makes several factual errors and is especially deficient in recounting Dyce's numerous friendships. The biography points up Dyce's great achievements in scholarship and serves as a testament of Forster's affection, but, lacking so much of Dyce's social and other extrascholarly activity, it fails to convey properly his genuine stature. What follows is but partial amends, for I have relied almost exclusively upon material in print, in order to supplement briefly what we learn in the "Reminiscences" themselves.

Major Alexander Dyce of the East India Company's service was wed to Miss Frederick Meredith Mary Campbell on 3 May 1797.[5] Their eldest son, Alexander, was born on 30 June 1798 in George Street, Edinburgh.[6] Of the Major's other children, I find notices of John Neil Dyce, graduate of Trinity College, member of the Faculty of Advocates, and Sheriff-Substitute of Lanark;[7] and of Archibald, with whom Alexander *fils* resided after the end of his academic and religious careers ("Sketch," xi, xvi). He was a cousin of William Dyce, the Pre-Raphaelite painter, but the records give no indication of a close friend-ship between them.[8]

Dyce's parents sailed for India in 1799, and from then until he en-tered the Edinburgh High School, he was left in the charge of two paternal aunts at Rosebank, a mansion in Aberdeen near the Bridge of Dee ("Sketch," ix). From these years we have his recollections of the local celebrities: Mercer, Beattie, Monboddo, and Gardenstone. When he moved back to Edinburgh, he was placed under the care of "Mrs. Smollett" while attending the High School ("Sketch," x). Dyce has much to say about her in the "Reminiscences," especially regarding her great attachment to the theater. From then on, that institution was to remain a large part of her ward's life.

His appearance during the High School years, as judged by Forster from a miniature, was "animated, intelligent, and handsome" ("Sketch," xi). His academic performance is less easy to gauge. Writes Forster: "The Gazetteer which Dyce kept to the last among his grander books . . . , with the inscription, 'Alex^r. Dyce received this book as a premium at the High School, August, 1811,' tells us all we know of him in the famous academy; and it may be feared that his scholastic achieve-ments in Edinburgh were somewhat eclipsed by his opportunity of in-dulgence in dramatic tastes and enjoyments" ("Sketch," x). But he did receive another such gift, a prize book inscribed "Puero Ingenuo Alex-andro Dyce" and signed by James Pillans, the rector, in 1811.[9] He was not awarded a major honor at the High School, nor was he thought dis-tinguished enough, even in 1849, to be listed by the academy's historian among "A Few of the Persons of Eminence and Rank Educated at the High School."[10] As Forster suggests, he may have spent more time than his classmates in the theaters of Edinburgh, but his "indulgence" seems not to have impaired his over-all education; and it probably engendered in him the enthusiasm that marks his later connections with the stage and with the editing of plays.

Dyce entered Exeter College, Oxford, on 27 February 1816 and took his B.A. in 1819.[11] Again, he appears not to have particularly distinguished himself in his studies, and he has left little information concerning his university career. The only contemporary he ever spoke of to Forster was Lord Yarmouth, afterwards Lord Hertford, "and very strange were the stories of him" ("Sketch," xiv). To others, however, he recounted Hartley Coleridge's oratorical displays at Oxford wine parties.[12] Forster writes of Dyce's curriculum: "He took up with much zeal the study of the classics, and was assiduous at lecture; but his earliest and strongest tastes remained" ("Sketch," xi). They led Dyce to make his first acquaintance with a famous family: he wrote to John Kemble asking which night was to be the great actor's last appearance. The reply, which Dyce includes in his essay on Kemble, "had the gravity and stateliness as of the utterance of a bishop, and was to the effect that he didn't know himself" ("Sketch," xii). It was to be in *Coriolanus,* 23 June 1817, and Dyce, among the hundreds of other *aficionados* who witnessed it, was fortunate enough to have a seat next to the orchestra. In June 1819 Dyce saw Mrs. Siddons's last performance, his account of which was borrowed by Thomas Campbell, and he always spoke of it "as a thing quite apart in his memory" ("Sketch," xii). His "Reminiscences" suggest that later he was to miss none of the major theatrical events of his time, and but few of the minor ones.

Upon graduating, Dyce was faced with a family crisis. His father, now a general in the Madras army, was anxious to see "Alick" advance himself in a similar manner ("Sketch," xi). This impulse no doubt derived from the notable military connections of both sides of the family. Dyce's uncle, General Sir Neil Campbell, was the British Commissioner with Napoleon at Elba and later the Governor of Sierra Leone; and his paternal grandmother, "Miss Ochterlony of Tillifrisky," was the guardian of young Sir David Ochterlony, who distinguished himself by military and diplomatic successes in India and for whom a column was erected at Calcutta.[13] Archibald Dyce became a general ("Sketch," xvi), and John served in the Madras Cavalry.[14] Their father offered Alexander the Church as an alternative, and he took orders after graduation ("Sketch," xi).

He served curacies at Llanteglos, near Fowey in Cornwall, and at Nayland in Suffolk, but the length of his ministry at each is a matter of dispute. Joseph Foster dates the first as 1821–25 and the second as 1825–27;[15] Forster, however, appears correct in claiming that both of Dyce's curacies were held between 1822 and 1825, when he began his literary life ("Sketch," xiv). While at Suffolk, Dyce collected anecdotes about the scholar and divine "Jones of Nayland" but engaged in no other scholarly tasks ("Sketch," xiv). As for religious inquiry, the *Handbook* notes that his library "not only shows that he had studied the usual theological books which young clergymen are supposed to read, but he possessed also good editions of the most important works of the Latin and Greek fathers" (14). He seems not to have been interested in the religious (or political) controversies of his lifetime—there are few books in his library that would indicate such interest[16]—and he involved himself chiefly in such disputes as those over Richard Bentley and John Payne Collier. Twenty years after Dyce abandoned his curacies Samuel Sharpe wrote, "Dyce and [John] Mitford are very little of clergymen, [William] Harness more so,"[17] and not much else is recorded of Dyce's religious life. During his London years he held no official position in the Church.[18]

Forster is alone in claiming 1825 for the year of Dyce's first residence in London ("Sketch," xiv); other sources are virtually unanimous for 1827, though without documentation.[19] Dyce probably resided at 72 Welbeck Street, Cavendish Square, at some time before October 1829,[20] but Forster makes no mention of it. The most prominent address of this period is 9 Gray's Inn Square, where Dyce resided until his mother's death in 1859 ("Sketch," xvi).

Dyce undertook his editorial career at once, and, perhaps on the strength of his early performance, he soon acquired the friendship of a generous patron of intellectual activity. Samuel Rogers was noted for his kindness to the most distant of his acquaintances.[21] Such persons frequently attended his celebrated breakfasts, and there had arisen as well the "Rogers Circle," a group that comprised the leading men of letters during Rogers's long life. Among these was Dyce, who joined the circle possibly as early as 1829, by which time Edward Moxon, the printer, was a member and thus came to know him.[22] By 1844, judging from the account of Charles Mackay, a poet and journalist,[23] Dyce was quite familiar with Rogers (" 'Perhaps you won't go down to posterity at all,' said Mr. Dyce, good-naturedly").[24] This breakfast took place a few days after Dyce and Mackay had attended the funeral of the poet Thomas Campbell, whom Rogers had succored, and the topics ranged from Campbell's penury to Shakespeare. Dyce, incidentally, must have known Campbell by 1834, when he contributed to the poet's *Mrs. Siddons*.[25]

Henry Crabb Robinson recorded other breakfasts and acquaintances from 1846 to 1853.[26] Among those mentioned with Dyce at Rogers's are his "venerable friend" William Maltby, the bibliographer who succeeded Richard Porson as principal librarian at the London Institution and who contributed the "Porsoniana" to Dyce's *Table-Talk of Samuel Rogers;* Dr. Alexander Henderson, a physician and student of literature; Rogers's nephew Samuel Sharpe, an Egyptologist and translator of the Bible; Dr. William Beattie, a poet; Rev. John Mitford, the editor of Gray and of the *Gentleman's Magazine;* and Henry Luttrell, a wit and poet who was one of Rogers's closest friends.

In a manuscript note in Sharpe's *Some Particulars of the Life of Samuel Rogers,* Dyce wrote, "Yes; such was undoubtedly the effect of intercourse with Mr. Rogers, it was indeed improving."[27] Most contemporary accounts say as much. William Jerdan, however, after attacking Dyce's recent and anonymous *Table-Talk,* writes, "I have used the word friend, but it did not appear that the nonogenarian (whatever he might have enjoyed half a century before) had any friends. I never saw about him any but acquaintances or toadies."[28] But in the "Addenda" included with the essay in a book ten years later, Jerdan states: "Upon the reperusal of this Character, and a knowledge of other circumstances communicated to me, I feel bound to acknowledge that I appear to have pressed rather severely upon Mr. Rogers. He was very irritable and not very amiable, but it may be too much to say that he had not 'any friends.' I am inclined to believe that he had at least one, and an independent one, in the Rev. Alexander Dyce, our pre-eminent Critic and Commentator . . ." (378). He goes on to praise further the elderly Dyce's scholarship, thus mitigating somewhat the con-descending tone of his apology. And there is little reason to doubt Dyce's sincerity, let alone his appraisal of Rogers's character: "Of his many acts of kindness and charity to the wholly obscure there is no memorial—at least on earth."[29]

Simultaneously, Dyce belonged to another literary circle, that of the novelist William Harrison Ainsworth. Among those who visited Ains-worth frequently at Kensal Lodge were Bulwer-Lytton, Forster, Disraeli, Dickens, Thackeray, and Maclise.[30] "The scholarly Dyce" is first recorded there about 1837.[31] Again the coterie was of a varied sort, and it included Samuel L. Blanchard, a writer and close friend of Ainsworth; William Jerdan, the aforementioned critic; Sir Theodore Martin, man of letters; George Cruikshank, the artist and caricaturist who illustrated Dickens; and Francis S. Mahony, the Cork satirist and ex-Jesuit most noted for *Fr. Prout's Reliques.* Dyce apparently joined the circle in the early thirties,[32] and he retained an acquaintance with most of these men for the rest of his life.

Forster's only remark on the extent of Dyce's friendships is that he "was a social man, had many friends, was welcome everywhere for the pleasure of his quiet talk, so full of varied knowledge made doubly de-lightful by old-world breeding and courtesy" ("Sketch," xvi). Dyce's obituary in *Notes & Queries* reports that "his intimate acquaintance with Sir Harris Nicolas, the Rev. John Mitford, the Kembles, and most of our living men of letters, must have made him the depository of much of the literary history of the present age."[33] But one must look elsewhere to learn of these associations; even his library catalogues are more helpful, in that they list scores of gifts and presentation copies from people now thoroughly forgotten.

Dyce's first close literary acquaintance appears to have been Euphra-sia Fanny Haworth, a friend of the Brownings.[34] He edited her anony-mous *The Pine Tree Dell, and Other Tales* (London, 1827) and noted in his copy: "These tales were written by my dear friend Miss Haworth, when she was quite a girl. I saw them through the press, and prefixed the 'Advertisement.' "[35] Another young lady, Fanny Kemble, also knew him at about this time. She notes in one of her autobiographies that the "arrangement of Massinger for the family library by my friend the

Reverend Alexander Dyce, the learned Shakespearian editor and commentator, was my first introduction to that mine of dramatic wealth which enriched the literature of [Renaissance] England. . . ."[36] This took place around 1830, and in a letter forty-four years later she states proudly that, having known Dyce, Collier, and other scholars, she cannot abide talk that Bacon wrote the plays attributed to Shakespeare.[37]

Still another lady writer became Dyce's lifelong friend in the years soon after his moving to London, and his method of ingratiation may provide a clue to the manner in which he came to know other such figures. Mary Russell Mitford met Dyce through the Reverend William Harness,[38] the liberal clergyman who was a friend of the Kembles, Kean, Byron, Dickens, Rogers, and Wordsworth, an influential reviewer of plays, and an editor of Shakespeare. Dyce at once began corresponding with Miss Mitford. She was "highly honored" by his approval of her *Rienzi*,[39] which was conveyed in a letter of 20 October 1828 wherein Dyce mentions the forwarding of his *Specimens of British Poetesses* (London, 1825) and the first volume of George Peele's *Works: Now First Collected* (London, 1828).[40] About the former he rather coyly asserts, "You will not, I trust, be very angry with me when you find that it contains some of your own verses. . . ." Campbell, Browning, Wordsworth, and Washington Irving were frequent callers at Miss Mitford's,[41] and Dyce and Harness are recorded there as late as 1850.[42]

Dyce's introduction to William Wordsworth was likewise brought about by a friend and a letter. John Mitford told Dyce that Wordsworth disagreed with the text of a poem in his edition of William Collins's *Poetical Works* (London, 1827), and on 13 October 1828 Dyce wrote to ask for the poet's reasons.[43] Wordsworth replied on 29 October to thank him for the book, and, as de Selincourt observes, this event "marks the beginning of a long and fruitful literary friendship."[44] Dyce informed Wordsworth on 9 January 1829 that he thought him correct in his evaluation of the faulty text, and he was to receive at least sixteen letters from the poet between that date and 5 January 1844.[45] They record Wordsworth's extremely high regard for Dyce's scholarship and some minor criticisms of the many editions that Dyce sent him over the years. He also expresses concern in the early thirties for Dyce's health, though the illnesses are not described.

Dyce provided some explanatory notes for Christopher Wordsworth's *Memoirs of William Wordsworth* (London, 1851), and among them is a brief insight into his active clerical days: "I had mentioned to Mr. W. that, when I had a curacy in Cornwall, I used frequently to carry 'The Excursion' down to the sea-shore, and read it there" (II, 226). What is recorded of Dyce's side of the correspondence reveals little else about him, apart from his dislike for Horace Walpole and an interesting comment on Sir Samuel Egerton Brydges: his mind "dwells on the 'minora sidera' of literature, . . . little twinkles of the last century, who were scarcely visible even in their own dark times: he writes me whole pages about the excellencies of Sneyd Davies, Bagshaw Stevens, and Capel Loft etc etc, and thinks they should enjoy places in the next Edition of the British Poets."[46]

Another letter brought him to the attention of Sir Walter Scott. On 4 March 1831 he sent Scott a copy of his edition of Robert Greene's *Dramatic Works, to Which are Added his Poems* (London, 1831), dedicated to Sir Walter, along with a note that dealt with such matters as a "shamefully careless" edition of Marlowe.[47] Scott sent his thanks and a book in return,[48] and on 31 March informed Dyce that he planned to use his edition for an article on Greene, Peele, and Webster in the *Quarterly Review*.[49] Lockhart notes of Scott's response to receiving the Greene, "It is proper to observe that he [Scott] had never met their editor, though two or three letters had formerly passed between them."[50] Dyce appears to have been surprised at his success: he wrote Scott on 5 April, "[I] had assuredly no hidden motives; of a critique on them [the plays] in the Quarterly Review I never for a moment dreamed"; and he goes on to discuss ghost stories, in which Scott was interested.[51] Dyce's stature was such in 1839 that Lockhart asked him to provide scholarly notes for the second edition of the biography of Scott. And in 1861 Dyce was not too shy to advertise his correspondence with Scott and his appearance in the original *Memoirs*.[52]

When he was first coming to know the greater names in English letters, Dyce must also have met John Forster, though the biographer has left no record of their first encounter. Forster was achieving a reputation at the same time as Dyce, having written for magazines in Newcastle and London by 1830.[53] He was also by that year a friend of

Leigh Hunt and Charles Lamb, and with them contributed to Moxon's
The Reflector in 1832. He appeared in the *Athenæum* and other such
journals from 1833 on. Like Dyce he became a lover of plays at an
early age;[54] the biography of his friend dwells upon theatrical anecdotes
and often digresses from the facts of Dyce's life to relate barely relevant
incidents of the stage. Renton observes that "no two men were ever
more intellectually alike" than these two and that they were "close
friends during the greater part of their lives."[55]

But of much greater importance for Dyce's early career was John
Mitford, who, as stated above, was a fellow member of the Rogers
circle and helped bring about Dyce's acquaintance with Wordsworth in
1828. When the gifted publisher William Pickering began his Aldine
Series in 1830, he called upon both Mitford and Dyce,[56] and Dyce
mentions the aid of Mitford in his 1831 edition of Greene (vi). The
two ministers were familiar enough by 1832 that Mitford could preface
his Aldine edition of Parnell with a dedicatory "Epistle to the Rev.
Alexander Dyce, A. B."—more than 750 lines in heroic couplets, filled
with echoes of Pope and Gray, which provide the first mention of Dyce's
proficiency in verse. He compares Parnell's friendship with Pope to his
with Dyce and writes:

> Oh, friend! as oft I hail thy taste refin'd,
> Thy gentle manners, thy congenial mind;
> Those studious hours that leave no page unknown,
> Of all that Rome or Athens call'd their own;
> Thine the fair flowers on Tiber's banks that smile,
> And thine a wreath from each Ægean isle,
> With many a violet mix'd from Britain's gothic pile;
> Secure of fame, thy future path I see,
> And mark another Parnell rise in thee.[57]

In a later and more candid missive, to Edward Jesse, Mitford says of
Dyce: "He has all the spite of a school-girl who means to tell her
governess that Miss Tottileplan in going upstairs, took two steps at
once, for which there is a heavy punishment at Kensington Gore and
the Hammersmith seminaries." But this was written in good humor, and
he goes on to praise Dyce's erudition.[58]

With William Harness he had "a long and uninterrupted friendship."[59] But Harness's biographer tells us little more than that "during this period [from the 1850s on], no one was a more frequent visitor in Mr. Harness's study than the well-known Shakespearian critic, Mr. Dyce. He was a tall thin man, with keen eyes and a strong Scotch accent. They had been literary friends through life. . . ."[60] Some of the other scholars he knew have left a record of Dyce, among them William Carew Hazlitt:

> The Rev. Alexander Dyce was invariably willing to afford any information to me on literary or bibliographical subjects. When my father was first acquainted with him he lived in Gray's Inn. He was a bachelor. I recollect that in a letter to my father or to myself he spoke of being engaged on a new English edition of Athenæus—a real want—but I never heard any more about it. I met him one day at Russell-Smith's, in Soho Square: a singularly huge, shambling, awkward, ungainly figure. He had come about an eighteenpenny book he required for use. There was some negotiation as to an abatement of the price, and ultimately he left the shop, book in hand. In a few moments he returned, and asked Smith if, when he had done with it, he would take the volume back at a reasonable reduction. On another occasion when I met Dyce, it was the Mitford sale in 1860, and he spoke of Mitford's handwriting as a curious mixture of neatness and illegibility—in fact, that the writer had come to him before then to ask him to assist in deciphering it. Dyce himself, although he wrote a fairly legible hand, was an interminable reviser of his own copy, and I heard that he almost threw his publishers and printers into despair. He was at one time intending to leave his library to one of the universities—the Bodleian, I believe, but he changed his plan.[61]

Samuel Sharpe writes that Dyce and Mitford "are simple, unaffected men, learned, full of conversation and literature."[62] There were many more: Dyce often acknowledges the aid of the bibliomaniac Richard Heber; he corresponded with David Laing and others of the trade.[63] The list goes on, and it includes the splendid eccentrics on whom he has lavished so many words in the "Reminiscences."

John Payne Collier was among his most spectacular friends, no less gifted than the others despite his propensity for forgery. Though E. K. Chambers condemns him as a "slovenly and dishonest antiquary,"[64] Collier was capable of sound scholarship when not inclined to vice. He too had extensive literary friendships. (He helped Dickens get his job on the *Morning Chronicle* and remained friends with him for life.)[65] Crabb Robinson provides the first record of Dyce in the company of Collier:

> April 6th [1833]. A Dinner at J. P. Collier's, where I met for the first time Dyce, whom I then thought agreeable. He is more than that, but by no means good-natured. He is a critic and too apt, as critics often are, to treat bad taste as bad morals. Woe be to the literary world if Pope's lie be true that
> Every bad author is as bad a friend.[66]

Robinson had no such reservations when he made the original diary entry, but when revising it for his reminiscences in light of the controversy over the integrity of his good friend Collier, he treated Dyce in the manner of several of Collier's sympathizers.

Before this conflict erupted in the fifties, Dyce was on good terms with Collier. To him he dedicated his *Works* (London, 1840) of Thomas Middleton, and in the preface to the Skelton (1843) he thanks Collier for assistance (I, viii). In 1846, after the first tremors had been felt, Dyce could still write to him familiarly:

> I have sent you the 11ᵗʰ vol. of B[eaumont]. & F[letcher]. together with the Memoir. The latter (which I myself consider as a wretched thing) I do not expect you to read through; I presume that you will only "trifle o'er it with the paper cutter," as Pope's young lady, when in the country, "trifles o'er her coffee with the spoon." . . .
>
> .   .   .   .
>
> Why do you persist in trying to render my old age unhappy by threatening to borrow my books for that [Shakespeare] Society (which you will make me hate)?[67]

But Dyce was less cordial in private: "Mr. Milman tells me Mr. Dyce is about to publish a volume on Shakespeare in which he proposes to 'knock Collier's head & Knights [sic] together, & shew that both are brainless.' "[68]

Before chronicling more fully Dyce's scholarly life, including his subsequent break with Collier, I shall provide some of the details recorded about Dyce's relations with the greater literary artists, apart from Wordsworth, known by him in middle life. He was familiar with several of these persons during his early years with Ainsworth, but none of their conversations at Kensal Lodge are in print. The best evidence of his intimacy with certain of them is a famous 1844 Maclise sketch of Dickens reading *The Chimes* from galley proofs to a gathering of his friends, among whom are Forster, Carlyle, Dyce, and Harness.[69] Aside from Forster, none of those pictured has left much in the way of an impression of Dyce. Dickens's sole published mention of him is in a diary entry for a dinner at Harness's, 5 February 1839: "Only three— Wordsworth—Dyce—Kenyon. Wordsworth (fils) decidedly *lumpish*. Copyrights need be hereditary, for genius isn't."[70] In the available letters Carlyle writes only once of being with Dyce, and that, much later. At Forster's on 4 December 1865 were Browning "and one Dyce (an Aberdeen *Ex*-Shovelhat, huge grey man, very good natured) who lives upon Shakespear; no other except ourselves,—poor Jane says she always sleeps *better* after such a thing!"[71]

Dyce was acquainted with dozens of other literary men, and he knew Tennyson (or Tennyson's publisher) well enough to have seen *The Princess* in advance of publication (1847).[72] He has left a memorandum of a conversation with Landor on 6 May 1850.[73] And Thackeray, toward the end of his life, notes in his diary a visit to Dyce (20 January 1863) and a gathering at which Dyce was present (24 September).[74]

To maintain such diverse friendships over a period of forty years required of Dyce more than judicious letters and the advice of intimates, not that these means are disreputable. By nearly all accounts, Dyce the man was worthy of this company. Moreover, while impressing them with his personality, he was also developing a genuinely brilliant record of scholarship that was likewise worthy of his eminent readers. In a career of nearly half a century, he published an imposing number of editions and, according to the *Times,* "numerous other works which appeared without his name."[75]

Shortly before his ordination, Dyce issued *Select Translations from the Greek of Quintus Smyrnaeus* (Oxford, 1821). He writes of this continuation of the *Iliad,* "I have made use of blank verse in preference to rhyme, thinking it impossible for the latter to convey to an English reader the most distant idea of the simple tone of Grecian poetry: I expect, therefore, to be told by the admirers of Pope's Homer that my lines are intolerably prosaic" (iv–v). His anthology of poetesses appeared in 1825 and again in 1827, only the second such work by Dyce's claim (v). With his edition of Collins (1827) he began his connection with William Pickering, without whose generosity several expensive undertakings would not have been possible ("Sketch," xv). And in order that his Aldine Series "should be textually of a high standard," Pickering selected Dyce, Mitford, and Sir Nicholas Harris Nicolas, the antiquarian, as editors.[76] For the series Dyce edited the *Poetical Works* (London, 1831) of James Beattie, who with Major Mercer had represented to the adolescent Dyce "all that was poetically conceivable of the beautiful and sublime" ("Sketch," ix); then Pope's *Poetical Works* (1831), Shakespeare's *Poems* (1832), and Mark Akenside's *Poetical Works* (1835). In the meantime he published editions of Peele (1828–39), Webster's *Works* (London, 1830–39), Fletcher's *Humourous Lieutenant* (London, 1830), and Greene (1831); completed James Shirley's *Dramatic Works and Poems* (London, 1833), begun by William Gifford; and edited *Specimens of English Sonnets* (London, 1833). The *Athenæum* praised his *Specimens,* and the *Quarterly Review* spoke of "his accustomed ability" in its notice of the Shirley.[77] The *Works* of Bentley, "to whom the success of his own earliest self-discipline had been largely due," appeared in three volumes from 1836 to 1838 and introduced him to the learned printer Charles Robson ("Sketch," xvii). Ending the furious activity of this decade, Dyce published Middleton's *Works* (1840).

It was natural for Dyce to incline toward the scholarly societies forming at this time. He was one of the first members of the Camden Society (founded in 1838) and was elected to its Council on 2 May 1839.[78] Dyce and others made the literary side of this group almost as important as the historical, but in a short time other organizations drained off most of their work. Dyce was a founder of the Percy Society (1840), along with James O. Halliwell-Phillipps, Thomas Wright, and Collier, and he sat on its first Council.[79] He was also on the original Council of the Shakespeare Society, which he helped to establish in 1840.[80] He dropped from all council lists in the later forties after publishing in the Camden series William Kemp's *Nine Daies Wonder* (London, 1840); in the Percy, Henry Porter's *The Two Angry Women of Abington* (1841), Sir Henry Wotton's *Poems* (1843), and Drayton's *The Harmony of the Church* (1843); and in the Shakespeare, *Timon* (1842) and *Sir Thomas More* (1844). Dyce was elected to the Athenaeum Club in 1842 but appears to have been inactive.[81]

This social and administrative torpor was most probably owed to Dyce's independent scholarly occupations. His Skelton came out in 1843, as did the first volumes of Beaumont and Fletcher (completed in 1846).[82] The complex problems posed by these three writers burdened him severely. Dyce claimed that his Memoir of the two playwrights occupied as much time as anything of similar length ever had. He wrote to Forster: "It extinguished everything else for me during the time. Of what has been passing lately I am entirely ignorant. Indeed I don't believe I am fully acquainted with anything that has happened later than the 29th of August, 1625, the day of Fletcher's burial" ("Sketch," xviii). The eleven volumes of this collection were published by his friend Moxon. Pickering published for Dyce Marlowe's *Works* (London, 1850), and there remained for him only Shakespeare and Ford.

But before the Shakespeare was completed, Samuel Rogers died, and Dyce felt at liberty to put out his friend's *Table-Talk* in 1856. It is only mentioned in parentheses by Forster ("Sketch," xx–xxi) and was a disaster for Moxon comparable to his own sonnets, Lamb's *Album Verse,* and the poetry of Browning.[83] The *Edinburgh Review* groaned that Rogers, who died on 18 December 1855, was "hardly cold in the grave" before the volume appeared (14 February 1856); "this book," it went on, "is in no one respect a creditable one," having "made Rogers use the very phraseology he notoriously disliked."[84] But, as Bishop observes, the brief delay is more an indication that the conversations were recorded when they occurred than that the whole book was written after Rogers's death.[85] Dyce affirms this in the preface to the third edition and claims to have terminated his memoranda at least five years before the death of Rogers (xii).

The attacks seem mostly to have been written by violent Rogers partisans. The *Times* charged that the poet was misrepresented and said, "We pity the task of the anonymous Boswell, but we cannot on this occasion remit a particle of his doom."[86] Referring to this review, Ainsworth wrote to Crossley in February: "*The Times,* you see, has come down upon poor Dyce (he must be a Dyce sombre, I think)[87] for his *Table Talk,* and says that it is a case for 'the literary police,' and that the executors 'ought to look to it' "; further, on 1 March: "Poor Dyce . . . is attacked again in *The Athenæum* of to-day. He will never survive it."[88] Crabb Robinson thought Dyce's treatment, especially by the *Times,* unfair, while concurring that his judgment in selection was not good.[89] And Jerdan, as if ignorant in 1866 of *Table-Talk's* editor, concludes his reappraisal of Rogers and Dyce by saying, "Should, here-after, any satisfactory memoirs of Rogers ever come to light, I might (if spared), and the public should look to the same eminent authority [Dyce] for the desirable work."[90]

Table-Talk also provides a clue regarding the state at that time of Dyce's relationship with Collier. In the preface to the third edition Dyce refers to "my old friend Mr. J. P. Collier," who, as "a proof of his kindly feeling towards me" has sent a letter to the *Athenæum* defend-ing the first edition (v). According to Collier, Dyce "is utterly incapable of the slightest intentional misrepresentation," despite their differences (vi). But regardless of the kind words, these differences had certainly resulted in a break by this time. Dyce first published his reservations about Collier's treatment of texts in the *Remarks* (1844). The book is justly critical of Collier but does not question his honesty. Neverthe-less, the *Athenæum* wrote: "Mr. Dyce is shrewd, subtle, well read, su-percilious, and confident. We agree with him that Shakespeare has suffered from the commentators; and the best apology for these 'Re-marks'—three hundred pages of additional trifling—is, that they are published in a substantive volume, apart from Shakespeare's works, and may therefore be 'squeezed' by those who have leizure, and then thrown into the fire."[91] As with the *Table-Talk* controversy, Dyce more often than not had to contend with those who were close friends with his sub-ject. Crabb Robinson, certain that Dyce was correct, nonetheless could never quite forgive him because he "was not kind to Collier in his criticisms."[92]

As was shown, Dyce and Collier were still outwardly friendly in 1846. In the biographical memoir of Beaumont and Fletcher his corrections of Collier's "very valuable" data concerning Shakespeare are gentle (I, xvii, n. o), even though some of the points he mentions had been less delicately handled by *Punch*.[93] But everything was in the open by the time Dyce published *A Few Notes on Shakespeare; with Occasional Remarks on the Emendations of the Manuscript-Corrector in Mr. Collier's Copy of the Folio 1632* (London, 1853). What must have particularly irked Dyce was that he and several other scholars had previously accepted and used Collier's fraudulent material without question.[94] Trading upon a well-earned reputation, Collier passed along Shakespearian forgeries and went so far as to compose obscene poems and ballads which he would then "discover" (without, of course, revealing the originals).[95] After Dyce's death Collier wrote: "we were intimate friends for about a quarter of a century; and it was only my engagement with a publisher to prepare an edition of Shakespeare in 1842, that occasioned the first difference between Mr. Dyce and myself. . . . Our paths from that date began to diverge, and, I deeply regret to add, never reapproached." He praises Dyce's scholarship, deplores his judgment, and says that "he was a gentleman in every respect—in birth, education, and deportment. He was the first to sever our long intimacy."[96] Significantly, in 1859, Dyce had written in contradiction to Collier's "artful misrepresentation" that "the main object of this little work [is] to expose the ungentlemanly treatment which I have received at the hands of one who seems to take a pleasure in proclaiming that he was once my friend."[97]

The first edition of Dyce's *The Works of William Shakespeare*, published by Moxon, appeared in 1857. The *Athenæum* generally approved the sparse annotation and conservative text, while lamenting the equally conservative Life.[98] The *Quarterly Review* called it "the best text of Shakespeare which has yet been given to the world."[99] The second edition (1864 [1863]–67) was dedicated to Forster and expanded the work to nine volumes, including extensive critical apparatus and a massive Glossary.[100] Carlyle's criticism of it is partly accurate: "Dyce's text, etc., seem to me fairly the best: at the same time for *use* it is simply intolerable. A wandering through the Gardens as of Para-

<u>William Wordsworth</u>

With this great man, whose genius has been was slowly but at last fully acknowledged by the multitude, and now exercises such a powerful influence on the more recent poetic literature of his country, I was on very intimate terms, the admiration I had expressed for his <u>Excursion</u> having led to our acquaintance; and several letters, which at various times he addressed to me, are printed in his Memoirs by his nephew; see vol. ii. pp. 214, 219, 220, 225, 274, 275, 278, 281, 284, 350. (Though he invited me over and over again to pass some days with him at Rydal Mount, I unfortunately could not make it convenient to do so; for at that period it was my duty, not my choice, to spend a large portion of the year in the north of Scotland: but whenever Wordsworth visited London, which latterly he occasionally did, we used to meet very frequently both at my Chambers in Gray's Inn and at the houses of our mutual friends.

This wife generally accompanied him to London, and sometimes their daughter Dora.— Mrs Wordsworth was the exemplar of all that is amiable in woman; and moreover is proved shown to have been endowed with true poetic genius by the fact, that, while Wordsworth was composing his verses on the Daffodils ("I wander'd lonely as a cloud", &c.), and had left a blank after the lines,

"For oft, when on my couch I lie
In vacant or in pensive mood",

uncertain how to complete the stanza, — Mrs Wordsworth filled up the lacuna thus,

"They flash upon that inward eye
Which is the bliss of solitude":

yet such was her modesty, that she positively forbade any mention being made, in any edition of her husband's Works, that these two lines (perhaps the best in the poem) were supplied by her.* —— Dora, the darling

* But the fact is noticed in the Memoirs of Wordsworth by his nephew.

FACSIMILE OF FOLIO 213^{r} IN THE MANUSCRIPT OF "REMINISCENCES," BY ALEXANDER DYCE, IN THE VICTORIA & ALBERT MUSEUM, SOUTH KENSINGTON (PRESSMARK D.26.E.9). REPRODUCED BY COURTESY OF THE VICTORIA & ALBERT MUSEUM.

dise,—accompanied everywhere as with a whirlpool of barking curs, unfortunate cats, apes, and irrational unclean creatures!—"[101] Dyce began work on a third, but it had to be finished by Forster in 1875. His last undertakings were the completion of Jervis's *Dictionary of the Language of Shakespeare* (London, 1868) and the revision of John Ford's *Works,* edited by Gifford (London, 1869), the latter published the year of his death.

Attacks on Dyce's scholarship per se were relatively infrequent. His confidence and self-satisfaction were found at times annoying, and the value of some of his work was questioned;[102] but by and large the quality of his texts and the ultimate usefulness of his notes (Carlyle notwithstanding) still command respect. His dedication to the task of scholarship is notable; he was not, as Wordsworth put it, "a man of leisure."[103] "I never hear anything, or of anything," Dyce wrote to Forster. "If the conflagration of the universe were to take place tomorrow, I should not know that it was going on till the flames had reached Gray's Inn gate" ("Sketch," xvi). His reserve in approaching the text is likewise praiseworthy, especially because he worked at a time when editors too often presumed to alter the author's word in accordance with their own tastes. He was fluent in Greek, Latin, Italian, and French and was renowned for his erudition. He was the first modern editor of Peele, Greene, Middleton, and Webster and the first to edit competently Marlowe and the plays of Beaumont and Fletcher; his Shakespeare was one of the century's best.[104] Of his Skelton, which remains standard at this writing, a modern critic gives the following appraisal: "Sometimes a scholar, through a loving and complete edition, can rescue a poet from obscurity and prepare the way for a critical revival, as the Reverend Alexander Dyce did with his magnificent edition of Skelton in 1843, a book that is a monument of erudition and appreciation and has required only slight correction in the century since."[105]

We have Forster's testimony that Dyce retained to the last an attractive personality and a handsome bearing, as well as his energy. Still the "gentle giant," a nickname that his height had earned him in youth, he stooped much and no longer paid such attention to dress as he had when once visiting his brother Archibald: the General told Forster that Dyce's luggage then consisted of "seven shirts and a 'Sophocles'"

("Sketch," xi). His interests remained constant, and despite his pre-occupation with editing he never lost his fondness for versifying. Begin-ning about the time of his work on Fletcher he translated Athenæus for amusement. The manuscript lies unfinished and unedited in his Col-lection, awaiting, as Forster says, "an enthusiast for the Deipnosoph-ists" ("Sketch," xx–xxii). Among the samples which Forster quotes:

> Befits not old man with young wife to yoke,
>   For she's a skiff which rudder cannot sway,
> Nor anchor hold: but oft, her cables broke,
>   At night she harbours in another bay.
>
> ("Sketch," xxi)

And too, the Collection has nine drawings by Dyce, including "Three NUDE FEMALE FIGURES, supporting a lotus flower with their out-stretched arms. In pencil."[106]

Dyce spent the last ten years of his life at 33 Oxford Terrace, Hyde Park, having been forced out of his chambers in Gray's Inn Square by Archibald; Dyce's books and art works, it seems, had left little dwelling space. Forster reports that it was often easier for Dyce to go to the British Museum than to unearth a book from his own scattered col-lection ("Sketch," xvi–xvii). He visited Aberdeen frequently and once offended certain of the town's Episcopalians by preaching on a text from the Apocrypha; but he was more remembered there as a "sporting" gentleman, causing a friend to wonder at his fondness for old plays while being able to fish so well with a fly ("Sketch," ix–x). He had inherited Rosebank from his aunt and seems to have been well off all his life, to judge from his Collection[107] and from Forster's intimations that he took upon himself much of the expense of his early editions ("Sketch," ix, xv).

Dyce suffered a painful illness in his final months. The last letter to Forster before his fatal attack of jaundice was in June 1868, when he reported that he was well and had been reading *Atalanta in Calydon,* written, as he said, by a "genuine singer" ("Sketch," xxii). At the be-ginning of August he wrote to tell Forster that "he might be shown by way of contrast to our old friend the Yellow Dwarf,[108] having become a

Yellow Giant. 'Being free from pain, which Horace Walpole defined to be the pleasure of old age, I ought to be satisfied; but I nevertheless am ill, ill, ill . . .' " ("Sketch," xxii). On 4 December he wrote, "I am . . . in the seventh month of my martyrdom. . . . I suspect that I am very gradually dying; and if such is the case, I certainly have no reason to make any childish lamentation, for I have lived a great deal longer than most people who are born into this world, and I look back on my past existence without much disapprobation" ("Sketch," xxii–xxiii). Dyce was still at work on the edition of Ford and notes in the preface (I, vii), dated 15 February 1869, that he was hampered by the "languor and weakness consequent on a very long and serious illness. . . ." He died on Saturday, 15 May 1869.[109]

Forster writes that Dyce left "a great many friends to deplore a loss which they could never replace, for all the qualities that give charm to private intercourse were his in abundant measure" ("Sketch," xxiii). Not the least of those who felt something of this loss was the "genuine singer" himself. Swinburne, who received Dyce's edition of Marlowe when he was thirteen, wrote Halliwell-Phillipps in 1880: "I have also to thank you for the cordial gratification I have received from the kind expression of your opinion on the subject of my poems, and your equally kind communication of the late Mr. Dyce's. Very few things could have given me more pleasure, as there are very few men of our time to whom I feel that I owe so much at once of enjoyment and of guidance as to yourself and to him."[110] Friends of all degrees, from Bulloch to Wordsworth, have left the same impression of Dyce.

---

1. "Rev. Alexander Dyce," *N&Q* Ser. 5, VIII (1877), 327. Like Dyce, Crossley was a friend of William Harrison Ainsworth, the novelist. A scholar, his library totaled more than 100,000 volumes. Biographical data on him and others are from the *Dictionary of National Biography* unless otherwise stated.

2. John Forster, "Alexander Dyce. A Biographical Sketch," in [John Kesson, comp.,] *Dyce Collection. A Catalogue of the Printed Books and Manuscripts Bequeathed by the Reverend Alexander Dyce* [to the South Kensington Museum] (London, 1875), I, vii–xxiv. In virtually the same form the essay appeared previously as "A Word on Alexander Dyce," *Fortnightly Review* N.S. XVIII (1875), 731–46. It was abridged and slightly amended in the *Handbook of the Dyce and Forster Collections in the South Kensington Museum* (London, 1880), pp. [1]–12 (hereafter, *Handbook*). Also, Forster's "Sketch" was the source for the *DNB* biography. Hereafter, references to Forster's biography will be cited as "Sketch."

3. "Rev. Alexander Dyce," p. 327. He also refers to Dyce's long and detailed letters to Sir Samuel Egerton Brydges (still unpublished), claiming that they are vital to any biography of Dyce. They would indeed be valuable, but I cannot locate them. William Powell Jones describes a collection of Egerton Brydges letters in the Harvard Library, but with no reference to Dyce ("New Light on Sir Egerton Brydges," *Harvard Library Bulletin* XI [1957], 102–16). For a reference to one such missive see William Bates, *The Maclise Portrait Gallery of Illustrious Literary Characters* (London, 1898), p. 19. In the British Museum are letters to Rev. Philip Bliss and William Carew Hazlitt.

4. A "Reply" to Crossley's querie, *N&Q* Ser. 5, VIII (1877), 374. Bulloch was an Aberdonian brass-finisher and *pari passu* a competent Shakespearian textual scholar.

5. *Register of Marriages of the City of Edinburgh 1751–1800,* ed. Francis J. Grant, Scottish Record Society, LIII (Edinburgh, 1922), 223.

6. "Sketch," p. viii ; *Times,* 20 May 1869, 11c (microfilm).

7. *The Faculty of Advocates in Scotland 1532–1943,* ed. Francis J. Grant, S.R.S., CXLV (Edinburgh, 1944), 64; *Alumni Cantabrigienses . . . Part II: From 1752 to 1900,* II, comp. J. A. Venn (Cambridge, 1944), 365.

8. None of William Dyce's paintings are part of the Dyce Collection, but this evidence is, in itself, not conclusive, because Daniel Maclise, whom Dyce knew fairly well, is also not represented. See *Dyce Collection. A Catalogue of the Paintings, Miniatures, Drawings, Engravings, Rings, and Miscellaneous Objects Bequeathed* [to the South Kensington Museum] *by the Reverend Alexander Dyce* (London, 1874).

9. The first inscribed volume is item 3983, the second 6071, in his library's *Catalogue.* His rector was Byron's "paltry Pillans" (*English Bards and Scotch Reviewers,* 515).

10. William Steven, *The History of the High School of Edinburgh* (Edinburgh, 1849), App., pp. 129 ff., 203 ff.

11. *Alumni Oxonienses . . . 1715–1886,* comp. Joseph Foster (London, 1888), I, 399. According to the "Sketch," p. xi, he entered in "the winter of 1815."

12. See the letter printed in *Poems by Hartley Coleridge, with a Memoir of his Life by his Brother* [Derwent], 2d ed. (London, 1851), I, lxix–lxx.

13. "Sketch," pp. viii–ix. On Sir David: C. E. Buckland, *Dictionary of Indian Biography* (London, 1906), p. 321.

14. *Faculty of Advocates,* p. 64.

15. *Alumni Oxonienses,* I, 399.

16. *Handbook,* pp. 14, 16. John Keble is represented by *The Christian Year* (Oxford, 1840) and *De Poeticae Vi Medica* (Oxford, 1844) ; Newman not at all.

17. From his diary, 22 December 1847, quoted in *Letters and Reminiscences of the Rev. John Mitford,* ed. C. M. [Mrs. Matilda C. Houstoun] (London, 1891), p. 208.

18. See the admittedly incomplete *Clergy List for 1841* (London, 1841), which excludes him, as does George Hennessy, *Novum Repertorium . . . or London Diocesan Clergy Succession from the Earliest Time to the Year 1898* (London, 1898).

19. See S. Austin Allibone, *A Critical Dictionary of English Literature and British and American Authors,* I (Philadelphia, 1886), 536; *Encyclopaedia Britannica,* 11th ed., VIII (New York, 1910), 743 ; and the *Times,* 20 May 1869, 11c.

20. From there he addressed a letter to Mary R. Mitford on 20 October 1828. Wordsworth wrote to that address on 12 January 1829, and then to 9 Gray's Inn Square on 16 October. See notes 40 and 43, below.

21. For a partisan character of Rogers, see the review of Dyce's *Recollections of the Table-Talk of Samuel Rogers. To Which is Added Porsoniana* (London, 1856) in the *Edinburgh Review* CIV (1856), 73–122.

22. Harold G. Merriam, *Edward Moxon: Publisher of Poets* (New York, 1939), p. 14.

23. "Bygone Celebrities and Literary Recollections, IV. The Rev. Henry Hart Milman—The Rev. Alexander Dyce—Thomas Miller," *Eclectic Magazine* N. S. XLI (1885), 169–72. The account is much the same in Mackay's *Through the Long Day* (London, 1887), I, 311 ff. Others who dined with Rogers have mentioned Dyce. See, for example, James T. Fields, *Yesterdays with Authors* (Boston, 1882), pp. 386–90.

24. Mackay, "Celebrities," p. 171.

25. Dyce was a member of "The Committee for the Campbell Monument": *Life and Letters of Thomas Campbell,* ed. William Beattie, 2d ed. (London, 1850), III, 441.

26. *Henry Crabb Robinson on Books and Their Writers,* ed. Edith J. Morley (London, 1938), II, 658, 693, 715, 729; *Diary, Reminiscences, and Correspondence of Henry Crabb Robinson,* ed. Thomas Sadler, 3d ed. (London and New York, 1872), II, 305.

27. Quoted in P. W. Clayden, *Rogers and His Contemporaries* (London, 1889), II, 220.

28. *Men I Have Known* (London, 1866), p. 375.

29. Preface to the first edition of *Table-Talk,* quoted from the third edition (London, 1856), p. xv.

30. Malcolm Elwin, *Victorian Wallflowers* (London, 1934), p. 163.

31. Stewart M. Ellis, *William Harrison Ainsworth and His Friends* (London, 1911), I, 272, 333.

32. See Edgar Johnson, *Charles Dickens: His Tragedy and Triumph* (New York, 1952), I, 103–4.

33. Ser. 4, III (1869), 495. The writer states that "he used, we believe, to keep a diary." Dyce heads his article on Cumnor Place "from my Diary." I have been assured that, wherever it is, it is not in the Library of the Victoria and Albert Museum. Mr. A. P. Burton, the Assistant Keeper, has written to me (2 April 1970): "There is evidence . . . that when Forster presented his collection to the Museum, a great amount of private papers and correspondence was destroyed by him or his executors, and I suspect that a similar fate may have befallen Dyce's private papers." On this subject he has directed me to K. J. Fielding, "New Letters from Charles Dickens to John Forster: How the Letters Were Found," *Boston University Studies in English,* II (1956), 140–49.

34. She is the "Eyebright" of *Sordello* III, 967.

35. Item 4523. Perhaps Dyce came to know her through the publisher of this book, John Andrews, who had printed Dyce's 1825 article on John Kemble in *The Album* (see the Preface to Chapter II, below). Miss Haworth presented Dyce with a copy of her *St. Sylvester's Day and Other Poems* twenty years later.

36. Frances Anne Kemble, *Records of a Girlhood,* 2d ed. (New York, 1879), p. 255.

37. To "H," 6 December 1874, in Frances Anne Kemble, *Further Records 1848–1883* (New York, 1891), p. 53.

38. *The Friendships of Mary Russell Mitford As Recorded in Letters from Her Literary Correspondents,* ed. A. G. L'Estrange (New York, 1882), p. 132 (ed. note).

39. Ibid.

40. Ibid., p. 131.

41. Caroline M. Duncan-Jones, *Miss Mitford and Mr. Harness: Records of a Friendship* (London, 1955), p. 29.

42. *Friendships of Mary Russell Mitford,* p. 364. See also *Mary Russell Mitford: Correspondence with Charles Boner & John Ruskin,* ed. Elizabeth Lee (London, 1914), p. 76.

43. *The Letters of William and Dorothy Wordsworth: The Later Years,* ed. Ernest de Selincourt (Oxford, 1939), I, 313 n. 2; for Dyce's two addresses: 345 n. 1, 423.

44. Ibid., I, 313 n. 2.

45. Ibid., I, 345 n. 1. See also II, 952; and *The Correspondence of Henry Crabb Robinson with the Wordsworth Circle (1808–1866)*, ed. Edith J. Morley (Oxford, 1927), I, 410.

46. *Letters of William and Dorothy Wordsworth*, I, 491 n. 1 (17 June 1830).

47. *The Letters of Sir Walter Scott*, [XII] *1831–32*, ed. Sir Herbert Grierson (London, 1937), 1 n. 1.

48. John Gibson Lockhart, *Memoirs of the Life of Sir Walter Scott, Bart.*, 2d ed. (Edinburgh, 1839), X, 53.

49. "Sketch," p. xv; Lockhart, *Memoirs*, X, 55–56. Grierson prints the letter but uses Lockhart's text (XII, 1). Sir Walter died before writing the article.

50. *Memoirs*, X, 53.

51. *Letters of Sir Walter Scott*, XII, 1 n. 1.

52. Quoted in *The Dramatic and Poetical Works of Robert Greene & George Peele* (New York, n.d.), p. [iii].

53. Henry Morley, "Biographical Sketch of Mr. Forster," *Handbook*, p. 57.

54. Ibid., p. 55.

55. Richard Renton, *John Forster and His Friendships* (New York, 1913), p. 197. Forster's works, from his adaptation of Fletcher's *The Elder Brother* (London, 1846) to his edition of Dyce's Shakespeare (London, 1875), are in the Dyce Collection.

56. Geoffrey Keynes, *William Pickering, Publisher* (London, 1924), p. 22.

57. *The Poetical Works of Thomas Parnell* (London, 1833), p. xviii. The poem is dated 1 September 1832. Earlier, he had praised Dyce's scholarship with comparable effusiveness in his edition of *The Poetical Works of John Milton* (London, n.d.), I, xx (the preface is dated 20 November 1831). Dyce dedicated to Mitford his *Remarks on Mr. J. P. Collier's and Mr. C. Knight's Editions of Shakespeare* (London, 1844).

58. *Mitford*, ed. C. M., pp. 225–26, 228–29; see also pp. 75–76, 80–81, 180, 209, 243. Dyce acquired over a hundred volumes from Mitford's collection, as well as five presentation copies.

59. Dedication to *The Works of Beaumont & Fletcher*, I (London, 1843).

60. A. G. L'Estrange, *The Literary Life of the Rev. William Harness* (London, 1871), p. 249. See p. 250 for Harness's criticism of Dyce's Shakespeare.

61. *The Hazlitts, Part the Second* (Edinburgh, 1912), pp. 282–83.

62. *Mitford*, ed. C. M., p. 208. Sharpe made gifts of presentation copies from 1844 to 1868.

63. For Heber see W. Carew Hazlitt, *The Book-Collector* (London, 1904), p. 40. Dyce mentions Heber's Skelton collection in his *Poetical Works of John Skelton* (London, 1843); quoted in the Boston, 1856, edition, I, vii. For Laing see Dyce's *Poetesses*, p. vi; *Skelton*, p. viii; and item 8955. Dyce received two presentation copies from Laing. He also corresponded with Sir Anthony Panizzi (item 1223) and received presentation copies from the American scholars Francis James Child and Richard G. White. Among the glimpses of Dyce afforded by the amazing E. H. Barker (see Dyce's article) is the report that he was forewarned of his father's stroke in 1835 by means of a dream (*Literary Anecdotes and Contemporary Reminiscences* [London, 1852], I, 60).

64. *The Mediaeval Stage* (Oxford, 1903), I, [v]. For an account of Collier's activities see Richard D. Altick, *The Scholar Adventurers*, rev. ed. (New York and London, 1966), pp. 144–60.

65. Henry B. Wheatley, "John Payne Collier and His Works," *Bibliographer* IV (1883), 156.

66. *Robinson on Books*, I, 424.

67. A hitherto unpublished letter (May 1846?) in the Ohio State University Li-

brary. Collier gave Dyce seventeen presentation copies and other gifts with publication dates of 1820 to 1856, some of which contain his spurious material.

68. Alan Lang Strout, "Some Unpublished Letters of John Gibson Lockhart to John Wilson Croker," *N&Q* CLXXXVII (1944), 136: a letter of 29 March 1844.

69. John Forster, *The Life of Charles Dickens,* I (London, 1908), opposite p. 372.

70. *The Letters of Charles Dickens, Volume One 1820–1839,* ed. Madeline House and Graham Storey (Oxford, 1965), p. 639. There is an autograph note from Dickens to Dyce in item 3056. John Kenyon, poet and philanthropist, was a close friend of Crabb Robinson, Landor, and Browning. Ticknor was at Kenyon's for a dinner party on 2 June 1838, and the company included Dyce, H. N. Coleridge, and T. N. Talfourd: *Life, Letters, and Journals of George Ticknor,* ed. George S. Hillard et al. (Boston and New York, 1909), II, 181.

71. *New Letters of Thomas Carlyle,* ed. Alexander Carlyle (New York, 1904), II, 233 (5 December 1865).

72. John Killham, *Tennyson and "The Princess": Reflections of an Age* (University of London, 1958), p. 13. (The work was printed by Dyce's friend Moxon.) William J. Fox gives an account of a dinner in 1846 at which Dyce and Tennyson were together: Richard Garnett, *The Life of W. J. Fox* (London and New York, 1910), pp. 283–84.

73. Used for biographical information by R. H. Super, *Walter Savage Landor: A Biography* (New York, 1954) and noted on pp. 515–16, 518, 525. Louis F. Peck, *A Life of Matthew G. Lewis* (Cambridge, Mass., 1961), pp. 66, 131, is another who uses MS notes Dyce inserted in his books.

74. *The Letters and Private Papers of William Makepeace Thackeray, Volume IV: 1857–1863,* ed. Gordon N. Ray (Cambridge, Mass., 1946), pp. 408, 414.

75. 20 May 1869, 11c.

76. Keynes, *Pickering,* p. 22.

77. *Athenaeum,* No. 308 (1833), 634; *Quarterly Review* XLIX (1833), 29. John Murray had asked Dyce to complete the Shirley, left unfinished at Gifford's death (Roy Benjamin Clark, *William Gifford: Tory Satirist, Critic, and Editor* [New York, 1930], p. 159). Crabb Robinson had vainly recommended Collier for the task (*Robinson on Books,* I, 344).

78. *Historie of the Arrivall of Edward IV. in England,* ed. John Bruce (London, 1838), p. 6 [58]; *The Political Songs of England,* ed. and trans. Thomas Wright (London, 1839), p. [v]; "Sketch," p. xviii; Charles Johnson, "The Camden Society, 1838–1938," *Transactions of the Royal Historical Society* Ser. 4, XXII (London, 1940), 26–27, 31–32.

79. *Encyclopaedia Britannica,* VIII (1910), 743; *Old Ballads from Early Printed Copies,* ed. J. Payne Collier (London, 1840), p. [v]; *Times,* 20 May 1869, 11c.

80. *Memoirs of Edward Alleyn,* ed. J. P. Collier (London, 1841), p. [vii].

81. Humphry Ward, *History of the Athenæum 1824–1925* (London, 1926), p. 135.

82. He was apparently at work on Skelton as early as 1835. See *Charles Lamb: His Life Recorded by His Contemporaries,* ed. Edmund Blunden (London, 1934), p. 256. In the preface Dyce notes that Southey "took a kind interest in the progress of the present edition" (I, vi, n. 1). For a "jest" in connection with the Beaumont and Fletcher see W. C. Hazlitt, *Jests, New and Old* (London, [1887]), p. 89, no. 315.

83. Merriam, *Moxon,* p. 80.

84. CIV (1856), 100, 101.

85. *Recollections of the Table-Talk of Samuel Rogers, First Collected by the Revd. Alexander Dyce,* ed. Morchard Bishop (Lawrence, Kans., 1953), p. viii.

86. "Rogers's Table Talk," 27 February 1856, 10d-e.

87. Ainsworth puns here on the name of David O. Dyce-Sombre, a notorious ec-

centric whose will caused extensive litigation from 1851 to 1856. The *Times* accounts of the legal struggles nowhere mention Dyce.

88. Ellis, *Ainsworth and His Friends,* II, 225.

89. *Robinson on Books,* II, 758, 760.

90. *Men I Have Known,* p. 378. P. W. Clayden in *The Early Life of Samuel Rogers* (London, 1887) blasts Dyce's "usual bald and half-remembered manner" (p. 162). According to Bishop, however, this work was done at the behest of Rogers's executors and attempts to deify the poet (*Recollections,* p. xii).

91. No. 865 (1844), 475.

92. *Robinson on Books,* I, 424–25; see also II, 643, 644.

93. VI (1844), 219; see *Robinson on Books,* II, 643.

94. Samuel A. Tannenbaum, *Shaksperian Scraps and Other Elizabethan Fragments* (New York, 1933), p. 1.

95. Samuel A. Tannenbaum, *Shakspere Forgeries in the Revels Accounts* (New York, 1928), p. 57.

96. *Trilogy: Conversations between Three Friends on the Emendations of Shakespeare's Text* (London, [1874]), I, [v]–vii; III, 92 (P. S.).

97. *Strictures on Mr. Collier's New Edition of Shakespeare, 1858* (London, 1859), pp. [v], vii. See *Robinson on Books,* II, 815, where Dyce is noted as speaking to Robinson of Collier on 31 January 1865.

98. No. 1577 (1858), 73.

99. CV (1859), 45. See Thomas Keightley's violent attack in *N&Q* Ser. 3, I (1862), 85–86.

100. The *Athenæum* was more or less appeased: No. 1889 (1864), 45.

101. Letter to Forster, 4 September 1872, in *New Letters of Thomas Carlyle,* II, 288.

102. See Allibone, *A Critical Dictionary,* I, 536, and the slighting of *Kemps Nine Daies Wonder* in the *Athenæum,* No. 650 (1840), 292.

103. *Letters of William and Dorothy Wordsworth,* III, 1170 (6 June 1843).

104. For such praise see the *Athenæum,* No. 1336 (1853), 672; *Handbook,* p. 16; *Mitford,* ed. C. M., p. 229; *Quarterly Review* CV (1859), 46–47; and "Sketch," pp. xvi, xix–xx.

105. Stanley E. Hyman, *The Armed Vision* (New York, 1948), p. 233.

106. Item 982 in *Catalogue of the Paintings;* the others are items 974–81.

107. The Dyce Collection remains intact with that of Forster at the Victoria and Albert Museum, formerly the South Kensington Museum. The *Catalogue* of his library lists 10,881 items, more than 14,000 volumes in all; the sixty-three manuscripts are mostly transcripts. The library, though "deficient" in topography, according to the *Handbook,* "abounds in the Greek and Latin classics; in the works of the scholars and critics of the sixteenth and seventeenth centuries . . . ; in English poetry and the drama, from the Elizabethan era to the present time; and in Italian poems, plays, and romances" (p. 13). All of the greater ancients, Greek and Latin, are there, along with many obscure ones, and they are usually represented by several editions (p. 15). Like Forster's, the Collection contains a multitude of plays. The "moderns" are also well represented: Austen, the Brownings, W. C. Bryant, Burns, Carlyle, Dickens, Eliot, Goethe (in translation), Rogers, Scott, Smollett, Thackeray, and Wordsworth comprise 166 items. Works on or by Shakespeare total eighty-five items. The catalogue of art works lists 3,347 entries. In addition to such masters as Sir Joshua Reynolds and Rubens, many lesser-known artists are represented by nearly 150 paintings and miniatures, as well as many prints, drawings, rings, and miscellaneous objects. There are numerous portraits of the Kembles, Kean, and, of course, Shakespeare. For relevant extracts from Dyce's will, see *Catalogue of the Printed Books,* I, v–vi; and Forster, "A Word," pp. 745–46 n. 1. For a description of

some choice items in the collections see F. G. Green, "The Dyce and Forster Collection at South Kensington," *Bookworm* III (1890), 273–76.

108. Dyce refers to Thomas F. Robson, who was quite successful some years before in the title role of Planché's *Yellow Dwarf*. See Renton, *Forster,* p. 201.

109. "Sketch," p. xxiii; *Times,* 19 May 1869, 1a.

110. Samuel C. Chew, *Swinburne* (Boston, 1929), p. 186; *The Swinburne Letters,* IV (New Haven, Conn., 1960), ed. Cecil Y. Lang, 151.

EDITORIAL
PRINCIPLES

The "Reminiscences" are comprised of 240 leaves (including material not in Dyce's hand) and an engraved portrait of Mrs. Siddons. Since the MS is not likely to be re-edited soon, I have chosen to err on the side of completeness in transcribing it. Dyce left the work unfinished and for the most part unrevised at his death; in fact, much of it is in the form of hasty scribbling on leaves varying in size and condition. Its present state also manifests considerable shuffling, though many of the articles are in alphabetical order. I have therefore put the MS into what I consider a logical form, while retaining the current enumeration of the leaves. The numbering was apparently done after the MS was disarranged and before it was received by the Museum. I indicate foliation at the head of each article, having found it burdensome and unnecessary always to signify within the text the beginning of a new leaf or a new side. I have further simplified matters by generally omitting recto and verso in stating the order of the leaves. Thus the notation "*ff. 188–205*" at the head of "Mrs. Siddons" should be understood to include all versos that contain writing (not all do). Except where stated otherwise, the leaves of an individual article are printed in their present order, and Dyce's footnotes appear on the same leaves as the text.

Dyce had the habit of writing an alternative word or phrase in or above the line. Where there are two readings, I have silently chosen the better, usually the afterthought. His placing of quotation marks was erratic, and so I have adopted American usage. Many abbreviations like "D'" are also modernized. Elsewhere his punctuation (which is sometimes difficult to decipher) is retained, along with occasional silent corrections consistent with his style. I have let stand his form for quoting long passages, using it also when printing letters that he did not transcribe. Spelling errors have been corrected without comment, both in Dyce's text and in other material included as part of the MS (e.g., the Mitford letters). I have generally made the spelling of proper names conform to that in the *Dictionary of National Biography*. Only in more important contexts, or when I had simply to guess, do I indicate difficult readings.

I have corrected the liberties Dyce took with the text of quotations only when they resulted in egregious errors. Usually he altered just capitalization, spelling, and punctuation, often for the better. He had the habit of his time of not always using ellipsis marks when an omission did not violate the sense; I generally ignored such "errors." For greater accuracy, I have adjusted some of his bibliographical references and have expanded others. This procedure also will aid those who wish to consult the Dyce Collection's *Catalogue,* which indicates the unpublished MS notes he placed in many of the volumes he referred to.

I have excluded insignificant marks and marginalia. Among these are the frequent "collated" next to a transcript; queries about a fact within an article; and such directions to the printer as the signal that ff. 66ᵛ and 67ʳ are to be transposed. I have not indicated where Dyce intended a note but gave none, and I have omitted incomplete cross-references ("See p."). His deletions go without comment except when they occupy space not otherwise accounted for.

Lacunae are indicated thus : [. . .]. Now and then I have ventured a guess as to Dyce's intention; hence most insertions in the text are not gratuitous but represent the filling in of a space left blank. Additions to the text and its notes are in brackets. Dyce's own brackets are preceded by an asterisk (*)—I have far more than he. The titles of the articles are Dyce's, but the headings and subheadings of the chapters are mine. To prevent excessive bracketing, I have not inserted first names or, for obscure literary works, the name of the author, unless clarity demanded it. The index provides all such information. On the other hand, to spare a footnote I have in a few places inserted such brief factual information as dates.

Biographical data seldom appeared necessary for persons of small stature. Pertinent remarks on the more important figures are to be found in my biography of Dyce and in the prefaces to each chapter. Nearly all the dramatis personae are in the *DNB,* and, unless otherwise indicated, all biographical material in the prefaces and notes is from that source.

THE REMINISCENCES

PREFACE
TO CHAPTER ONE

THE TWO "ODDITIES" in the first article were both judges. The amazing James Burnett, Lord Monboddo (1714–99), always sat beneath the bench with the clerks. His *Origin and Progress of Language* (1773–92) claims that the speechlessness of orangutans was accidental (they being members of the human species). Though more charitable to this proto-Darwin on other occasions, Dr. Johnson once remarked, apropos of Rousseau, "Why, Sir, a man who talks nonsense so well, must know that he is talking nonsense. But I am *afraid,* (chuckling and laughing,) Monboddo does *not* know that he is talking nonsense" (30 Sept. 1769). For a very different estimate of Monboddo see Hans Aarsleff, *The Study of Language in England, 1780–1860* (Princeton, N. J., 1967), pp. 36–41. The other justice, Francis Garden, Lord Gardenstone (1721–93), was remembered in Dyce's time for his *Travelling Memorandums* of Europe (1791–95) and for his attachment to the pigs that roamed his house.

James Beattie (1735–1803) counted this singular pair and Thomas Gray among his literary friends. Dyce's reserved praise for *The Minstrel* (1771–74) has been seconded by the majority of critics since, and his notice of Beattie's prose works is equally just. The most ambitious of them, the *Essay on Truth* (1770), was a popular and unsuccessful attempt to explode Hume. The "earlier-deceased brother" of Montagu was James Hay Beattie (1768–90), the successor to his father in the chair of moral philosophy and logic at Marischal College, Aberdeen. The unfortunate Montagu died in 1796.

James Mercer (1734–1804), another friend of Beattie, achieved modest distinction for the *Lyric Poems* from which Dyce selected the "specimens" I have omitted. His biography in the *DNB* ends with the eerie fact that, having nearly suffocated in a chest as a boy, he directed that his heart be pierced with a gold pin before he was buried.

The fragmentary article on Mary Ann Paton (1802–64) relates an incident of about 1810, for she began her public appearances at eight by singing, playing the harp and pianoforte, and reciting Collins's "Ode to the Passions" as well as the poem that so pleased the young Dyce. She went on to enjoy considerable success as a singer.

Regrettably, the letter by Sir David Ochterlony (1758–1825) makes no mention of the campaign beginning at the time of its writing: Sir David was soon to leave Ludhiana and become "The Conqueror of Nepal." One of England's most distinguished soldiers, he served nearly fifty years in India. His "celebrity" indeed justifies the inclusion of a statement contrasting so much with the portrait that the reader is likely to get elsewhere.

For an understanding of the author, the article on Mrs. Smollett is the most significant in this chapter. We find in it the source of the enthusiasm that was to shape Dyce's career. Dyce tells us that her sister (Mrs. Sharp) was the "Miss Renton" of *Humphry Clinker;* yet, according to received opinion, Tobias Smollett had in mind Cecilia Renton, the wife of Alexander Telfer-Smollett. "Miss Renton," then, would be Dyce's "Mrs. Smollett." See *The Letters of Tobias Smollett, M.D.,* ed. Edward S. Noyes (Cambridge, Mass., 1926), p. 228.

Like the encounter with Walter Scott in "Mrs. Smollett," the anecdotes in "Strawberry-Hill" give evidence for Dyce's lifelong knack of crossing paths with luminaries of varying stature, sometimes not by design. After a hundred years, one cannot easily judge the degree of finesse with which he drops names, or the impact of some of those names on the intended audience. However, the occasionally incisive gossip and such rhetoric as the long parenthesis on Twickenham prevent Dyce's chatter from being purely idle. He is entitled, I think, to exemption from the category likewise denied the sensitive Bishop Percy by Dr. Johnson: "A mere antiquarian is a rugged being" (23 April 1778).

The final article, "Cumnor Place," contributes new folklore to an old libel. Lady Amy Dudley died on 8 September 1560. According to the anonymous *Leicester's Commonwealth* (1584)—a source of *Kenilworth*—she was pushed down a staircase by Anthony Forster and Sir Richard Verney, thereby clearing the way for the hopeful Robert Dudley, Earl of Leicester, to marry Elizabeth. That Forster "drove a nail into Lady Dudley's head" is an attractive embellishment, even if apocryphal. The curious will find this motif also in *Judges* IV, 21, *The Canterbury Tales* (I, 2007; III, 769–70), and *The Tempest* (III, ii).

CHAPTER ONE ✤
EARLY YEARS

S C O T L A N D [*ff. 1–2ʳ*]

During the earlier part of my boyhood I lived with some very near relations at Aberdeen,—

> "la bella Aberdona
> Che del gran fiume Dea in riva è posta";[1]—

where I was in the habit of hearing much talk about Lord Monboddo, Lord Gardenstone, Dr. Beattie, and Major Mercer,—the three first being personages then very celebrated in the north, and the fourth a well-known resident at Aberdeen.

I was often in the company of the daughter and grandchildren of Lord Monboddo; but I do not remember to have heard any anecdotes about that truly profound thinker and learned writer, though very frequent allusions were made to his belief that men were originally furnished with tails, and he was very generally described as being "an oddity."[2]

Lord Gardenstone—far inferior in intellect and acquirements to Lord Monboddo—greatly surpassed him as "an oddity": when he ate fish, he always used his fingers instead of a knife and fork; and when he had occasion to travel from Edinburgh to Aberdeen, or vice versa, he invariably went round about by Stirling rather than expose himself to the dangers of crossing the Queen's Ferry.[3]

Dr. Beattie was a good deal over-rated by his fellow-citizens of Aberdeen: but, though his prose essays are now not undeservedly forgotten, his *Minstrel*—at least the First Book of it—will continue to be read with pleasure and to secure for him a respectable place among our minor poets. He was truly unfortunate in his domestic circumstances,—in the insanity of his wife, and in the death of his two beloved sons—his only children. It is, therefore, the less to be wondered at that he was occasionally tempted to have recourse to wine for relief from his afflictions, and that he should have been seen—as Mr. Peter Mylne, the member for Aberdeen, declared that he had seen him—kneeling in a state of intoxication before the Duchess of Gordon. When, during his last illness, he was deprived of the power of speech and motion by repeated fits of paralysis, with an almost total loss of memory and of his mental faculties generally, his niece Mrs. Glennie tried in vain to make him understand that his old friend Sir William Forbes had come from Edinburgh to see him; nor did he recognize Sir William.

There is nothing of poetical fiction in the following passage of *The Minstrel* which expresses his intense dislike of the crowing of the cock: I have heard his intimate acquaintances say that it invariably affected his nerves in a most violent and painful degree;

> "Fell chanticleer, who oft hast reft away
> My fancied good, and brought substantial ill,
> O, to thy cursed scream, discordant still,
> Let harmony aye shut her gentle ear," &c. Book i. st. xxxvi.

Beattie's younger son Montagu (so named after the authoress of *The Essay on Shakespeare*), who died in his eighteenth year, though much inferior in acquirements to his earlier-deceased brother, was endowed with no ordinary talents. The late Dr. Brown [?] [. . .] was one of his youthful companions, and told me that, while they were making together a botanical excursion in Scotland, Montagu "discovered a new species of grass."

The name of Major Mercer is now, I presume, scarcely remembered even at Aberdeen: but he was a highly accomplished gentleman, and composed verses which rose considerably above mediocrity. A collection of his *Lyric Poems* was published by Sylvester Douglas Lord Glenbervie, whose sister was his wife. They reached a third and enlarged edition in 1806. The Memoir prefixed to them informs us that "His eldest daughter was now married to a gentleman of good family and fortune in the county; and for some years both he and Mrs. Mercer and his other daughter passed a considerable part of the year with them"; and that at a later period he was visited "by a severe domestic misfortune, which, notwithstanding the consolations of friendship, philosophy, and religion, clouded the remaining days both of himself and Mrs. Mercer." p[p]. xlii[-iii]. The "gentleman of good family and fortune in the county" was Mr. Gordon of Wardhouse. His wife, Mercer's eldest daughter, a lady of exquisite beauty, several years after her marriage ran away from her husband and children with Colonel Woodford: this was the "severe domestic misfortune which clouded the remaining days of Major and Mrs. Mercer."

As it is more than probable that the readers of the present work have not the slightest acquaintance with Major Mercer's compositions, I adduce the following specimens of his poetry. . . .[4]

[MARY ANN PATON; *f.* 5ʳ]

But no record exists of his having written a farce called *The Schivas*[5] *Carrier,* which, though never printed, was acted at the theatre in Aberdeen. It must have been a difficult matter to form a collection of old pictures in that northern region: he, however, possessed a whole roomful of them—such as they were—in his house in Castle-street; where, as also in a sort of arbour which he had erected in a wood on the banks of the Dee in the neighbourhood of Aberdeen, I have frequently breakfasted with him, and always found him an entertaining and instructive host. The last time I ever saw him was at a small evening-party to which we were invited by a gentleman in Aberdeen to hear the singing of Miss Paton and of her mother, who happened to be on a visit to that city. Miss

Paton was then a little girl, and had not yet appeared in public; but she was wonderfully precocious and confident, and gave full promise of the excellence which she afterwards attained:[6] she concluded her performances by reciting, with a superabundance of gesticulation, Dryden's *Alexander's Feast,* and towards the end of the ode, she scampered round the room, leading on the Macedonian conqueror to fire the palace of the Persian kings. Mrs. Paton was an accomplished musician, with a powerful voice, and sung—somewhat in the manner of Catalani—Italian songs of the highest class.—

SIR DAVID OCHTERLONY [*ff. 9–10*^r]

This very distinguished man was nearly related to my paternal grandmother, Mrs. Dyce—née Miss Ochterlony of Tillifrisky in [. . .],—who took him into her house at Aberdeen during his boyhood, treated him as one of her own children, and equipped him when he sailed for India as a cadet.[7] Though he never returned to Britain, he retained the warmest affection for my grandmother and her daughters; as is proved by the following long letter addressed to my aunt Miss May Dyce,—a letter which, if written by a person of less celebrity, would perhaps be hardly worth printing.

"I have this instant, my dear cousin, received yours of the 12th Oct^r, and very much fear I did not keep my promise of writing to you more fully subsequent to my letter of Nov. 1812. I am a shocking procrastinator, and so readily find excuses that are *satisfactory to myself* for not engaging in so terrific an employment as writing, that I am afraid your expectations of a letter have been disappointed. If I have, however, been by some accident a good boy, and told you how welcome, though undeserved, your letters are to me, and how happy I am to hear of all of you, but more particularly of your esteemed and respected mother, still a line in corroboration will not be unwelcome. If you look at the map, my dear cousin, you will find me at the very John O'Groat's House of Hindostan; and I send my letters to Calcutta without knowing that a ship is under dispatch, and seldom know by what conveyance they have been sent; and as I do not keep copies or memoranda for reference, I would not venture to assert that I have written to you *once,* though you may have received many more proofs that Aberdeen, my beloved old friend your mother, and all those who talk of leading-strings[8] are remembered with regard.

Thank you, my kind cousin, for your purse, which, I suppose, is a kind hint to me to economize and fill it as soon as possible; but I fear, my dear friend, you did not consult mamma in this present, or she would have told you that it was quite needless to send one to an Ochterlony, whose spendthrift dispositions may be traced in the Family Pedigree duly by the sale of estates from the large Barony of that name now Kelly to the last remnants of Tulerfrosky [*sic*] and Pitforthy, which I sincerely wish had been purchased by Alexander;[9] that one or other or both might have belonged to a descendant of the name; as I am sure I shall never be able to call them mine, or even return to *look at* the domains of my ancestors.

When I tell you, my dear cousin, that *long* before you receive this, my eldest daughter will be married to a young officer of cavalry, and that I have marriage-portions to provide for five more, beside the expense of education and their equipment to India, your worthy and beloved mother will not expect I shall have the happiness of personally expressing my sincere and affectionate regard. If I have not hinted at these circumstances before, it is from that natural unwillingness that we feel to disclose our transgressions;[10] though, had I sent them to Scotland, I know no one to whose liberality, kindness, and humanity I would have confided them with greater confidence. They are not the less entitled to my affection for being what they are, and I have only to hope and trust that the sins of the father will not be visited on his offspring.

In the last dispatch of shawls[11] I have taken such precautions that it is next to impossible they should not be received; and I beg you will never *thank me* by saying anything about them more than acknowledging their receipt; for I can assure you, if you think them worthy of acceptance, I shall be the party obliged.

Believe me, my dear cousin, affectionately interested in the welfare of the whole family of Rosebank, and that Alexander's[12] riches are not so much an object of my envy as the happiness he may have enjoyed in the society, and promoting the welfare and comfort, of your mother, whom I have ever regarded with filial affection.

Your sincere friend and affectionate cousin,

Da. Ochterlony.

Ludianeh, 1ˢᵗ Augᵗ 1814."

MRS. SMOLLETT [*f. 13*]

While a boy at Edinburgh, I was occasionally in the company of this old lady, with whom my mother, from her childhood, had been well acquainted. She was the daughter of Mr. Renton and of Lady Susanna Renton (daughter to the Earl of Eglinton), and the widow of Mr. Alexander Telfer-Smollet of Bonhill, nephew to the famous novellist. She was very spritely in conversation; and that she had a love of the higher kind of literature was evident from the books which I have seen her reading,—such as *Percy's Reliques of Ancient English Poetry,* &c &c.[13] But what gave her a sort of notoriety was her fondness for the drama, which had reached such an excess, that (unless prevented by illness or some particular engagement) she went to the play every evening; to the horror of her more rigid presbyterian neighbours, who opined that a woman on the verge of 80 should have long ago renounced such vanities. Regularly, about twenty minutes before the curtain rose, a hackney-coach drew up to her door in Princess Street to convey her to the theatre; whither she was generally accompanied by her daughter; but frequently she went alone. Even when the house was half empty (which was usually the case, if there was not the attraction of some London "star"), Mrs. Smollett might be seen the lonely and attentive occupant of the box next the stage, looking the very picture of a perfect gentlewoman, in her black dress of a rather obsolete fashion, with a large fan in her hand.

To my great delight I was now and then allowed to join her at the theatre; and once when I and several other boys were with her in the stage-box during the performance of Blue-beard, and when, owing to

our position and the crowd upon the stage, we had not a full view of the
paste-board elephant with its rolling eyes,—Mrs. Smollett tapped with
her fan on the edge of the box, and motioned to the Bashaw's Attendants
to stand back a little,—which they immediately did.

Another night I was in her box along with Mr. and Mrs. (afterwards Sir Walter and Lady) Scott, when John Kemble acted Brutus
in *Julius Cæsar*. On the conclusion of the play, he was announced for
Sir Giles Overreach (a part which at that time neither Cooke nor Kemble had been able to render so popular as it was made by Edmund Kean
at a considerably later period); and I distinctly recollect hearing Scott
remark to Mrs. Smollett that "Sir Giles was Richard the Third in lower
life,"—a criticism which, if I mistake not, he has somewhere repeated
in his works.[14]

Mrs. Smollett was on terms of intimacy with the manager of the
theatre Henry Siddons and his charming wife; who mingled very little
in Edinburgh society, most of the northern gentry of those days looking
down with contempt on players. She was also the patroness of Terry,
who was then a favourite member of the Edinburgh company; as is
noticed in the following passage of Lockhart's *Life of Sir W. Scott*,—
the readers of which memoir are doubtless quite in the dark as to who
"old Mrs. Smollett" was: "A perforated cross," writes Scott in a letter
to Terry, speaking of Abbotsford, "the spoils of the old kirk of Gala-
shiels, decorates an advanced door, and looks very well. This little sly
bit of sacrilege has given our spare rooms the name of *the chapel*. I
earnestly invite you to a *pew* there, which you will find as commodious
for the purpose of a nap as you have ever experienced when, under the
guidance of *old Mrs. Smollett*, you were led to St. George's, Edinburgh."[15]

A sister of Mrs. Smollett was alive during my boyhood,—Mrs.
Sharp of Hoddam, who, under her maiden name of Renton, figures in
Smollett's *Humphry Clinker*, where Miss Lydia Melford writes to her
friend Miss Lætitia Willis thus: "I contracted some friendships at
Edinburgh, which is a large and lofty city, full of gay company; and, in
particular, commenced an intimate correspondence with one *Miss
R—t—n,* an amiable young lady of my own age, whose charms seemed

to soften and even to subdue the stubborn heart of my brother Jery; but he no sooner left the place than he relapsed into his former insensibility."[16]

STRAWBERRY-HILL; LORD WALDEGRAVE [*f. 224*]

"Carter, the draughtsman, designed many of the Gothic ornaments for Strawberry-Hill: and he told me that, during his residence there, he was obliged to have all his meals brought to him from Twickenham; Horace Walpole forbidding the servants to supply him with potatoes, or even to allow him to boil his tea-kettle on the kitchen-fire." *Mr. Adair Hawkins.*

In 1816 I passed some time at Strawberry-Hill, accompanying my uncle Sir Neil Campbell thither on a visit to his friend and fellow-soldier Lord Waldegrave, who was a Lieutenant-Colonel in the army, and had been present at the battle of Waterloo. The house was then exactly in the condition in which it had been left by Horace Walpole,—a strange gim-crack half-wooden Gothic castle, crammed with very costly works of art and "curiosities" of every description. A portion of these—the more valuable of the miniatures, &c.—was kept under lock and key, and not exhibited to the sight-seeing strangers who on certain days, to the great inconvenience of the family, were permitted to wander through the apartments. We used to breakfast in the Library, to which the dingy volumes on the open shelves gave rather a gloomy air. After breakfast we sauntered awhile about the grounds; where we were occasionally joined by old Baroness Howe, who, "bearded like the pard," had walked over from Pope's famous residence at Twickenham which she had bought, and who, I believe, was almost the only lady-visitor to Strawberry-Hill, its mistress being under a cloud; for she had lived with her lord before marriage, and their eldest son was unfortunately illegitimate. (In 1812 Baroness Howe married Mr. Wathen Phipps, an oculist of note, who subsequently was raised to the dignity of Sir Wathen Waller Baronet, his pretension to the name of Waller being through his maternal grandmother. This marriage was, on the part of the Baroness, a comparatively innocent freak. But not such was her

barbarously levelling Pope's house to the ground, altering and mutilat-
ing his garden, and erecting at the extremity of his property that house
which is now occupied as two tenements,—a desecration only inferior to
the felling of Shakespeare's mulberry-tree by parson Gastrell at Strat-
ford:[17] the obelisk erected by Pope to his mother's memory, with the
affecting inscription, *"Ah Editha! matrum optuma! mulierum amantis-
sima! vale!"* has been whisked away to Gopsall, Lord Howe's mansion
in Leicestershire—what business has it to be there?) My seat in the
dining-room at Strawberry-Hill was opposite to Sir Joshua's picture
of the three Ladies Waldegrave, which I had never seen before, and
which completely fascinated me.

Lord Waldegrave, who in features bore a considerable resemblance
to the portraits of Horace Walpole, was a gentlemanly soldier-looking
person, of rather reserved manners. He did not pretend to any knowledge of literature: and it was said that he felt greatly disappointed that
no money had been found in the box which, in accordance with the terms
of Horace Walpole's Will, was to be opened when he had "attained the
age of twenty-five years" and was then to "be delivered to him for his
own." The contents of the said box—*Memoires of the last ten years of
the reign of George the Second* and various other manuscripts—were,
during my stay at Strawberry-Hill, unpublished; and it would seem that
they had not yet been submitted to the inspection of any one who could
estimate them properly; for when I ventured to ask Lord Waldegrave
"What they were?" he replied in these very words, "A mass of worth-
less political papers."

CUMNOR PLACE (*from my Diary*) [*f. 231ʳ*]

"Oxford, May 16, 1821. I walked to day with my friend George
Sandby to the village of Cumnor, about three miles from Oxford, now
rendered an object of curiosity by the novel of *Kenilworth*. We saw the
tomb of Antony Foster [*sic*], which is erected close to the altar in the
church, and on which is inscribed a copy of Latin verses (written probably by some erudite Oxonian) in memory of himself and wife, whose
figures are placed above them engraved on brass plates. Nothing remains

of Cumnor Place, which stood very near the church, except the foundations.

We were informed by the clerk that the story of the murder of Lady Dudley was a common subject of conversation among the inhabitants of Cumnor, the circumstances of it having been handed down from father to son. He himself had been told the story by his father-in-law, who died about eight years ago, at the age of eighty-seven, and who had learned the particulars from his grandfather. The tradition is, that Foster, having dispatched the servants to a neighbouring fair, assisted by his confidential attendant, drove a nail into Lady Dudley's head, and left the body lying at the bottom of the stairs, that it might be imagined that her death was occasioned by a fall. Her ladyship's ghost, the clerk further informed us, was very troublesome, paying frequent visits to Cumnor Place, till at last by means of several clergymen, it was laid in a pond at no great distance from the spot of the murder."

1. Fortiguerra's *Ricciardetto,* C. XXIX. 53.

2. It appears to me that his countrymen undervalue Lord Monboddo as a literary character; they seem to consider him less eminent in that respect than his contemporaries Lord Kames, Lord Woodhouselee, and Henry Mackenzie: but surely he excelled them immeasurably in learning, and, unless I am much mistaken, in abilities also.

3. There is a memoir of Lord Gardenstone in Chalmers's *Biog. Dict.* [*The General Biographical Dictionary.* . . . A New Edition, Revised and Enlarged by Alexander Chalmers, XV (London, 1814), s.v. "Francis Garden."]

4. [Mercer's rehabilitation will have to await another editor. Four poems occupy the remainder of f. 2 as well as ff. 3–4: "To a Fountain," "The Invitation," "To the Vine," and "To Folly." All are in the *Lyric Poems.*]

5. Schivas [was] an estate belonging to Mr. Irvine of Drum. [At the top of the leaf, in a hand possibly not Dyce's, is written, "Qy to whom this relates? probably not Major M." I find the following in *Boswell's Life of Johnson,* ed. George B. Hill, rev. L. F. Powell, V, 2d ed. (Oxford, 1964), 496: "Mr. Irvine of Drum was Alexander, 18th Laird of Drum, 1754–1844. '. . . Married a daughter of Forbes of Shivas, niece of Gardenstone's, who directs him . . . ,' says the confidential report made in 1788."]

6. Though her style was never of the purest kind, she undoubtedly ranked as one of the best and most attractive of English singers; and during several years drew a large salary at Covent-Garden Theatre, "which," said Charles Kemble to me, "she very well deserved." But the deterioration of her singing on returning from engagements in America was piteous,—it had become coarse and vulgar.

7. [I cannot locate Tillifrisky.] In *The Gentleman's Magazine* for March 1826 [XCVI, N.S. 19, 275–76], is a Memoir of Sir David, in which though the writer mentions that he "went to India when eighteen," nothing is said about his residence at Aberdeen under the roof of my grandmother.

8. I do not understand the allusion here.

9. My father,—afterwards Lieut. General Dyce. [The Memoir in the *Gentleman's Magazine* states that Sir David's "paternal great-grandfather, Alexander Ochterlony, was Laird of Petforthy, in the county of Angus" (275–76).]

10. His children were all illegitimate.

11. A present to my three aunts of three shawls apiece,—the largest and the most costly that the looms of India could furnish.

12. See above, note [9.]

13. The education of young Scotch ladies, the contemporaries of Mrs. Smollett, was generally very imperfect: few of them could spell tolerably.— The Honourable Mrs. Boyd, an Englishwoman, who died at an advanced age, told me that when in company with her husband (a brother of Lord Errol) she first visited Edinburgh, she went to an evening party at the residence of a person of distinction; that, on entering the room, she seated herself beside two ladies of high fashion, who were in earnest conversation about the annoyance of vermin in a house, and that one of them said to the other, "Yes, Mem, nae dout, boags *[bugs] is bad, but, troth, Mem, I almost think that flechs *[fleas] is waur *[worse]."

14. ["Life of Kemble," *The Miscellaneous Prose Works* (Edinburgh, 1841), I, 814: "That singular character [Sir Giles] is Richard in ordinary life, as extortioner and oppressor, confident in his art and in his audacity. . . ."]

15. Vol. iii. p. 311, first ed. [London and Edinburgh, 1837.]

16. Vol. iii. p. 59, [3d] ed. 1783.

17. But the disfigurement of Pope's villa was begun by Sir William Stanhope, who at the poet's death became by purchase possessor of his estate. [*DNB*, s.v. "Pope, Alexander": "After his death the house was sold to Sir William Stanhope, Lord Chesterfield's brother. In 1807 it came into the possession of the Baroness Howe, daughter of the admiral. She destroyed the house and stubbed up the trees." The destruction of "Pope's famous residence" occurred before Dyce's visit to Strawberry Hill.]

PREFACE
TO CHAPTER TWO

MRS. SMOLLETT'S VICE OF PLAYGOING, which so appalled her Presbyterian neighbors, apparently infected Dyce. The young man who marveled at Colman's pasteboard elephants acquired an addiction to worthier spectacles, and he became associated with scores of actors, playwrights, and others involved with nineteenth-century theater. His account of this tribe will alter no reputations; rather, it is a vademecum displaying the variety of talent and temperament in this crucial period of British stage-history.

I have divided the articles into "Major Characters" (the Kembles and Keans) and "Minor Characters" (the rest). For the first group, Dyce's capsule biographies will suffice; his summary treatment of the others must also suffice, though at least one of them, Dora Jordan, is considerably more than minor. Nearly all the persons in this chapter are in the *DNB,* and further information can be derived from the basic bibliography that I have appended below. It supplements Dyce's notes, the titles in which were generally "standard" in their time. I refer to this bibliography with short titles in my own notes.

This chapter is valuable primarily for its elaboration of Dyce's expert judgment. At the same time, he has left us a great deal of new factual information. Hillebrand (see below) does not record Edmund Kean's drunken fit over his son's body; the American letters of Charles Kean supplement those in Carson; the Kenney epistles show the timeless stratagems employed in backstage finagling; and so on. As Dyce ingenuously says of Raymond's *Memoirs of Elliston,* these essays will be "entertaining to those who are interested in the biography of players."

Dyce's observations began when the precise and artificial "neoclassicism" of Kemble was giving way to Kean's "naturalism." The latter style is exemplified by the amazing boast of Kean's son: "We shall have in one scene [of *King John*] 150 persons on the stage." (Not surprisingly, the younger Kean also derides an attempt by Samuel Phelps to perform *Richard III* as Shakespeare wrote it.) Although fair to both sides, Dyce's appreciation of Kemble is perhaps heightened by his personal antipathy to Edmund Kean ("a low blackguard") and by nostalgia owing to the manifest and progressive theatrical decay in his lifetime.

Much of "John Kemble," chiefly the remarks on Kemble's acting, first appeared in *The Album* IV, no. 8 (April 1825), 253–72, an essay signed "D." Dyce has added several anecdotes, while altering or excising many others. I do not know why he failed to credit his previous article, nor can I explain his evident intention not to indicate that Mrs. Charles Kemble's letters were to William Harness. In the latter case, it should be noted that his over-all intention is unclear.

Some comment is necessary on two of the "minor" articles. The current opinion of Mrs. Piozzi's letters to Conway is that they are a "diabolical fabrication" (James L. Clifford, *Hester Lynch Piozzi (Mrs. Thrale)* [Oxford, 1941], p. 470). Clifford cites Percival Merritt, *The True Story of the So-called Love Letters of Mrs. Piozzi: "In Defense of an Elderly Lady"* (Cambridge, Mass., 1927). And Merritt, in turn, reprints an important review of the *Letters* from the *Athenæum,* no. 1815 (9 Aug. 1862), 169–72, the thesis of which is that the letters were distorted by the anonymous editor. Dyce has overlooked the *Athenæum* review; Merritt does not take into account the article in the *New Monthly Magazine* cited by Dyce; and with that I will let the matter rest.

Finally, "George Raymond" is the fullest piece on this author that I have been able to locate. The *DNB,* that house of many mansions, has seen fit to exclude him, and in ascribing the *Lone Hut* Nicoll wavers between him and one "Richard John Raymond" (*English Drama,* IV, 389, 606). Nicoll does not list *More Plots Than One.*

Baker, Herschel. *John Philip Kemble: The Actor in His Theatre.* Cambridge, Mass., 1942.

Boaden, James. *Memoirs of Mrs. Siddons. Interspersed with Anecdotes of Authors and Actors.* 2d ed. 2 vols. London, 1831.

Carson, William G. B., ed. *Letters of Mr. and Mrs. Charles Kean Relating to Their American Tours.* St. Louis, 1945.

Cole, John William. *The Life and Theatrical Times of Charles Kean.* 2d ed. 2 vols. London, 1859.

Downer, Alan S. "Nature to Advantage Dressed: Eighteenth-Century Acting," *PMLA* LVIII (1943), 1002–37.

———. "Players and Painted Stage: Nineteenth-Century Acting," *PMLA* LXI (1946), 522–76.

Genest, John. *Some Account of the English Stage from the Restoration in 1660 to 1830.* 10 vols. Bath, 1832.

Hillebrand, Harold N. *Edmund Kean.* New York, 1933.

Nicoll, Allardyce. *A History of English Drama 1660–1900.* 2d ed. Vols. III–V [Drama from 1750 to 1900]. Cambridge, 1952–59.

Williamson, Jane. *Charles Kemble, Man of the Theatre.* Lincoln, Neb., 1970. [This book came to my attention too late to be consulted.]

CHAPTER TWO ❖
THE STAGE

PART I: MAJOR CHARACTERS

EDMUND KEAN AND HIS WIFE [*ff. 60–65, 62(b)*]

I saw little of Edmund Kean except in public: but for years I was intimately acquainted with his widow; who, though she had been heart-
lessly thrown off by him to the mercy of strangers, was, in her later
days, surrounded by all the comforts and elegancies of life, supplied to
her by the affectionate son who had been the companion of her poverty.
She was a woman of the kindliest disposition, and possessed of a
superior natural intelligence. I felt for her a most sincere regard; and I
know that it was mutual.— Her maiden name was Mary Chambers: she
was a native of Waterford, and respectably connected. In consequence
of some family embarrassments, she, along with a sister, had taken to
the stage as a means of subsistence; and she was acting (as an amateur,
I believe) at the Gloucester Theatre when she first met with Kean. They
were married at Stroud in 1808, she being somewhat older than her
husband, who then [was] under twenty; and she continued to perform
with him at various places in the provinces, having had a few lessons
in elocution from Mrs. Mason, a sister of Mrs. Siddons. I remember
her telling me that at some country theatre she played Almeria to the
Zara of Mrs. Siddons in Congreve's *Mourning Bride;* and that, after
the performance, Mrs. Siddons said to her, "My dear, you did well
enough,—only you fainted too soon."[1] In spite of her strong good

sense, her acting, I suspect, was but so-so; nor was it likely to have been rendered more attractive by her decided Irish brogue.

She has frequently assured me that she did not know who was her husband's father or who was his mother; and that, to the best of her belief, he himself was equally ignorant on both points.[2]

She was inclined to think that he had a touch of insanity; in proof of which,—besides the marvellous anecdote of "Cooke's toe-bone,"[3]—she would cite his behaviour on the death of their eldest son, Howard, a remarkably beautiful and precocious boy, who died of water on the brain at Dorchester in his fifth year, in Nov.[r] 1813. Kean was deeply attached to Howard: yet when the child was lying a corpse in its little bed, and Mrs. Kean was sitting sadly beside it, he suddenly rushed into the room, frightfully excited,—ran to a cupboard,—took out a bottle of beer,—poured the contents over the dead body,—and then fell down on the floor in a state of utter exhaustion. But this would seem to have been a sort of madness produced by intoxication; for he had just come from a tavern, where, in the hope of forgetting his grief, he had been swallowing quantities of brandy.

The above-mentioned child, Howard, had once or twice appeared on the stage with Kean, in pieces which required an infant performer. Moreover, from hearing his father rehearse at home, he had caught sundry fragments of speeches and songs, with which he used to gratify his admiring parents in private: among other things, he would imitate very amusingly Kean's striking manner of giving a portion of a song in Arnold's opera of *The Devil's Bridge,*—

> "And here stands the murderous wretch—
> But, mark me!—'tis but fancy's sketch."

Now, it happened that for one of his benefits at Exeter, Kean was to enact a "savage" in some melodramatic after-piece; and Howard, carefully tutored for the part, was to exhibit himself as the savage's son.[4] The night arrived, and all promised to go off well. Howard, in his first scene, was, on entering, to cross the stage, and kneel to his father on the opposite side; and, at the proper moment, Mrs. Kean, standing at the wing, launched on the boards her infant savage (*dressed in blue and silver*) with a particular injunction "to walk straight to his papa." Loud applause followed his entrance; whereupon Howard, thinking that it would be meritorious to do "more than was set down for him," instead of crossing the stage, marched boldly up to the foot-lights, and throwing himself into an attitude, spouted out at the top of his tiny voice,—

"Here stands the *mudrous* wretch."

The dismay of the parents, and the surprise of the audience, may be conceived. (After Kean had risen to the height of fame, he played Count Belino in *The Devil's Bridge* at Drurylane Theatre, and was rapturously encored in the song, with a scrap of which poor little Howard had astonished the Exeter audience. The whole runs as follows. . . .[5] Braham—the original Count Belino—was greatly taken by Kean's mode of giving the concluding couplets of these two stanzas, and requested as an especial favour that he would teach him how to give them in the same way. Kean readily consented. Braham came to Clarges Street, received the wished-for lesson, and desired instruction, and went away quite convinced that when he next played Count Belino, he should be able to introduce "the Kean effect." But, no! the Clarges Street lesson proved abortive, and Braham involuntarily relapsed into his old manner of singing the song.)

A bundle of play-bills of the Exeter Theatre, dated Dec' 1812, and Jan', Feb', and March 1813, now lying before me, are not a little curious as showing the variety of characters which Kean used to perform while his talents were as yet confined to the provinces. . . .[6]

Kean was always a sincere admirer of John Kemble's acting, though it differed in style so essentially from his own; and whoever had expressed any contempt for it in Kean's presence with a view of gratifying him would quickly have found out his mistake. Mr. Procter (*Life of Kean*, vol. i. p. 163) notices the "delight" which Kemble and Mrs. Siddons afforded Kean, when he and his wife, in passing through London in the days of their wandering, went to Covent-Garden Theatre to see *Henry the Eighth;* and Mrs. Kean told me that, during the trial scene, she having whispered to her husband some remark, he was so angry at her for distracting his attention from the stage, that "he gave her a punch with his elbow which almost took away her breath."

The first character in which I saw Kean was Richard the Third, when he performed it for about the sixth time in London. The crowd was enormous: the slowly-moving line of carriages on their way to Drurylane Theatre extended from Coventry Street (Piccadilly) to Brydges Street; and, no doubt, the thronging from the city was proportionably great. With all its novelty of conception and unflagging spirit, I must confess that I think Kean's Richard the Third was not unjustly described by John Taylor (the author of *Monsieur Tonson*) as "a pot-house Richard." In it so far from being "every inch a king," he was not even one inch a king. It began with a clap-trap of the worst taste imaginable; for in speaking the passage,—

> "But I, that am not shap'd for sportive tricks,
> I, that am curtail'd of man's *[so Cibber] fair proportion,
> Deform'd, unfinish'd, sent before my time
> Into this breathing world, scarce half made up,
> And that so lamely and unfashionable,
> That *dogs bark at me as I halt by 'em*,"—

Kean most absurdly started, and pointed to the side-scene, as if the dogs were actually barking at him: and it concluded (at least as he originally played it, while his bodily strength was unimpaired) with a melodramatic feat, of prodigious difficulty no doubt, but altogether unworthy of a great tragedian; for after he had fallen on receiving his death-wound, Kean continued to fight, recumbent, round and round the stage, during several minutes, moving himself along by means of his left hand, and thrusting at Richmond with the sword in his right.[7]

Soon after Kean came out as Othello at Drurylane Theatre [5 May 1814], knowing that Mrs. Siddons had been there to see him in that part, he sent his wife to Northcote, to learn from him, if possible, how Mrs. Siddons liked the performance. The answer was, that Mrs. Siddons had made no remarks on it to the painter. This, of course, did not satisfy Kean. "Mary," he said, "you must go back to Northcote, and particularly request that, when Mrs. Siddons next visits him, he will endeavour to ascertain what she thinks of my Othello." Away went his ever-obedient wife on her second mission: and the opinion of the great actress—given, I believe, very reluctantly—was at last obtained, viz.

"that Mr. Kean's Othello was, on the whole, far too violent, but that he delivered the farewell[8] with genuine pathos."— Many years after, when Kean played Othello at Covent-Garden Theatre (Young being the Iago, and Charles Kemble the Cassio), I sat beside Mrs. Charles Kemble; who, though not disposed to recognize much merit in Kean, declared to me that his speaking of the words "And so she did,"[9] was so exactly the voice of nature, that "it made her jump."— I once saw Kean play Othello at Edinburgh to the very graceful and lady-like Desdemona of Mrs. Henry Siddons; whom he said he preferred to all the Desdemonas he had ever acted with; and no doubt she was incomparably superior to his London Desdemonas, Mrs. Bartley, Miss Smithson, &c. (As early as May 1805, Mrs. Henry Siddons was the Desdemona in a rather memorable performance of *Othello* at Convent-Garden Theatre, —memorable, because it did much towards checking the absurd mania of the public for the Young Roscius, and recalling their attention to those excellent full-grown actors whom they had of late so unjustly neglected. On that occasion Othello was played by John Kemble, Iago by Cooke, Cassio by Charles Kemble, and Emilia by Mrs. Litchfield, for whose benefit the performance took place, and at whose particular request John Kemble—whom Betty had for some time completely shelved —was induced to appear as the noble Moor.)

Mr. Procter, in his critique on Kean's Sir Giles Overreach, remarks; "The conclusion was as terrific as anything that has been seen upon the stage. It threw ladies in the side-boxes into hysterics, and Lord Byron himself into a 'convulsion fit.' One veteran actress was so overpowered by the last dying speech of Sir Giles, that she absolutely fainted upon the stage." *Life of Kean,* vol. ii. p. 141. The actress alluded to by Mr. Procter was Mrs. Glover: but is there not some exaggeration in the statement that "she absolutely fainted"? I can, however, myself bear witness to the effect which in the last scene of *A New Way to Pay Old Debts* was produced by Kean on an actress whose experience of the stage exceeded that of Mrs. Glover. It was at the Edinburgh Theatre, when Mrs. Renaud (well known in London for so many years as Mrs. Powell) was playing Lady Allworth to his Sir Giles: I believe she had never seen him act till that night; and I distinctly recollect the fixed gaze with which she regarded him in the tempest of his passion,—the real astonishment expressed in her countenance which time had not yet wholly robbed of its original beauty.[10] (Mrs. Renaud, having been dismissed from Covent-Garden Theatre for refusing the part of Helen Macgregor in *Rob Roy,* accepted an engagement in Edinburgh, where she continued to perform till age and decrepitude had rendered her a painful spectacle, and where she died in such destitution that she had been compelled to part with some of her scanty wardrobe for a subsistence. Too many of the children of Thespis have ended their days in a similar condition,—suddenly exchanging the glare and tinsel of the stage for the gloom and squalor of poverty.)

For the sake of variety Kean appeared in sundry plays, which being comparatively inferior productions, added little or nothing to his reputation. Yet in these he generally contrived to render certain scenes highly effective: so when he acted Oroonoko in Southern's disagreeable and unpoetical drama of that name, he threw into the concluding scene an intense pathos.

A great deal of nonsense has been put in print about Kean as an actor. We have been told that "he was such a genius" and that "acting came to him so naturally," that, beyond getting the words by heart, he scarcely needed to study the characters he performed; and, moreover, that he used to deliver particular passages sometimes in one way, and sometimes in another, according to the impulse of the moment. Now, the very reverse of this was the truth. Before appearing in a new part, he never failed to bestow on it the most careful consideration; and he used to consult his wife, of whose judgment he thought highly, about "the points" he intended "to make" in it. When he and Mrs. Kean were alone together of an evening, he would place the candles on the floor, in imitation of the stage-lights; and after going through a speech, or a portion of a scene, in more ways than one, he would ask, "Well, Mary, which of these do you prefer?" and he was generally guided by her opinion. Having once fully made up his mind about the best mode of giving certain passages, he, as it were, stereotyped them, and never deviated into any other manner.

The greatest actors are seldom free from mannerisms; and Kean had a mannerism which he carried to such excess that it became rather offensive,—a sudden change from measured declamation to rapid and familiar utterance, accompanied with a quick jerking walk over part of the stage. Yet this invariably elicited rapturous applause, the true value of which may be estimated from what Kean told Charles Kemble. "More than once," he said, "I have amused myself by playing tricks with the audience: on coming to one of those passages in which I am accustomed to pass suddenly from slow to rapid speaking, I sometimes, instead of giving the words, have substituted an indistinct 'bow-wow-wow,' and crossed the stage as usual; and—would you believe it?—the usual applause has always followed."[11]

From my general recollection of Kean's acting I should say that he was seldom uniformly excellent throughout any one character; but that in portions of certain plays he was truly admirable; for instance, in the third act of *The Merchant of Venice,* in the third act of *Othello,* and in the last act of *A New Way to Pay Old Debts,* his every tone, his every look, his every gesture, was perfection, his energy tremendous.

Macready—who used to speak of Kean as an actor "with whom none of us can pretend to cope"—thought that one of his finest performances was Sir Edward Mortimer in Colman's *Iron Chest,* as he originally played the part, before it had lost its freshness by repetition, and while his powers were in all their vigour.[12] Indeed, that piece (which ranks among the best of a not good kind) was excellently cast at Drurylane Theatre in those days, when Adam Winterton was acted by Munden, Blanch by Mrs. Orger, Barbara by Mrs. Bland (with her flute-like voice unimpaired by age), Wilford by Wallack, and Samson by Harley.

Though fully conscious of his own extraordinary talents, Kean lived in the dread of being eclipsed by some new tragedian; and he was so alarmed on hearing that David Fisher, who had acquired great fame in Norfolk and Suffolk, was engaged at Drurylane Theatre, that, according to Mrs. Kean's account, it

> "took from him
> His stomach, pleasure, and his golden sleep."

But his fears proved vain; for the clever actor who had charmed the audiences of Beccles, Bungay, &c, was unable to make the slightest sensation in the metropolis.

When Kean joined the Drurylane company, one of its most prominent members was Rae, who, if overpraised by [Richard] Cumberland in his *Memoirs* [London, 1807] (vol. [II,] p[p. 383–84]), is undervalued by Mr. Procter in his *Life of Kean* (vol. i. p.p. 56, 65). Rae was, in fact, a second-rate actor, playing very respectably a variety of characters, and having the advantage of a handsome face and person. During their boyhood he and Kean had been intimate; but, on Kean's coming to Drurylane, Rae, it appears, chose almost to "cut" his old companion, and Kean ever after disliked him mortally. When Rae, afflicted with a painful disease, and in great poverty, was lying on his death-bed, Kean, then in the receipt of a large income, swore by all the gods and goddesses that "he would not give him a single farthing": Mrs. Kean, however, at last prevailed on him to assist in relieving the wants of the dying man:—how far was she then from suspecting that at no very distant time she herself would need the intercession of a friend (Charles Young the tragedian) to force a few pounds from her unworthy husband to furnish her and her son with the necessaries of life!

Drinking had always been Kean's besetting sin; and many were the disagreeable adventures in which it involved him. While "starring" at Norwich, he, one night after the play, got dreadfully drunk, had a battle royal in the street, and fell into the hands of the watchmen. He was to have dined next day with the Bishop of Norwich (Bathurst); but he was so disfigured by the blows he had received on his face, that he was compelled to send an apology to his lordship. A large bump on his nose threatened to be permanent: "No matter, Mary," said Kean to his wife; "I shall now have a Roman nose as well as John Kemble."

Kean's performance of Count Belino in *The Devil's Bridge* has been already noticed ([pp. 56–57]); and on one or two other occasions during his London career—as, for instance, when he played Tom Tug in *The Waterman*—he gave proof to the audience that besides being a great tragedian, he had considerable talents as a singer, who, however unscientific, possessed a sweet voice and a correct ear. But the public were not aware that he could sing sacred music in a style far superior to that of most amateur vocalists: his "Comfort ye my people," accompanied by himself on the piano, was full of feeling and expression.

The reckless course of profligacy which Kean had been pursuing for several years not only injured his health, but—a usual consequence—hardened his heart. He conceived a hatred of his unoffending wife, and showed it by an extravagance of behaviour, which kept her in constant alarm: for instance, once, at their house in the island of Bute, he, in the middle of the night, drew a dagger from under his pillow, and brandished it as if about to stab her: upon which, she softly slid out of bed, and retreated to the room of her sister, Miss Chambers (a clever woman, who always resided with them, and who, it appears, was able at times to exercise some influence, for good, over the mind of her brother-in-law). At last, he entirely separated himself from his wife; nor did she see him again till upwards of seven years had elapsed, when, shortly before the death of Kean, a sort of reconciliation took place between them through the kindly offices of their son, who, with true filial affection, had adhered to the fortunes of his mother during all her trials.— Edmund Kean died May 15, 1833.

[ƒ. 62(b)ʳ]¹³ A Mr. F. W. Hawkins in a *Life of Edmund Kean, 2* vols., 1869, allows that "there were flaws in his private life" [II, 427]. Flaws, quoth 'a? My extreme intimacy with the great actor's wife and son has made me much better acquainted with "his private life" than Mr. F. W. Hawkins can possibly be; and I say decidedly that Edmund Kean was a bad husband and a bad father, in short, a thoroughly bad man, who at last degenerated into a low blackguard.

CHARLES KEAN [ƒƒ. 66–71]

I had scarcely finished writing the preceding article on Edmund Kean, when I read, with the deepest regret, the newspaper-announcement of the death of his son Charles [22 Jan. 1868], with whom, both long before and long after his marriage, I had been on the most intimate terms, till, in evil hour, an unfortunate circumstance—which need not be related here—completely estranged us from each other. I had not seen him for many years, when I suddenly and unexpectedly found myself beside him at the door of the Athenæum: "Mr. Dyce," he said—and the formal "Mr." sounded strange to me—"I start for Australia two days hence [6 July 1863], perhaps never to return; and I now wish to shake hands with you as one of my oldest friends." I heartily wished him all health and happiness; and, after talking together for a few minutes, we parted to meet no more.

Charles Kean made his first appearance on any stage at Drurylane Theatre, which was then under the management of Price, Octr 1, 1827, as Young Norval in Home's tragedy of *Douglas*. His youth—for he was not yet eighteen,—his name, and the notorious fact that he came forward with the view of earning a subsistence for his mother as well as for himself, drew together a very crowded audience on the occasion: but from his want of stage-experience he was unable to produce the effect at which he aimed; and the most that could be said of his inartistic acting was, that it gave a promise of something better,—nor were the newspaper critics willing to allow even *that*. Though he continued at the theatre during the remainder of the season, repeating Norval several times, and playing some other parts, his reception by the audience was always more or less cold, and his treatment by the public press invariably unmerciful.

In 1833, soon after his return from America, Charles Kean having been engaged, with a salary of thirty pounds a week, by Laporte then manager of Covent-Garden Theatre, and having acted there a few nights with indifferent success,—it occurred to Laporte that if Charles and his father were to perform together in the same piece,[14] a novel and a powerful attraction would be produced. He accordingly entered into arrangements for that purpose with the elder Kean, whose health at that time, in consequence of his excesses, was miserably and incurably impaired; and the play selected for their first appearance in conjunction, March 25th, was *Othello*,—the Moor by Edmund Kean, Iago by Charles, and Desdemona by Ellen Tree. That in the third act of the tragedy the elder Kean, utterly exhausted, dropt his head on his son's shoulder, and was carried off the stage (never again to appear before an audience), and that Warde (who had been in readiness to take up the part) acted Othello in the subsequent scenes, are particulars which are related with minute detail in various publications: but a circumstance connected with that night's performance which I have now to add on the authority of Charles Kean himself, has never found its way into print. After the sad catastrophe in the third act he was naturally desirous that

some other actor should be substituted for him in the rest of the tragedy:
"Surely, sir," he said to Bartley the stage-manager, "you do not expect
me to finish Iago, when in all probability my father is at the point of
death." "Sir," replied Bartley, "you are bound by your engagement to
play Iago, and play it out you must." This reply was neither feeling nor
courteous; but Charles Kean had not yet attained a position which ensured him the respect of the officials of the theatre.— Many years
after, when that same Bartley was visited with a succession of domestic
calamities, he received from Charles Kean and his wife the most
friendly and unremitted attentions.

The reputation and success of Charles Kean date from his re-appearance in London, Jan^r 8, 1838, at Drurylane Theatre, then managed
by Bunn, who,—in consequence of the applause he was known to have
met with in the provinces, while labouring hard at his profession,—
engaged him to perform twenty nights at a salary of fifty pounds a
night. He now chose Hamlet for his debut; and how enthusiastically he
was received, and how greatly he was admired during the whole of that
engagement (which was continued for forty-three nights, and would
have been still further extended, but for an engagement[?] which
Charles had accepted at the Edinburgh Theatre) are matters of stage-
history.

Vanity is not unfrequently the innocent weakness of actors, as it is of
poets, painters, and musicians: and Charles Kean was assuredly far
from being the consummate performer which he believed himself to be,
and which, indeed, some obsequious critics latterly endeavoured to per-
suade the public that he really was: though in voice and manner he bore
a strong resemblance to his father, he was only an Edmund Kean shorn
of his beams. Yet, on the other hand, he certainly had much more
dramatic talent than was acknowledged by those—and they were not a
few—who envied his success,—for, bating occasional disappointments,
his career was a highly successful one; and after Macready had retired
from the scene, he had no rival as a tragedian.— But whatever was
thought of Charles Kean as an actor, there could be but one opinion
about him as a man. His conduct in private life—the very reverse of his
father's—was not only irreproachable, but exemplary; and his manners
were those of a polished gentleman.

There are some persons, unless I am mistaken, who will read not without interest what I now subjoin from the mass of letters which were addressed to me at various dates both by Charles Kean and his mother, and which in consequence of the deep regard I felt both for him and (as already mentioned) for her, I have always been unwilling to destroy.

"My dear Sir,
I have had bad, very bad news from Scotland; disappointments of all sorts. I will tell you all on Sunday next, when I hope to see you. Poor Charles is quite desponding: it has made me really melancholy. He has had a good deal of sunshine, and must bear clouds and darkness,—for, I trust, only a little time. I long for Sunday to tell you all my troubles. God bless you!

M*[ary] Kean.

Wednesday 29th
*[London, Park Street]"

"My dear Sir,
I am about to ask a great favour of you; which if you refuse, I shall feel hurt and very much mortified. It is to accept, as a testimony of my son's and my regard and esteem for you, the pictures in my dressing-room,—Hamlet and Macbeth. You will keep them for our sake, and remember, when you look at them, you have two sincere, very sincere friends * * * *

Yours very truly
Mary Kean.

Tuesday Morning,
Decr 7, 1841.
*[London, Park Street]"

"My dear Sir,
Do not forget Sunday: it would not be Sunday to me if you were absent.
I have had a letter from Ireland: things are going on tolerably,—I

mean, theatricals; as to the other affair, he says it will end in nothing; I hope so * * * * * *

Yours very truly,
Mary Kean.

January 19, 1842.
*[London, Park Street]"

"My dear Dyce,

My mother received your letter just as we were starting for Brighton, where we are now all ensconced at Harrison's Hotel. Her hand is so bad, she has requested me to write for her, and to say she hopes next summer to see you at Keydell,[15] being quite sure the air there would benefit you quite as much as Ramsgate. Why don't you run down and see her while we are away? You would find a comfortable room, board and lodging, a hearty welcome; and you might write and criticize there quite as well as in that wretched, lonely, suffocating square. Go and stay a fortnight with her on her return next week. At any rate you are engaged to us next summer.

We find Brighton very dull, for all our people are dead, buried, married, or gone. The Horace Smith family, our last tie, have fled to Leamington.

After this engagement, we proceed to Birmingham, Liverpool, and Dublin; which will occupy us until 1st January. Little or nothing shall we see of our home before next spring!

I think on the whole both my mother and wife are better. (My mother says, that's not true,—she will never be better.) * * * * * *

Your sincere friend
Charles Kean

Brighton, Harrison's Hotel,
6 October, 1844."

"Sheffield,
7 April, 1845.

My dear Dyce,

* * * * * * My address is always *the theatre,* wherever I may be.
* * * * I saw *Richard 3d* at Sadler's Wells * * * Clarence's dream was

an awful bore; the swearing of Queen Margaret very revolting; and the whole play very dull and heavy, more especially the last act, which is not to be compared in effect to Colley Cibber's. The *two* tents were ludicrous, and looked very like two large shower-baths[16] * * * * I only got to London at 5 o'clock, and saw *Richard,* and left the next morning at 8; so I could not call on you * * *

> I remain, Ever Yours,
>
> Charles Kean."

> "Philadelphia,
>
> 30 Dec. 1845

My dear Dyce,

Rehearsals every morning, and acting every night, leave me little time for correspondence; but thinking you are one of those who will most rejoice at my success, I scribble this hasty despatch to let you know that two or three years more of this 'fun,' and I may hang up my hat at Keydell. Pounds, shillings and pence always tell the *true* history of an actor's success. We commenced here on the 1ˢᵗ of September, and have already *sent home* three thousand, five hundred pounds sterling! - - - - - - Of course, with such prospects before us, we shall not dream of returning before the summer of 1847, and it will be a glorious two years. I have not ventured yet to tell my mother of our intended long absence, though I believe she suspects it. I wish you would run down to see her in the summer: there is no one she would be so happy to see.

We return to New York next week to bring out *Richard the Third,* as you saw me do it at Drurylane, and as they never had an exhibition of the kind in this country, we anticipate great results. After that we proceed to the South, viz. Charleston, New Orleans, &c.

I wish you would write to me and tell me how you are going on. Entrust your letter to the care of Mr. Miller, bookseller, in Henrietta St., Covent-garden: he forwards all letters to me from our home, from whence, thank God, we hear nothing but good news.

My dear Dyce, we shall receive, God giving us health, and *no war,* this year alone £10,000, and I believe nearly as much the next. But I dread this Oregon question. The feeling here is so anti-English and so belligerent. My hope of peace is entirely placed in the coolness of *our* Ministry.

I shall be so anxious to hear from you! Remember me very kindly to Harness; and believe me ever

Your sincere friend,
Charles Kean.

P. S. We commenced our *third* engagement here last night to a house crowded to the roof. *Ion* was the play, and *I* acted Adrastus!!

Write a line to my mother: it would be such a comfort to her in her solitude."

"Boston,
31ˢᵗ Oct. 1846

My dear Dyce,

The Mail Steamer leaves this place to-morrow for England, so I will scribble a few lines to let you know that our bark continues to 'sail freely both with wind and stream.' We have added to our list the new five-act play which you may remember I purchased of the author, George Lovell, before I left England. (He wrote *The Provost of Bruges,* and *Love's Sacrifice.*) It is called *The Wife's Secret,* and has made a great hit. Indeed, but one opinion seems to prevail about its merits, and that is unqualified praise. It is a sweet play, and has the great merit of being very short. Wherever we act it, its attraction increases nightly.

We have just concluded here a most brilliant engagement, and last evening on the occasion of my benefit the theatre was choke full, and crowds went away disappointed. *The Merchant of Venice* was the play; and I don't think I ever received so much applause in Shylock before. Our very great attraction is the more wonderful, as the opposition is so powerful. There are no less than three theatres now open in this city - - - - - - The country is now over-run with tragedy heroes - - - - - Mr. Forrest had a very successful fortnight as a welcome home again, and a public dinner at the end of it. I hear that he prays Macready may be some day induced to revisit the States, that he may resent the injuries done to him in London by the 'clique.' He ascribes his failure,[17] and above all the interruptions, hissing, &c to that gentleman's party; and seriously I don't think his 'eminence' could attempt an appearance in N. York again in consequence.

We are re-engaged for another week here, and then return to New York to re-produce *The Wife's Secret;* and, after that, we bring out *King John* in a manner that has never been seen here, or indeed any where else, for Macready was outrageously wrong in his costume. We shall have in one scene 150 persons on the stage. I find the wardrobe and the manager the scenery. Every dress will be from authority, and each authority will be published. We expect it will run some weeks, commencing on the 16ᵗʰ November: it will deserve to do so.

We continue to hear most excellent accounts from Keydell; but have not heard as yet about *your visit there.*

If you can spare me a letter, need I say how much pleasure it will give me? but be sure you pay the postage, or it will never leave England. The Mail leaves on the 1ˢᵗ of every month. Now tell me as much about yourself as I have written on the subject of

Your very sincere friend,

Charles Kean."

"My dear Mr. Dyce,

What would I not give to be back in my solitary retreat in Park-street—you coming every now and then to visit me! I feel here quite out of my element. But the place is very pretty, and will be prettier - - - I am glad you do not come till next year, when you will see it in perfection.

Sir Charles Napier is, I may say, next door to us - - - in short, the neighbourhood is full of naval people - - - How delighted I should be to see you walking up the avenue! I should not know how to make you comfortable enough. Take care of yourself till we meet. God bless you!

Mary Kean.

P. S. Charles says your book is a treasure. He talks of you continually. *[Not dated. Written from Keydell.]"

"My dear Dyce,

Your letter,[18] directed to Leeds, has followed me here, and I hasten to reply to its contents.

In the first place, I have an engagement at the Haymarket commencing about the same time that this Benefit is proposed; and therefore to direct the public attention to the *one* night by such increased attraction would be to the prejudice of *the rest*. Such an arrangement is never to the advantage of an engagement, but especially prejudicial when advertized at its *commencement;* and were I, therefore, ever disposed to comply, it would assuredly not be until *I had finished all previous arrangements*.

Independent of this, however, I have private motives which induce me at once to decline the proposal altogether: but that the Committee may be assured that the object of this Benefit has my best wishes, I enclose you a cheque for ten pounds, which I beg you will hand to them in my name.

I remain, My dear Dyce,
Ever Yours sincerely,
Charles Kean.

Manchester, 7ᵗʰ May,
  1848."

("Dear Mr. Dyce,

I fear your old friend Mrs. Kean is breaking fast. She has been very ill, and *now lies dangerously ill:* indeed, my dear sir, I do not think there is a chance of her ultimate recovery; and I have thought it right, in the midst of my troubles, to let you know this much, lest you should be shocked by some sudden news.

Yours faithfully
Ellen Kean.

*[Not dated. Written from Keydell.]")

"My dear Dyce,

I have been very anxious to see you for some time past. I hope you are not laid up again.

We go down to Keydell every Saturday since my poor mother's illness, returning on the Sunday evening. She cannot now, poor soul, last more than three weeks. Yesterday she received with me the holy sacrament. Her mind was perfectly clear, and she thoroughly understood what was going on. She has not tasted food for three weeks.

That I should lose her now is in the natural course of events; but, my dear friend, it is a hard struggle. We have been so together all our lives, so inseparably connected one with the other, and under such peculiar circumstances, that it is more difficult to bow to the will of God with that resignation which I feel I ought, than it would be under ordinary circumstances.

My heart is so full I can write no more. Come and see me, and I will tell you all.

Ever Yours,
Charles Kean.

Athenæum Club,
  11 March, 1849."

"My dear Dyce,
My beloved mother expired calmly and quietly at ½ past one o'clock to-day.

Your afflicted friend
C. Kean.

Keydell, near Horndean, Hants,
  Friday 30ᵗʰ March, 1849."

JOHN KEMBLE [*ff. 73–85ʳ, 85Aʳ*]

When we see upon the stage the representatives of kings and heroes, we generally feel that they do not fully realize, in their personal appearance, our ideas of the illustrious dead; but Kemble, in this respect, completely satisfied the demands of the most extravagant imagination. His face and form were such as poetry and sculpture have attributed to the chiefs of the heroic times. If his features, from being so strongly marked, were seen to less advantage in a private room, they were, on that account, more admirably adapted to the stage: the prevailing expression of his countenance was one of gentle melancholy, and his full dark eyes were radiant with a dreamy brightness. His dignity of man-

ner was natural, not assumed; and in his lofty carriage and his measured step you might read his consciousness of the physical advantages
he possessed;

> "Like a Titan stepped he,
> Proud of his divinity."

If Mrs. Siddons was worthy of being painted as the Tragic Muse,
Kemble might as fitly have sat to Sir Joshua as the male personifica-
tion of Tragedy. Though his voice was not powerful, yet so exquisitely
did he manage it, and so distinct was his enunciation in passages of the
most rapid delivery, that scarce one word of what he uttered was lost
by that portion of the audience who were farthest from the stage, even
in the overgrown theatres of the metropolis.[19]

Coriolanus was undoubtedly his greatest performance. It was a piece
of acting, of which (as of his sister's Lady Macbeth or Queen Katharine) the theatres cannot now present a shadow; and we believe that
those who have seen it derive a pleasure from reading that tragedy
which the most ardent admirer of Shakespeare, who has never witnessed it, can hardly feel. How striking was his first coming on the
stage! We have it before us at this moment: we see the Roman mob, in
all their dirt and raggedness, headed by little Simmons,—now they
are running out to kill Marcius, but perceiving him approach, they retreat in terror, and huddling together like sheep, squeeze themselves up
to the opposite wing,—and now, after a pause, in rushes Kemble, wrapt
in the graceful foldings of his scarlet robe, an antique Roman from top
to toe! During the first three acts, his proud patrician bearing con-
trasted admirably with the vulgar insolence of the rabble, who kept
thronging about him, and then retiring, like the waves of the sea dash-
ing about some stately rock. To enumerate all the *points* he made,
would require whole pages, though, no doubt, he thought less of them
than of the general effect of the performance. His appearance, as he
stood, covered by a black mantle, beneath the statue of Mars in the
dwelling of Aufidius, has been well preserved by the friendly pencil
of Lawrence. How touching was the scene, where he sat, with heaving
breast and averted face, listening to the supplications of his wife and

mother, till nature's holiest feelings overcame the thirst for vengeance on his ungrateful country! His acting grew more and more excellent towards the conclusion of the play. When Aufidius said to him, "You may depart in safety," with what indignation he drew back his lofty form, and slowly surveyed him from head to foot,—what scorn flashed from his eye and quivered on his lip, ere he deigned an answer to the insult! When the Volscian leader called him "boy of tears," the manner in which he rushed up to him and spoke the following lines, while the veins of his neck seemed bursting with the effort,—

> "If you have writ your annals true, 'tis there,
> That, like an eagle in a dove-cote, I
> Flutter'd your Volsces in Corioli;
> Alone I did it—boy!"—

and, above all, the checking of his vehemence at the word *boy,* and the triumphant sneer with which he uttered it, composed the *ne plus ultra* of histrionic art.

Brutus is a Roman of a very different stamp from Coriolanus, and the part does not afford such scope to the talents of an actor; but no one could have made more of it than Kemble did. In the orchard-scene he spoke the short soliloquies like a man whose mind was really busied about "the acting of a dreadful thing"; and his tenderness to Portia never went beyond what we may suppose the stoic patriot would have allowed himself to show. The truly classical imagination of Akenside could not have presented to him, when he composed the following passage, a grander figure and attitude than Kemble displayed, as he held his dagger over the body of him "who bled for justice' sake";

> "When Brutus rose
> Refulgent from the stroke of Cæsar's fate,
> Amid the crowd of patriots, and his arm
> Aloft extending like eternal Jove
> When guilt brings down the thunder, call'd aloud
> On Tully's name, and shook his crimson steel,
> And bade the father of his country hail,
> For, lo! the tyrant prostrate in the dust,
> And Rome again is free."[20]

In the famous tent-scene we thought he expressed his contempt of Cassius with too much bitterness; and his rising from his seat, and walking carefully on tiptoe, to take the lute from the sleeping Lucius, appeared to us to be a little out of character. "Talk no more of her" (Portia), he spoke in the true tones of that sorrow which lies too deep for tears, and the words fell upon the heart with an icy coldness.

When I saw Kemble in Hamlet, so many years had passed over him, that he wore an aspect too aged for the royal Dane: but his accomplished mind remained unchanged, and he exhibited in his own unequalled style the *soul* of Hamlet, and all the irresolution of the melancholy, meditative prince. As Boaden has given a detailed account of this performance,[21] I shall merely observe that Kemble was the only actor I have ever seen, who kept up the high-bred dignity of the part from beginning to end.

Wolsey never had so good a representative as Kemble. His dressing of the part was rich in pictorial beauty. He did not appear, as Wolsey has appeared of late, an old man with sallow face, creeping along with stealthy tottering steps; but he was indeed the aspiring Cardinal, with florid cheeks and arrogant demeanor, who dined each day from plate of gold, and to whom, when he washed his hands, a nobleman of England held the towel. His agitation on perusing the fatal papers—the sinking of his soul under the calamity—his lamentation over his vanished greatness—the rising of his proud spirit at the taunts of the courtiers, and the rage and sarcasm of his replies—were all most true to nature. His look and attitude, as he exclaimed,

> "My robe and my integrity to heaven
> Are all I now can call mine own,"

while his eyes were cast upwards, his left hand slightly raising his crimson gown, and his right arm extended above his head, composed a truly beautiful picture. In the banquet scene his beckoning to Campeius to take precedence of him, and then brushing out before that grave personage who was about to obey the sign, was, perhaps, a stage-trick unworthy of Kemble; as was also the *whit!* he uttered, and his imitation of snuffing a candle with his fingers at the words

"This candle burns not clear : 'tis I must snuff it ;
Then out it goes !"

Kemble's Macbeth was equal in finish to his best pieces of acting. In the murder scene he was more frozen with terror, more bewildered, and less noisy, than his successors in the part: "Wake Duncan with thy knocking! [I] would thou couldst!" he uttered in the piercing accents of despair. At the banquet, on the vanishing of the Ghost, he exclaimed, "So, being gone, I am a man again," like one who had really been delivered suddenly from some intolerable burden that weighed down his very soul. In the recitation of "tomorrow and tomorrow," &c his voice sounded like a soft and mournful music; and his horror on hearing that Birnam wood was on its way to Dunsinane—the vain effort of his terror-palsied arm to draw his sword & stab the bearer of such dreadful tidings—and his tremulous tones when he recovered the use of speech —all showed the consummate artist.[22]

Though Young's *Revenge* was written when nature was banished from the stage, and, as a whole, is stiff and bombastic, it contains one or two passages of great power, and some situations eminently striking. In Zanga there is something grand, which Kemble rendered absolutely sublime: he maintained excellently the solemn mysteriousness of the part, from his first appearance under the archway in the glare of the lightning, till he trampled on the body of his swooning master. Young's turgid lines enabled him to display that elaborate declamation in which he was unrivalled, and which he now and then relieved by some exquisite touch of nature the more admired because unlooked for. "Know, then, twas I!" [V, ii] was one of his most successful bursts: it was not very loud, but given with an energy indescribable: well might Alonzo fall senseless to the ground, for, as Kemble spoke it, the effect was blasting,—each word was like a poisoned arrow winged with certain death! His minute attention to propriety of costume was seen in this play: when he wrote on his tablets [II, i], instead of holding the pencil between his fingers and thumb, he clutched it in his hand in the oriental style.

To those who have never seen Kemble as Penruddock in *The W[heel] of [Fortune]*, Cumberland's [. . .][23] sketch can convey no idea of the picture into which the actor worked it up. To point out the excellencies of this performance, it would be necessary to mention particularly every scene. His remark to Henry W[oodville,] "You bear a strong resemblance to your mother" [IV, ii], has been often & justly praised, but I thought it less affecting than his reply to Mrs. Woodville, "You see, madam, what a philosopher I am" [V], during which he burst into tears, & buried his face in his handkerchief. . . .[24]

In his zeal to form a collection of old English plays, Kemble gave prices which were then unprecedented, but which (I too well know) were trifling in comparison of the prices given for copies of the same plays by more recent collectors. This excited an ill-natured attack from Gifford in the following passage of *The Baviad;*

> "Others, like Kemble, on black-letter pore,
> And what they do not understand, adore;
> Buy at vast sums the *trash* of ancient days,
> And draw on prodigality for praise.
> These, when some lucky hit, or lucky price,
> Has bless'd them with *'The Boke of gode advice,'*
> For *ekes* and *algates* only deign to seek,
> And live upon a *whilome* for a week."

"Note. Others, like Kemble, &c. Though no great catalogue-hunter, I love to look into such marked ones as fall in my way. That of poor Dodd's books amused me not a little. It exhibited many instances of black-letter mania; and, what is more to my purpose, a transfer of much 'trash of ancient days' to the fortunate Mr. Kemble. For example,—

	£.	s.	d.
First Part of the tragicall Raigne of Selimus Emperour of the Turks . . .	1	11	6
Jacob and Esau, a Mery and Whittie Comedie	3	5	0
Look About You, a comedie . .	5	7	6
The tragedie of Nero, Rome's Greatest Tyraunte, &c &c . . .	1	4	0

How are we ruined!"[25]

The reader will naturally think that such satire comes with a bad grace from a man who, in illustrating the drama of the reigns of Elizabeth and James, has himself not unfrequently had recourse to "the trash of ancient days." Now, the truth is, that when Gifford wrote *The Baviad* he had not yet taken to the study of our early play-wrights; and that he afterwards regretted this attack on Kemble is beyond a doubt. When he reprinted *The [Baviad]*²⁶ in 1811 [8th ed.], he was careful to omit the note just quoted, in [. . .] "the trash of ancient days" might not be understood as [?] containing any allusion to dramatic pieces: and in an "Advertisement" prefixed to the second edition of Massinger's *Works,* 1813, speaking of the above lines of *The Baviad,* he is disingenuous enough to say,—"That I ridiculed the purchase of old plays, is a mere conceit of the Edinburgh Reviewers - - - - - I have even specified the object of my satire, the *'Boke of gode advice,'*²⁷ which happens not to be a play" [I, iv, v] :—very true, Mr. Gifford,—it is a [. . .]; but *Selimus,* and *Look About You,* and *Nero* "happen to be plays," and moreover, are perhaps hardly such trash as you pronounce them to be!

Soon after quitting the stage, Kemble sold his collection of dramas to the late Duke of Devonshire. Previous to their removal to Devonshire House, they were lying on the floor of Mess⁽ˢ⁾ Payne and Foss's shop in Pall-Mall, when several persons, including Joe Kelly (the ex-singer and composer) came in to look at them.²⁸ A gentleman, examining a volume which consisted partly of very old and partly of very modern pieces, remarked that he considered it injudicious to bind up together plays of such different dates. "O," cried Irish Joe, "what does it matter? Fifty years hence, the one will be as ould as the other."

That Kemble was an excellent actor is certain. That he was very far from excellent as a writer is equally certain, though his education (unlike that of players in general) had been what is called classical, and he possessed a knowledge of Latinity which had some pretensions to critical exactness. "To those," says Boaden, "who remember Mr. Kemble's latter diffidence as an author, it may excite surprise that, on his just attaining manhood, he should venture before an audience a tragedy of his own composition. On the 29ᵗʰ of December, this year *[1778], he brought out his tragedy of Belisarius for his own benefit *[at Hull]. As I have never seen a line of this play, I cannot speak to its merits: it appears to have been well received, to have been thought creditable to his talents, and to have acquired for him both money and reputation" [*Life of Kemble*, I, 22]. *Belisarius* was never printed: but many years ago I read it in a manuscript copy (then belonging to Mr. J. P. Collier) which had been sent in to the licenser: and I could not but wonder that so poor an attempt at dramatic composition should have met with anything like success even at a country theatre, and with an audience predisposed in favour of the author.[29]

Towards the end of 1816, when it was generally understood that Kemble would ere long take leave of the public, I wrote to him from Exeter College, Oxford, requesting to be informed of the exact time of his final performance, that I might make such arrangements as would enable me to be present on that occasion. He replied to me as follows:

"Sir,

If I knew on what day I am to appear on the stage for the last time, it would give me great pleasure to acquaint you with it. I believe nothing is at present determined about it: when it is fixed, the public advertisements will inform the town of it, as soon as I shall have heard of it myself.

With many thanks for your obliging note, I am, Sir,

Your obedient servant,

J. P. Kemble.

Saturday.

P.S. Your letter was left, as letters to me sometimes are, at the Theatre, and was not sent till just now."

For[30] his last performance, June 23ᵈ, 1817, he selected the part of Coriolanus. Wishing to be as near the stage as possible on that night, I stationed myself, a little before one o'clock P.M., at the pit-door of Covent-Garden Theatre, to wait patiently till it should be opened at half-past six. About a dozen persons were already assembled there; and before the time of admittance arrived, I was wedged in among a crowd more numerous by some hundreds than the pit could hold. When the door opened, the rush along the lobby was fearful: but I attained my object,

—a place next to the orchestra; and just as I was sitting down, I saw several gentlemen—among whom was my friend Harness with young Dallas in his arms—drop from the lower tier of boxes into the pit, they having bribed the attendants to let them in. Before the commencement of the overture, Talma, accompanied by Horace Twiss, entered the orchestra, where places were reserved for some of Kemble's particular friends; and I, being quite close to them, heard Talma say in very good English, as he surveyed the densely packed house, "Ah, he well deserves such an audience!" Deafening and prolonged applause greeted the first appearance of Kemble; who probably never played Coriolanus more exquisitely than he did that night: it was, indeed, a performance of which—now that tragic acting is a lost art—the play-goers of the present day cannot form a conception.

[. . .] were[31] eagerly applied by the spectators to the representative of Coriolanus, and the more vehemently applauded because they [had] not forgotten that certain partisans of Kean, with disgusting want of feeling and of good taste, had gone so far as to hiss Kemble both in Richard the Third and in Sir Giles Overreach.

In the closing scene Kemble—who more recently when acting Coriolanus had been caught in the arms of the conspirators after they had stabbed him—fell at full length on the boards, thinking it now unnecessary to husband his strength.

On the conclusion of the play there was a loud cry of "No farewell from Kemble!" and a satin scroll on a roller containing, as I understood, a written request that he would sometimes gratify his admirers by re-appearing in some of his favourite characters, was handed to Talma, who threw it from the orchestra on the stage. Kemble, however, had wisely made up his mind to act no more: and, under the conviction, as he expressed it, that "some little parting word would be expected from him on that occasion," he came forward, and took leave of the public in a short, simple, and touching prose-address. While he spoke, his agitation was extreme: he kept nervously twisting his pocket-handkerchief round and round his fingers, and now and then used it, with a trembling hand, to wipe away the tears that trickled down his cheeks. The most enthusiastic cheers followed him, as with profound obeisances and faltering steps, he retired from the view of the audience; who, in compliment to him, unanimously determined that they would have no afterpiece that night: in consequence of which, though the curtain rose and discovered Mrs. Gibbs and Miss Carew ready to begin *The Portrait of Cervantes,* it descended again almost immediately, and before they had uttered a single word.

Kemble was generally most attentive to the business of the scene, and whether the spectators were few or numerous, went through his part to the utmost of his ability. Not so, however, on a particular occasion at Limerick, while he was acting Zanga in *The Revenge:* the house was all but empty—the very scanty audience vulgar, riotous, and evidently incapable of comprehending the play; and Kemble was so disgusted with their rudeness and their ignorance, that he turned the conclusion of the tragedy into a sheer burlesque, giving the prostrate Alonzo a kick, and bidding him "get up!" This I was told by Lady Becher (Miss O'Neill), the Leonora of that night. (She was then a provincial actress, never dreaming of the laurels which awaited her in Covent-Garden.)

A Miss Douglas—a woman neither young nor handsome, but a tolerable actress, who had performed in London and elsewhere—happened to belong to the Edinburgh company while Kemble was playing an engagement there; and being a person of great eccentricity (or, in plain terms, *maddish*), she chose to fall violently in love with him, not concealing her romantic passion either from him or from others. To all this tenderness he showed himself utterly insensible, not taking the slightest notice of it by word or look; till one evening, just before the curtain rose, when he was in the green-room dressed for Coriolanus, and when she (his Volumnia), after vainly endeavouring to attract his attention, had declared aloud that "she had rather be treated with indifference by Mr. Kemble than courted by others"—he, standing before the mirror, and arranging the folds of his scarlet robe, glanced at her over his shoulder, and said in a careless tone, "You must be very drunk indeed."

About [. . .] years before his retirement, Kemble was announced at the bottom of the bills for the character of Falstaff in *The First Part of King Henry IV.;* and he certainly rehearsed it (perhaps several times), for I know that during one rehearsal, while he was going through a scene with unusual sluggishness, he said to Conway, who was cast for the Prince, "Mr. Conway, you understand, of course, that I intend to be much more jocose in the evening than I am at present." But he never appeared as the fat knight; nor were the public ever informed why he did not. He alleged, indeed, to a friend of mine, that his chief reason for not attempting the character was his dread of the "stuffing" which was necessary to make up the figure of Sir John: "I was in terror," he said, "of dropping down on the stage under the weight of the wicker and the padding." There might have been some truth in this, for he was very asthmatic: but I apprehend that he was deterred more by the intellectual than by the corporeal requisites of Falstaff, and that he was afraid of failing in a part which so few actors have been able to master. Yet Kemble, with his grand tragic face and form, undoubtedly possessed very considerable comic powers; an evidence of which was his ludicrous assumption of idiotcy, as Don Leon, in the earlier scenes of Fletcher's *Rule a Wife and Have a Wife*.

Kemble was always courteous towards debutants; and if he saw anything faulty in their performances, he would notice it to them in the most delicate manner. He not unfrequently, however, found them impracticable. When Sinclair the singer (who had served as a common soldier in Scotland) first came out at Covent-Garden Theatre and with great success, he was intolerably awkward in his gestures and gait. Hence Kemble took occasion to say to him; "It appears to me, Sinclair, that you are sometimes at a loss to know what to do with your arms; which, indeed, was the case with myself when a young actor: now, I got over that difficulty by taking lessons in stage-deportment from Le Picq; and I would particularly recommend you to put yourself under the tuition of a ballet-master." "O," replied Sinclair in his semi-Scottish dialect, "I'm much obleeged to you, Mr. Kemble, for the advice; but I raly can't see any reason why I should follow it; for I'm encored every night, and my freends assure me that I'm verra graceful."

Chiefly owing to an asth[matic] complaint, Kemble's acting of a particular part would be very different at one time from what it would be at another. I once was at Covent-Garden Theatre when he acted Penruddock in Cumberland's *Wheel of Fortune* with a tameness at which Mrs. Powell and Abbot[32] (Mrs. [. . .]) were scarcely able to conceal their surprise: but, long after that date, I have seen him play

Penruddock in his finest style. So too, from the same cause, he would sometimes be utterly spiritless in the earlier scenes of a tragedy and all animation in the later ones. I remember Macready's saying to me, "The last time I saw Kemble in Macbeth, he seemed, during the first three acts, to be half asleep; but in the fourth and fifth acts he *did* blaze out indeed."

When Kemble and Mrs. Siddons, after quitting the stage, were staying for a while at Paris, some members of the T[héâtre] Fran[çais] (not including Talma), paid them a visit at their lodgings, and made it a particular request to be favoured with a specimen of English acting. Accordingly, Kemble and Mrs. Siddons recited a short scene; which was greatly applauded by the foreign artists, though they ventured to mention, in the politest manner possible, what appeared to them objectionable,—"*Vous parlez trop vite.*" Whereupon (as I was told by Thomas Campbell, who was present), Kemble turned to his sister, and said with a smile, "Well, Sally, this is the first time that *we* were ever blamed for too-fast speaking!"

[*f. 85A^r*][33] The following anecdote rests on the authority of Kemble's nephew, the late Horace Twiss, who related it to me as a fact.— From some passage or lobby in the old Drurylane Theatre it was possible to get a partial view of the interior of Kemble's dressing-room by looking through some sort of aperture; which, during the run of *Pizarro,* used to be nightly besieged by ladies of a certain description, whose constant cry was, "Do, Kemble, like a good fellow, come a little forward when you have dressed yourself, and let us have a sight of you." But Kemble continued to turn a deaf ear to their importunities; with an account of which he regularly amused his wife on returning from the theatre. One night, however, he came home seemingly in rather low spirits. "What's the matter?" asked Mrs. Kemble: "has anything happened? or have the ladies ceased their flattering requests to see you?"— "No, P[riscilla]," he replied, "no; not exactly: but there has been a-a-a slight mistake."— "How so?"— "Why, to-night, after dressing myself, I was foolish enough to comply with their wishes by coming a little forward before leaving the room; when immediately I heard a shrill voice exclaim in a tone of disappointment, "Law, girls, we're all wrong! it isn't Charles! *it's only the old 'un!*"

[*f. 75*]³⁴ Of Kemble's conviviality we have received the following anecdote from unquestionable authority. A medical gentleman was asked to dine at the house of a friend in order to meet the tragic hero, but was unable to accept the invitation. He, however, called on the entertainer, about 12 o'clock in the forenoon of the day after the dinner, *and found the party still at table.* "You have lost much," said the host to him, "by being absent, for Mr. K., last night, favoured us with Collins's *Ode on the Passions.*" Our friend, of course, expressed his regret. "Nay," said K., "you sha'nt lose it, for I'll speak it again"; &, accordingly, having first washed his face to refresh himself, he once more recited the whole ode with admirable spirit.

MRS. CHARLES KEMBLE (MISS DE CAMP) [*ff. 72ʳ, 90–95*]

In the society of this very intelligent lady, and most accomplished actress, who was equally at home in ballet, opera, comedy, and farce, I have passed many pleasant hours.

When only six years old, she was engaged at the Opera-house, Haymarket, to play Cupid and other fairy personages in ballets; and I have heard her mention, that a grand ballet on the story of Bacchus and Ariadne having been brought out, in which she figured as the little god of love, the chief dancer of the day who represented Bacchus *wore his hair in full curl, pomatumed and powdered, and surmounted by a wreath of grapes and vine-leaves.*— Her Irene in Colman's *Blue Beard,* a part she acted originally to the Fatima of Mrs. Crouch, and many years after to the Fatima of Miss Stephens, enabled her to display to advantage both her melodramatic and her vocal powers; and few things were more amusing than her assumption of consequence as the sister-in-law of the bashaw,—for instance, in the illuminated garden-scene, as she passed by the kneeling slaves, her pushing down their heads to increase their prostration. In another melodrama by Colman, *The Forty Thieves,* her performance of Morgiana, ending with the tambourine-dance and the stabbing of the robber-chief, fascinated the town for many a night. But her melodramatic *chef-d['oeuvre]* was Julio in *Deaf and Dumb,* a five-act drama, taken from the French of Bouilly by Holcroft, in which, without the aid of language, she carried mimetic gesture and expression of countenance to the utmost perfection: "The novelty of the task imposed upon Miss De Camp," says Holcroft in his Preface, "and the admirable manner in which she executed it, would make it inexcusable, not individually to mention her merits."[35]— Her Lucy in Gay's *Beggar's Opera* was a very striking picture of that shrewish damsel.— Of Miss Sterling in Colman and Garrick's *Clandestine Marriage,* she made, I believe, much more than any actress ever did: the scene [I, ii] in which she tries to mortify her sister Fanny by displaying her jewels and by describing the grandeur that awaits her when she marries Sir John Melvil invariably drew down the heartiest applause.— To conclude this imperfect list of her performances with the notice of a very important character,—I have no hesitation in saying that her Beatrice in Shakespeare's *Much Ado About Nothing* was, beyond all comparison, the best which the stage could boast of in my recollection.

[*f 93ʳ/95ʳ*][36] "Weybridge
Sept[r] 5th, 1825

I wish you had learnt to write, and I to read before we had both become grey headed. I need not then have requir'd the combin'd assistance of all my family to enable me to decypher your Epistle; we have but lamely made it out amongst us; but I *gather,* that you are well and happy, and I assure you, we were all truly glad to hear it. Your mind must indeed have been in a pitiable state of disorganization had it been otherwise, surrounded as you are by every thing which can charm the eye, and captivate the understanding. Is there a house in England (or elsewhere) in which so rare a combination of beauty, taste and intellect, is to be met with?[37] but shall you not henceforward, deem all ordinary society, stale, flat and unprofitable? and what is to become of us?— I heard of your calling in Soho Square,[38] where you no doubt were inform'd of my residence here and Charles's departure for Germany—he wish'd very much that I had accompanied him, and indeed seeing so little of him as I do thro' the Winter the temptation was a strong one— but with my boys and girls growing up into men and women, I thought it neither prudent nor affectionate to absent myself; so here have we

been rusticating, and I hope getting in a stock of health to carry us thro'
the ensuing season. I am glad you like Miss Mitford's play.[39] I hope
it possesses *movement*. The subject is a fine one but I am afraid will
want incident—she must not dare to invent any; and all which are historical are so well known, that there can be no surprise excited. The
pathetic however there is great scope for—and if she can make the people cry, the play will no doubt answer the purpose well. I shou'd like
to have read it, but I shall be obliged to suspend my curiosity 'till my
husband returns, as I have determin'd to keep my mind clear from all
theatricals (which God knows I have had enough of) 'till he comes
back. I know not whether it has arriv'd or not, for I have heard nothing about it—but I conclude it has, and is by this time ranged in order
amongst a dozen others which have been sent for *'early* inspection.' I
shall be in town on Wednesday to receive Mrs. Kemble[40] when if it
shou'd not be amongst the rest, I will write to let you know.— Charles
shall hear your message about Mr. Fitzharris—but I confess I do not
think he will obtain an engagement—I know that unseen, unheard, and
untried, *I* shou'd not give him one! We are overstock'd with mediocrity, and unless the gentleman possess very first rate qualifications, it
were useless to saddle the concern with an additional salary. It is
true he is very well spoken of by his friends of Reading and the Isle
of White [*sic*]—but are they competent to judge? I assure you that
with all my long experience upon these matters, I shou'd mistrust my
own opinion were I to see Mr. Fitzharris or any other person in a mere
Provincial company—they are all generally so very bad in country
theatres, that if there be one but decently tolerable, he is deem'd at once
a great actor—you know not how often Mrs. Siddons herself has been
deceiv'd under the same circumstances—however all this is merely from
myself and will in no way operate against Mr. Fitzharris, as I have for
some time past, made up my mind never to offer an opinion upon any
of the measures of Covent Garden. I think you will be surprised to hear
that Charles Eckersall[41] row'd himself up the river one day, and dined
with us! I wish you cou'd be persuaded to do the same. John[42] is now
gone to Dr. Malkin's [?], and we cou'd give you a tidy bedchamber for
a night or two. We have but poor *indoor* accommodation—but the

country is beautiful, and we almost wholly live under the canopy of heaven, which I invite you to, with the sincerity of a very true friend.

M. Thérèse Kemble

Mrs. Whitlock has been with us, and speaks of Mrs. Siddons (with whom she pass'd several days) in a most deplorable manner!—

The Rev.ᵈ William Harness
  Thomas Hope's Esqrᵉ·ˢ
    Dorking
      Surrey"[43]

"Two songs apiece, and a duet will do—but there's no objection to more, if the situations will admit of them. The performers you speak of are popular, and songs by them (provided they are not brought in by the neck and shoulders) cannot but serve a piece. If it is any consolation to you, *we* are as ill, as you can be, and my poor husband was compelled to fag thro' Hamlet on Monday when in fact he ought to have been in Bed. I agree with you about Archer [in *The Beaux' Stratagem*]. I think the *whole* play well done—(Mrs. Sullen might be better, but Miss Chester makes up in looks for her deficiencies as an actress) and that it is that renders it so popular—it is not necessary to give every body *much* to do, but to give them that, which they *can* do—it is that attention to *well fitting,* in Paris, that makes their Comedies so excellent a treat. I send you an order for tomorrow, but if you fancy you are to see Miss Byfield, you are mistaken; the new piece is however a very pretty one, and you will at any rate, be amused. My best remembrances to Miss Harness, and[44] Believe me always,

Very sincerely Yours

M. Thérèse Kemble

Wednesday—"

MRS. SIDDONS [*ff. 188–205ʳ*]

It was only towards the close of her career that I had the never-to-be-forgotten pleasure of seeing this incomparable woman perform her chief characters: but time had certainly not impaired the excellence of her acting; indeed, I believe that during her latter seasons, her Lady Macbeth, Queen Katharine, &c were finer than ever.

There are few circumstances which have impressed my memory more vividly than my first introduction to Mrs. Siddons, some years after she had quitted the stage, by my friend William Harness, at her house in Upper Baker Street. When we were ushered into her drawing-room, she had no one with her except her daughter Cecilia (afterwards Mrs. Combe); and she was sitting on a sofa, over which hung Harlow's sketch in oil for his well-known picture of the Kemble Family. Her attire was extremely plain and neat: she wore an umber-coloured gown, a muslin cap with her white hair parted on her forehead, and black kid gloves cut down so as to leave her delicate taper fingers bare. She looked somewhat thinner in the face than when I last had seen her on the stage; but her hazel eyes had lost nothing of their brilliancy and really seemed at times to send forth sparks. She spoke in a deep clear tone of voice, articulating each word distinctly; and she illustrated what she happened to be saying by a little more—a very little more—gesticulation than is usual in private society. Her whole manner and bearing were the perfection of dignity and grace. When the introduction was over, she said to me, "I will confess I was unwilling to become acquainted with you, for, though so much of my life has been spent in public, I have always had a nervous dread of being formally introduced to strangers; but *now that you have made my acquaintance,* I hope you will do me the favour to call frequently."— She used to maintain that those who had lived much with persons of celebrity, would never wish to attain celebrity themselves, because they must have witnessed the annoyances to which these [?] persons was [sic] subjected by the eagerness of strangers pressing for introductions to them.

Mrs. Whitlock,[45] a younger sister of Mrs. Siddons, used often to relate an anecdote of the girlhood of the great actress. One night, somewhere in the provinces, when Roger Kemble and his wife were busy at the theatre, their children were left at home together in the parlour; and the eldest of them, Sarah (Mrs. Siddons), in order to amuse the others, undertook to show them how

> "the sheeted dead
> Did squeak and gibber in the Roman streets";[46]

which, having let down her hair about her ears, she did so effectively, that her brothers and sisters were almost afraid to move till the return of their parents from the theatre.

It is well known that Mrs. Siddons's engagement by Garrick in 1775–6 proved altogether unsuccessful; and that it was not till her re-appearance at Drurylane Theatre in 1782 that she was at once acknowledged as the greatest female tragedian of her time.— A report goes, that during the thunders of applause elicited by one of Mrs. Siddons's performances in 1782, George Steevens exclaimed, "This is enough to make Garrick turn in his coffin!": and Mrs. Piozzi, the intimate friend of Mrs. Siddons, declares that "Siddons hated the little great man [Garrick] to her heart."[47] It appears at least that she felt more indignation at his treatment of her than she has chosen to express in those interesting Memoranda which are printed in her *Life* by Campbell, and which are intended to show that Garrick behaved to her with an odd mixture of courtesy and neglect, ending in his "letting her down in the most humiliating manner."[48] We must remember, however, that the Mrs. Siddons of those days was a timid inexperienced actress, very different from the Mrs. Siddons of 1782, and that if Garrick had brought her out in some important part, there is every probability that she would have failed to make an impression on the public.— It is [a] matter of regret that in the ample Memoranda just mentioned she has entered into no criticism on Garrick's acting, though, besides playing with him in two pieces, *Richard the Third* and Hoadley's *Suspicious Husband,* "she had seen him in his great characters from one of the boxes."[49] And I remember Charles Kemble's once remarking to me, not without surprise, that, notwithstanding Mrs. Siddons's admiration of Garrick's talents, what he had heard her say concerning his acting amounted to little more than this,—viz. that his action was frequently angular (that is, that he jerked his elbows in a peculiar manner), and that the expression of his eyes was marvellous, having a sort of fascination like that attributed to those of the snake.

I possess a few play-bills of the Liverpool Theatre, which by some chance have escaped destruction, and which curiously show how various were the characters performed there by Mrs. Siddons during the earlier portion of the period between her dismissal from Drurylane Theatre in 1776 and her return to London & triumphal success in 1782. . . .[50]

Dr. Beattie, in a letter to his niece, dated Edinburgh, 28th May, 1784, writes thus: "Nothing here is spoken or thought of but Mrs. Siddons. I have seen this wonderful person not only on the stage, but in private company; for I passed two days with her at the Earl of Buchan's. . . . . . She loves music, and is fond of the Scotch tunes; many of which I played to her on the violoncello. One of them ('She rose and let me in,' which you know is a favourite of mine) made the tears start from her eyes. 'Go on,' said she to me, 'and you will soon have your revenge'; meaning, that I would draw as many tears from her as she had drawn from me. *She sung 'Queen Mary's Complaint' to admiration; and I had the honour to accompany her on the bass.*"[51] Now, Mrs. Siddons, not long before her death, assured me that the statement in the last sentence of the above extract is *utterly false,*— that, when it was pointed out to her on the publication of Forbes's book, *she was struck with astonishment.* "I should as soon," she said, "have stood up and danced for the amusement of the party, as have attempted to sing a song to Beattie's accompaniment."— Since, on the one hand, it is not to be supposed that the author of the *Essay on Truth* would violate truth even in a matter of so little moment as the present; and since, on the other hand, I see no reason to doubt the fidelity of Mrs. Siddons's memory; I can only account for such conflicting evidence by the hypothesis, that when Beattie's letter was transcribed for the press, the passage in question was by some chance inaccurately copied,—an accident which I know by experience is far from uncommon.

Two parts which she used to mention as "having afforded her particular pleasure in the acting," were Athenais in Lee's *Theodosius,* and Zara in Congreve's *Mourning Bride.* The former part, which she first acted in 1797, and in which she was always well received by the public, soon dropped from her repertoire; but the latter she continued to play from an early period of her career down to the time of her retirement from the boards,—and wonderfully she played it, infusing true passion into its stilted and bombastic speeches, to say nothing of her most majestic and picturesque appearance as the captive queen: indeed, the late William Godwin,—who was the most constant frequenter of the theatre I ever met with, being in his old age as unwilling to miss the performances of Kean and Miss O'Neill as he had been in his youth unwilling to miss those of Garrick and Mrs. Yates—did not scruple to say that "it was worth taking a day's journey merely to see Mrs. Siddons walk down the stage as Zara."[52]

That her Euphrasia in Murphy's *Grecian Daughter,* her Hermione in Phil[ips's] *Distressed Mother,* her Elvira in Kotzebue's and Sheridan's *Pizarro,* and her Arpasia in Rowe's *Tamerlane,* should invariably have proved attractive performances, will perhaps seem strange to persons who are acquainted with those pieces only in the closet, and who are not aware what the powers of Mrs. Siddons were able to effect in dramas of an inferior order.— An early publication of Leigh Hunt furnishes the following remarks: "Of the force of such mere action I recollect a sublime instance displayed by Mrs. Siddons in the insipid tragedy of *The Grecian Daughter.* This heroine has obtained for her aged and imprisoned father some unexpected assistance from the guard Philotas [II, i]: transported with gratitude, but having nothing from the poet to give expression to her feelings, she starts with extended arms and casts herself in mute prostration at his feet. I shall never forget the glow which rushed to my cheeks at this sublime action."[53] Here, too, may be quoted the words of another accomplished theatrical critic, Mrs. Inchbald; "The Arpasia of Mrs. Siddons *[in Rowe's *Tamerlane*] has, indeed, the power of inspiring a degree of horrible wonder in the dying scene; when, dropping down dead at the Sultan's feet, she gives, by the manner and disposition of her fall, such assurance of her having suddenly expired, that an auditor of a lively imagination casts up his eyes to heaven, as if to catch a view of her departed spirit."[54]

But the characters in tragedies *not written by Shakespeare,* which Mrs. Siddons rendered the most fascinating to the public, were Isabella in Southern's *Fatal Marriage,* Calista in Rowe's *Fair Penitent,* Belvidera in Otway's *Venice Preserved,* Jane Shore in Rowe's tragedy of that name, Lady Randolph in Home's *Douglas,* Mrs. Beverley in Moor[e's] *Gamester,* and (the already mentioned) Zara in Congreve's *Mourning Bride.*— Tom Davies, an old stager, and certainly not disposed to overrate her acting, bears witness to the intense feeling she displayed in Calista, her complexion actually changing under the conflicting emotions excited by the scene.[55]— As to her Belvidera, it appeared to have lost little of its charm even when her age and figure were such that Jaffeir no longer dared to address her as his [. . .]

With respect to Mrs. Siddons's performances in the plays of our great dramatist,—though, during her long professional life, she at various times and in various places had appeared, with more or less success, as Portia in *The Merchant of Venice,* Lady Anne in *Richard the Third,* Olivia in *Twelfth-Night,* Rosalind in *As You Like It,*[56] Juliet in *Romeo and Juliet,* Desdemona in *Othello,* Ophelia in *Hamlet,* Cordelia in *King Lear* (as altered by Tate), Queen Elizabeth in *Richard the Third,* Portia in *Julius Cæsar,*[57] Beatrice in *Much Ado About Nothing,*[58] and Katharine in the farce taken from *The Taming of the Shrew,*—yet in none of these characters, though she played some of them excellently (more particularly Desdemona), can she be said to have produced, nor indeed did they admit of her producing, a deep and permanent impression on the public mind. Her fame, as the matchless representative of Shakespeare's matchless heroines, is mainly founded on her Lady Macbeth, her Queen Katharine in *Henry the Eighth,* her Constance in *King John,* her Volumnia in *Coriolanus,* her Imogen in *Cymbeline,* her Hermione in *The Winter's Tale,* and her Isabella in *Measure for Measure.* Nor was it any wonder that audiences, all over Britain, were never weary of seeing her in the parts just enumerated; for by continual study, even down to the period of her quitting the stage, she had elaborated them to a perfection which baffles description, and which cannot be conceived by those who have only seen them embodied by her feeble successors.[59]

With some of her youthful performances she felt dissatisfied in her later years; her maturer judgment condemning what then appeared to her the bad taste of certain things she had done on the stage, which, however, had been applauded to the very echo.

Several times, while she was "starring it" at different provincial theatres, the manifest superiority of some individual actor to the rest of the wretched company had deceived her into a belief that he was really a person of histrionic talent; and if, after the play, she happened to bestow on him a few words of praise, they were immediately followed by a request that she would make his fortune by recommending him to the manager of Covent-Garden or Drurylane. "I have done so," she said, "in the case of more persons than one; and when I saw them on the London stage, I felt quite ashamed of my recommendation,— their acting was so very bad."

Mrs. Siddons took a formal leave of the public 29th June, 1812, after performing Lady Macbeth. But few or none know that she originally had selected the part of Hermione in the *Winter's Tale* for her farewell performance, and that it was chiefly owing to the repeated suggestions of the late Henry Foss of Pall Mall—conveyed to her through her brother John Kemble—that she finally acquiesced in the more judicious choice of Lady Macbeth. The audience would not suffer the tragedy to proceed after the sleep-walking scene,—Lady Macbeth having nothing to do in the remainder of the play; and Mrs. Siddons presently, in plain modern attire, spoke the Address written for her— and not badly written—by her nephew Horace Twiss.[60] The long white kid gloves which she then had on, and the small bouquet which she wore at her bosom, were carefully preserved by her faithful companion Miss Wilkinson;[61] who bequeathed them to her niece Mrs. Groom; and by the latter lady they were presented to a friend of mine, an enthusiastic admirer of Mrs. Siddons, who still treasures them—the bouquet being now almost withered to dust—as interesting relics.

Memoirs of Mrs. Siddons. Interspersed with Anecdotes of Authors and Actors was written and published by Boaden in 18[27], while she was yet alive. She had but a slight acquaintance with that gentleman (though he was on intimate terms with her brother John Kemble); and she was so annoyed by the announcement of the book, that she at first determined to print a letter in the newspapers, declaring that it

had been composed and published without her knowledge or con-
currence. She forbore doing so, however, on learning the embarrassed
circumstances of the author: and, after reading the work, she probably
ceased to feel offended at the liberty he had taken; for from beginning
to end, it is a hymn of praise on her and her acting.— Boaden[62] has
noticed some of the few occasions on which, after formally bidding the
public farewell, Mrs. Siddons was induced (not reluctantly) to re-
appear on the stage: but, either by an oversight or through ignorance,
he omits all mention of her very last performance, June 9th, 1819, when
she played Lady Randolph in Home's *Douglas* for the benefit of her
brother Charles and his wife; and when Norval was acted by C. Kemble,
The Stranger by Young, Glenalvon (excellently) by Macready, and
Anna by Miss Foote (Lady Harrington). Accompanied by two college-
friends, I came up from Oxford expressly to be present at that last
performance of Mrs. Siddons; and I furnished Campbell with an
account of it, which he printed verbatim in his unfortunate *Life*[63] of
the great actress, and which I now transcribe. "The part *[Lady
Randolph], I think, was injudiciously chosen: it is long and laborious,
it brings the actress almost constantly before the audience, and is
not, like Lady Macbeth or Queen Katharine, equally striking in every
scene. Her action in the greater part of the play was thought to be
somewhat redundant, and to want that grand repose for which she had
been so celebrated. In many pasages, however, she was still herself;—
particularly in the threatening injunction to Glenalvon to beware of
injuring Young Norval, when she uttered the words,

> 'Thou look'st at me as if thou fain wouldst pry
> Into my heart—'tis open as my speech' [II, iii],

and when she swept past him with an indignant wave of her arm. She
was also great in her final exit, when, exclaiming,

> 'For such a son,
> And such a husband, drive me to my fate' [V],

she rushed distractedly from the stage.— The audience showed their
devotion for her: at the question of Young Norval,

> 'But did my sire surpass the rest of men,
> As thou excellest all of womankind?' [IV]

they applied the words to Mrs. Siddons by three rounds of applause."[64]
A good many years after, Macready, the Glenalvon of that night,
assured me, that when Mrs. Siddons (as above described) crossed the
stage at " 'tis open as my speech," he was so startled by her tones,
look, and gesture, that for the moment he forgot himself: "the woman,"
he added, "who could do *that,* must have done many wonderful things."
(A similar effect was once produced on Macready by an actress of a
very different kind, viz. Mrs. Glover, while playing Mrs. Candour to
his Joseph Surface in *The School for Scandal:* the perfect *naturalness*
with which she said to him, "By the by, I hope 'tis not true that your
brother is absolutely ruined" [I, i], so took him by surprise that for the
instant he felt uncomfortable, his thoughts turning away to "his own
brother, Major Macready.")

Though in her readings from Shakespeare Mrs. Siddons did not
attempt to rise to the loudness of stage-declamation,—for she fully
agreed with her brother John Kemble in thinking that *reading* and
acting ought always to be kept distinct,—she nevertheless contrived
by the skilful management of her voice and the lightning of her eyes
to give to passion all its intensity. When she read the scenes between
Othello and Iago, you seemed to hear the latter, with his head on the
shoulder of the former, pouring in low whispers the poison into Othello's
ear; nor was the rage of the Moor the less affective because it was less
noisy than it usually is on the boards. In reading *Antony and Cleopatra,*
which she did only to her friends in private, she displayed marvellous
power. Indeed, she once intended to have acted the Egyptian queen;
but abandoned the design, "because, as throughout a great portion of
the tragedy Cleopatra is *playing a part,* she was afraid that the audience
would not have thoroughly understood the performance." She always
read with an eye-glass in her hand, which she occasionally used to
assist her sight while glancing at the book, and which she sometimes
employed to heighten the effect of her reading: it served for the dagger
in *Macbeth,*—

"like *this* which now I draw";

and with it, as she repeated in an unearthly tone,—

"double, double toil and trouble," &c

she stirred the contents of the enchanted caldron.

But Mrs. Siddons in her readings did not always confine herself to the tragedies of Shakespeare: she would occasionally read, at least to her friends in private, some of his richest comic scenes,[65]—for instance, the scene between Falstaff, Prince Henry, Pointz, &c (*First Part of Henry IV,* act ii. sc. 4),—and evidently no less to her own enjoyment than to that of her auditors.— She had, indeed, a keen relish for the ludicrous. I have heard her relate with much humour an anecdote of a provincial actress, whom the manager scolded for throwing herself on the stage without a due care of her white sat[in] dress: "Sir," answered the lady in high indignation, "Mrs. Siddons never minds where *she* flumps herself."[66] And on one of the last occasions I ever saw her, she described very comically and dramatically an innocent ruse of which she had recently been made the victim: "Two nights ago," she said, "I was at my brother's *[Charles Kemble's] house in St. J[ames's at Park Place] to meet a small party; when Mrs. Charles said to me, 'As, I believe, you are fond of Scotch ballads, I wish to introduce you to a lady here, Miss Hamilton, who sings them charmingly.' I, of course, replied that I should be happy to become acquainted with her and to hear her sing. On which, Mrs. Charles, with great formality, introduced me to a tall strange-looking woman, who, having made an awkward curtsey, forthwith sat down to the piano and sang, in a Stentorian voice, a queer song—'My love he is so cru-*el,*' and so on. I was all astonishment; nor, till some time had elapsed, did I discover that this Miss Hamilton was no other than my nephew Henry Kemble[67] in woman's clothes."

After quitting the stage, Mrs. Siddons—as, I believe, is more or less the case with all players in like circumstances—suffered extremely from the want of excitement: she was not fond of cards; she was far from a devourer of books; and, on a review of the past, she fancied—

though unwilling to confess it—that the duties of the profession she had abandoned, which formerly appeared so irksome, would now afford her a pleasing recreation. I have seen a letter to her friend Mrs. Fitz Hugh, in which, alluding to John Kemble's return to the stage after a temporary absence, she writes; "Coriolanus was glorious, and gloriously received: but, alas, where was Volumnia? sitting in an upper box, and sadly gazing on her substitute!"[68]

Mrs. Siddons understood no language but her own; and her acquaintance with literature was comparatively very limited. "I believe," said Mrs. C. Kemble to me, "that, with the exception of the Bible, Shakespeare, and Milton, she scarcely ever looks into a book."— It must be allowed that she could not have "looked into" three better.

It not unfrequently happens that theatrical performers, when in what is called "good society," look and talk as if they were on the defensive; conscious that their profession is not universally regarded as an honourable one, they seem unable to get rid of the suspicion that some slight may be offered them. But in the case of Mrs. Siddons, who had been so much caressed and flattered by persons of the highest rank, even by royalty itself, such a feeling, if it ever existed, had long passed away. She was, however, though very unassuming, not without a proper sense of the respect that was her due; and resented any violation of it. Accordingly, at a party given by Lady Milbanke (some time before Lord Byron married Miss M.), she took offence at the behavior of Lovell Edgeworth; though, I believe, he was far from intending to treat her rudely. She had no acquaintance with him: yet, to her surprise, he came up to her without having been introduced, and, rubbing his hands together, said abruptly and as familiarly as if he had been one of her oldest friends, "Madam, I had the pleasure of seeing you many years ago act the part of Millamant[69] in the little town of T——."[70] "Sir," replied Mrs. Siddons in her most dignified and solemn manner, "I never played Millamant in any theatre, and I never was at the little town of T—— during the whole course of my life." Edgeworth, however, continuing to insist that he was not mistaken,[71] she rose from [her] seat, and walked to the other side of the room. "Really," said she to Harness, as he was handing her, not long after, to her carriage, "Really, that Mr. Edgeworth is a very ungentlemanly gentleman."

Among the admirers of Mrs. Siddons none was more ardent than Talma : and one night at Lord Glenbervie's he carried his admiration to an excess which rather discomposed her. After talking to her for some time in a strain of the highest compliment, he suddenly exclaimed, "Ah, Madame, il faut que je vous embrasse,"—suiting the action to the word.

It is well known that John Kemble was publicly feted when he bade farewell to the stage, that a grand dinner was given to him, and that he was presented with a piece of plate, while an Ode, composed for the occasion by Thomas Campbell, was recited by Young the tragedian. These honours paid to a brother whom she dearly loved afforded much pleasure to Mrs. Siddons : but she could not help recollecting at the same time that she (the greater performer of the two) had received no such testimonies of public approbation when she took leave of the stage. "I trust," she said, "that in the next world women will be more valued and respected than they are in this."[72]

Her sensibility was exquisite. Miss Kell[y], in an "entertainment" which once proved very attractive, took occasion to inform the public, that when, during her juvenile days, she played Prince Arthur to the Constance of Mrs. Siddons, the linen collar worn by her as the young prince used to be wet through and through with the tears shed on it by the great actress in the course of the tragedy. Even while reading passages of Milton to her friends in private, the tears would sometimes trickle down her cheeks. But the most remarkable instance of her extreme sensibility—one which some readers will probably treat with ridicule—was often related by the late Mrs. Groom, who, when Miss Wilkinson, was for several seasons well known to the musical world of London as an accomplished concert-singer, and who, eventually, after the ruin of her husband's affairs, nobly supported her family by becoming a teacher of singing, and could boast of numbering among her pupils the children of Queen Victoria. Being niece to the Miss Wilkinson, who lived for many years as companion to Mrs. Siddons, she consequently was very often in the society of the latter even from her childhood. One morning, when a little girl, as she was puzzling over a story-book, Mrs. Siddons inquired what was the subject of it ; and on learning that it was *The Life, Death and Burial of Cock Robin*, rejoined, "Well, my dear, I will read it to you." Accordingly, she proceeded to do so in her most careful and artistic style; and so completely was she carried away by the narrative, that, at its close, she could not restrain her tears for Robin's untimely fate![73]— Some readers, as I have observed above, will probably treat this anecdote with ridicule, thinking that it equals in absurdity what Madame D'Arblay and Mrs. Piozzi have recorded of Sophy Streatfield's marvellous readiness "to cry"[74]: nevertheless, as it [is] highly characteristic and of unquestionable authenticity, I have not chosen to omit it.

When a young portrait-painter (whose fame soon died away) was extolled by his London admirers as superior to Sir Thomas Lawrence,[75] Mrs. Siddons observed; "The public have a sort of pleasure in mortifying their old favourites by setting up new idols. I know it by my own experience; for I have been three times threatened with an eclipse,— first, by means of Miss Brunton (afterwards Mrs. Merry[76]), secondly by means of Miss Smith (afterwards Mrs. Bartley), and lastly by Miss O'Neill. Nevertheless," she added, "I am not yet extinguished." Of the three ladies in question, one only could be considered as a really eminent performer,—viz. Miss O'Neill (now Lady Becher).

I remember Mrs. Siddons saying, "Liston now receives as much per week as the united salaries of myself, my brother John, and my brother Charles amounted to."

She always maintained that a constant residence in London and London society had a decided tendency to harden the heart.

Mrs. Siddons died June 8, 1831.

PART 2: MINOR CHARACTERS

[GIOVANNI B.] BELZONI [*f. 22*]

Long before he was known to the world as the indefatigable explorer of Egyptian antiquities, he used to act melodramatic (or rather, pantomimic) parts, and exhibit feats of strength at various theatres in England and Scotland. He was of gigantic stature—seven feet in height, if not more, and possessing extraordinary physical power. When a boy,

I saw him, at the Edinburgh Theatre, play Orson in *Valentine and Orson;* and I have a vivid recollection of his striking appearance on his first entrance in that piece, when he rushed from the back-scene down to the foot-lights, strangling a hare. He concluded his performances of the evening by carrying about the stage eight men; two of them on his shoulders; others hanging upon him with their feet resting on an iron girdle attached to straps which depended from his neck; and some supported by means of his hands.

MRS. [MARY ANN] DAVENPORT; [WILLIAM] FARREN, &C. [*f. 36*]

In the parts of old women—whether jolly dames, pompous matrons, starched ancient maidens, or feeble crones—Mrs. Davenport had no equal during my acquaintance with the stage. Mrs. Glover, who latterly took to parts of the same kind, was very inferior : in order to produce a laugh, she would unscrupulously vulgarize certain characters far beyond what the authors intended, and even cockneyfy their language : an instance of this was her Mrs. Heidelberg in *The Clandestine Marriage;* and yet after all her efforts to render it ludicrous, it was not so truly comic as the Mrs. Heidelberg of Mrs. Davenport.

In *The Clandestine Marriage,* when played at Covent-Garden theatre, Mrs. Davenport was associated with Farren as Lord Ogleby, Charles Kemble as Lovewell, Fawcett as Sterling, Jones as Brush, [Farley] as Canton, Mrs. Charles Kemble as Miss Sterling, and Miss Brunton (Mrs. Yates) as Fanny. All these performers did ample justice to their respective parts : but Farren carried away the chief applause, and very deservedly; for a more finished piece of acting than his Lord Ogleby could not well be conceived. From beginning to end it was elaborated to perfection : in the earlier scene [II, i] where the battered old beau appears at his toilet, making himself up for the day; in act iv. sc. 3, where, in the dialogue with Lovewell, he chuckles over the idea that Fanny has conceived a passion for him; and in act v. sc. 2, where, on Sterling's threatening to turn Fanny and Lovewell out of doors directly, he declares, with a burst of generous feeling, that, should Sterling do so, he will receive them into his own house;—Farren displayed in all such consummate ability as seemed sufficient to refute the allegations of his theatrical brethren that he was a man endowed with very little mind; unless, indeed, we choose to agree with those writers who maintain that acting is an imitative art almost independent of the intellectual powers.

Strange that Farren, who was so completely the polished gentleman in Lord Ogleby, should have been rather the reverse in Sir Peter Teazle: yet it is a fact that Mrs. Nisbett, when his Lady Teazle at the Haymarket Theatre, complained of his vulgarity to the manager: "I am far," she said, "from affecting any airs of over-delicacy; but the way in which Mr. Farren *runs* [*amourously*] *at me* in *The School for Scandal* is so very offensive, that I must beg you will interfere to prevent his doing so in future."

Lord Ogleby as well as Sir Peter Teazle was originally performed by King. The elder Charles Mathews had seen him in both parts; and, on my asking how he played them, Mathews replied, "Sir, he grimaced throughout like a monkey."[77]

MRS. GIBBS [*f. 44*]

Though not "a star," Mrs. Gibbs was a very valuable addition to any theatrical company. She was excellent as the representative of the waiting-maids of Congreve and of the dramatists of that class; nor was she less successful in various other characters,—Mrs. Candour in *The School for Scandal,* Charlotte in *The Stranger,* Tilburina in *The Critic,* &c &c. How trifling soever might be the parts she played, she was sure to make them "tell" by her neat and pointed delivery, her joyous manner, and her exhilarating laugh. The effect of her acting was heightened by her personal appearance; for on my first seeing her she was still much more than comely, and must have been beautiful in her youth. When a pageant in honour of Shakespeare was produced at Covent-Garden theatre, in which Miss O'Neill figured as the Tragic Muse, the managers very properly assigned her Comic sister to Mrs. Gibbs.

Somewhat late in her career she married George Colman the

Younger (with whom she had long lived *par amours*) ; and a very affectionate and prudent wife she proved. His circumstances made it necessary for him to reside within the rules of the King's Bench;[78] and many a night, after performing at the theatre, would Mrs. Gibbs (as she continued to be called), in order to save the expense of coach-hire, put on her cloak and pattens, and trudge home over Blackfriars Bridge, regardless of the weather.

To an actress who has remained on the stage till considerably advanced in years, it is generally a trial (and the more severe, if she has once been beautiful) to be compelled to take the parts of old women: it was, therefore, with extreme reluctance, and, I believe, not without shedding tears, that Mrs. Gibbs, on the retirement of Mrs. Davenport, acted the Nurse to Fanny Kemble's Juliet,—and did not act it well, for it was unsuited to her style.

MRS. [DOROTHY] JORDAN [*ff. 58–59ʳ*]

Was assuredly one of the most popular comic actresses that ever trod the British boards : and what added to the pleasure of her audience was the evident pleasure she herself took in the parts she played; for instance, it was plain how thoroughly she relished the brilliant wit of Shakespeare's Rosalind; in which character, by the by, I may mention, as an instance of stage-trick now long obsolete, that when, with delightful archness, she sung into the ear of Orlando (Barrymore[79]) the burden "Cuckoo, cuckoo,"[80] she at the same time made the powder fall from his wig by giving it a smart brush with the back of her hand.— Nor was she less charming in another romantic part of our great poet,—Viola in *Twelfth-Night*.

But Peggy in *The Country Girl* (an alteration by Garrick of Wycherley's *Country Wife*),—the character which she selected for her debut in London, and which laid the foundation of her fame,—was perhaps her *chef d'oeuvre*. No description can convey an adequate idea of the fascination which she threw into the part: as the play proceeded, the audience were more and more enraptured with the exquisite picture of rustic simplicity combined with a cunning which enables her to out-

wit her surly guardian, till the crowning point of all, when, on the exclamation of Moody, "She's my wife, and I demand her" [V, ii], Peggy
suddenly appears in the balcony, and rejoins, "No, but I an't,"—words
which came from the mouth of Mrs. Jordan in a tone so perfectly natural
that one could hardly think she was only acting.

Another piece which afforded her an opportunity of showing off
her peculiar talent to the best advantage, and which may be considered
as having died with her, was that strange production *The Devil to Pay*
(an alteration from Coffey's farce of that name, which he founded on
Jevons' *Devil of a Wife*) wherein a cobbler's spouse, Nell,[81] is meta-
morphosed by a magician into Lady Loverule, while the latter is changed
into the cobbler's wife. Nothing in its kind could be more truthful or
amusing than Mrs. Jordan's representation of the bewilderment of Nell,
when, waking in bed as Lady Loverule, she holds a dialogue with her
attendant Lettice, part of which runs thus [II, vi] ;

> "*Lettice*. Your ladyship's chocolate is ready.
>
> *Nell* *[aside]. Mercy on me! what's that? Some garment, I sup-
> pose.— *Put it on, then,* sweetheart.
>
> *Lettice*. Put it on! Madam, I have taken it off; 'tis ready to drink.
>
> *Nell. I mean, put it by:* I don't care for drinking now."

That none of the great triumphs of this favourite daughter of Thalia
were in modern genteel comedy must be attributed to a want of refine-
ment in her acting, which has been allowed even by her most ardent
admirers. And it seems certain that at times—though, I presume, very
rarely—she was tempted to overdo her part; for I have heard Charles
Kemble frequently relate that one night in *The Wonder* when he played
Felix to her Violante, she was so carried away by the impulse of the
moment that she absolutely bullied him, following him round the stage
while he awkwardly kept retreating before her;[82] and so great was his
indignation that, on their making their exit, he said, "Mrs. Jordan, if
a real Donna Violante had treated a real Don Felix with such intolerable rudeness, he would surely have stabbed her."

Latterly, of course, the effect of her performances was marred by the extreme unfitness of her figure for the juvenile parts, of which a large portion of her repertoire consisted: yet there was such a charm about her, that when an elderly, fat, dumpy woman,—and having some sort of string attached to her wig and passed tightly under her chin, to make a distinction between the said chin and her neck,—she continued to play youthful belles, and even hoydens of sixteen, to crowded and applauding houses. This was the case on the last occasion of my seeing her—in 1816 [i.e., 1814], when my friend Kenney brought out a new comedy called *Debtor and Creditor,* in which, though looking like a respectable grandmother, she acted with great sprightliness a very young lady. She was well supported in that comedy by Liston, Terry, Jones, Emery, and Mrs. Powell.

Nor in any account of Mrs. Jordan ought her merits as a singer to be passed over without notice: though not much of a musician, she had a very correct ear, and warbled ballads with ravishing sweetness and expression.

[JAMES] KENNEY AND HIS LAST DRAMATIC PRODUCTION [ff. 86–89]

"12 Cork Street[83]

23ᵈ Octʳ 1844

My dear Mr. Dyce,

When I met you some time ago you may remember I express'd a wish that you would take the trouble to read the play which had made so much stir between the actors & last management of C. G. Theatre. That wish, as Moxon may possibly have apprized you, I have not abandoned—first, because it would be a great satisfaction to me to have an opinion in which I should have so much Confidence and Secondly for a Reason more especial which I will explain.— From the Circumstances of my having lent myself to one or two Experiments [?] to oblige Macready, and in the Certainty of getting the pieces acted, tho' avowedly without faith in their Success, which the Events justified, it strikes me that I have lost more of my Estimation with Managers than I deserve, and I should say with Webster in particular, who in two or

three instances latterly has treated my overtures with strange inatten-
tion. But as you have been one of his judicial Committee in the Case [?]
of the prize Comedies, it strikes me that if the play came to his hands
thro' you, & with your Recommendation, the author being no otherwise
identified than generally, as a *Friend of yours,* he would give it special
attention, and if he should take the Same Sanguine impression of it,
which *[Charles] Kemble did, & also his Cabinet Advisers, he might
be induced to make a temporary Engagement or two to do it justice,
for I do not see how that could be accomplished, as regards the two
characters of the Duchess & Laroche in the present state of his Company. This favour of course would imply your approbation of the play,
and not that your Candour should suffer any violence in granting it.
The chief objection of the Actors, made under the perverse & discon-
tented State of their feelings, was to the general position of the Duchess
& the Construction of the last act. With all allowance for the fallibility
of their opinions, I have nevertheless, amended the play in a careful
re-consideration, and no objection I think in either of these Cases will
now remain.—

Relying on your Kindness I venture to send the M. S. herewith, and
should request to be favoured with your Sentiments about it, previous
to any [?] further proceedings.

> I am,
> D' Mr. D.
> Yrs very truly
> Ja' Kenney

My original title was Infatuation, or a Tale of the French Empire but
as that Name appear'd in the papers I should send it in under another.
As a *Drama,* it is quite original.—"

> "12 Cork Street,
> Sat'

My dear Mr. Dyce,
*   *   *   *   *   *   *   *   *

I am anxious you should stipulate that Webster should not pass the
play into the hands of any adviser, as I hear Mr. Boursicault [*sic*],

the author of the forthcoming comedy, is much in his counsels, if not altogether; and he is notoriously a man to distrust: and pray use your own time and convenience in the matter, as I am not at all impatient, nor could there be any need of it at the theatre at this moment.

Yours very truly,

J. Kenney."

Thinking the play more than tolerably good, I wrote to Webster, asking if he would read it. He replied :—

"My dear Sir,

I shall feel great pleasure in perusing the play you speak of, especially when so highly recommended.

I am,

My dear Sir,

At all times

Your obliged obed^t Servt,

B. Webster.

The Revd Alex^r Dyce.

*[n. d.]."

I accordingly sent the play to Webster, who having delayed for several months to signify his decision on it, Kenney became so restless and impatient that I heartily regretted having meddled in the matter.

"12 Cork Street,

15 Mar. 1845.

My dear Mr. Dyce,

Having had recent confirmation, and that on unquestionable authority, of what I stated to you when you last wrote to Mr. Webster, that he had repeatedly declared his intention of acting no more plays of serious interest, and also that his arrangement with Vestris would bar his engagement of any such actress as my heroine would require, I must again beg of you to request from him an immediate return of the M. S. I have now waited much longer than in kindness you advised, and with many thanks for whatever trouble I have given both you and Mr. Webster, be it distinctly understood that my request now amounts to a requisition that you will obtain the play for me *at once* under all and any circumstances.

I am,
My dear Mr. Dyce,
Yours ever truly,
J. Kenney.

P. S. I have written what precedes that you might quote it to Webster if you could spare so much trouble, which I am really ashamed to give; and pray add an earnest word or two representing the propriety of my demand and urging compliance, 'or that you will get into disgrace,' &c, &c."

I was now forced to reclaim the play from the Haymarket-manager, who returned it to me with the following letter :

"T. R. Haymarket,
March 26, 1845.

My dear Sir,

Until my Easter pieces were launched I could not pay proper attention to your note : let this, I beg, be my excuse for not having ere this answered it. I have devoted the whole of this day to the careful perusal of your friend's play, and think it highly dramatic and most effective. Successful it must be; but I know of no actress except Miss Helen Faucit who could do adequate justice to the Duchess de Bracciano : certainly no one of my company. This is fatal to its representation here. Then for the elite of the talent here there are no parts, except perhaps Gobert for C. Matthews [*sic*]. Gobert is a delightful fellow : I could almost have wished he had had another scene. My forces are essentially comic; a five-act play without them would go for nothing : people would cry 'where's Farren,' &c? The author would suffer by it, saying nothing of the injury it would do your humble servant in pocket.   *   *   *   *

I am, My dear Sir,
Your obliged Servt,
B. Webster.

The Revd Alex^r Dyce."

The play, under the title of *Infatuation,* was afterwards acted, for a night or two, at the Princess's Theatre, Miss Cushman and James Wallack taking the chief parts.

Subsequent to Kenney's death, Miss Cushman told me, at one of Rogers's breakfasts, that she possessed the original MS. of *Infatuation* with my remarks on the margins.

[J O H N] H E N D E R S O N ' S A N D [C H A R L E S] M A C K - L I N ' S S H Y L O C K ; [G E O R G E F .] C O O K E ' S R I C H A R D T H E T H I R D , S I R P E R T I N A X M A C S Y C O P H A N T , A N D S I R A R C H Y M A C S A R C A S M ; M A C K L I N A N D D [. . .] [*f. 119ʳ*]

"My brother *[John Kemble] thought very very highly of Henderson's Shylock: but he said that in the fourth act of the play Macklin was superior to Henderson on account of the natural rigidity and stern expression of his countenance.

"I saw Cooke make his first appearance at [. . .] in Richard the Third.[84] It went off, on the whole, rather flatly till he gave the words, 'Well, as you guess,' which drew down thunders of applause; and from that speech to the end of the tragedy the audience were in raptures. His Richard was not free from coarseness: but he was a great actor; so great, that I have no hesitation in saying, that his Sir Pertinax Macsycophant[85] and his Sir Archy Macsarcasm[86] might rank, as artistic performances, with my sister's Lady Macbeth and my brother's Coriolanus.

"When Macklin was very old and his memory much impaired, he was stopped in the street by an actor named D[. . .] (not the well-known Tom Davies), who said to him, 'Mr. Macklin, you perhaps don't remember me; but I used long ago to play to you boys' parts in various pieces.' 'O, ay,' replied Macklin, 'I remember: I'm glad to see you, Dav[. . .]: good-by: *you're very much grown, Dav*[. . .].' "

C. Kemble.

MADEMOISELLE [ANNE-FRANÇOISE-HIPPOLYTE] MARS [*f. 120ʳ*]

An exquisitely refined actress, who was perfectly natural without even for a moment sinking into vulgar familiarity. I was once talking about her to Mrs. Jamieson at the house of Charles Kemble, when Charles broke in with the remark, "She has not an equal in Europe." Though properly a comic actress, her pathos was intense, quite free from any hysterical exaggeration; and in the *Fille d'honneur* and in the slight melodrame of *Valérie* she drew as many tears from the audience as were ever shed at the deepest tragedy. Her acting as the heartless and satirical Célimène in the *Misanthrope* was one of the most brilliant specimens of genteel comedy which can well be conceived.

One night at Paris, after seeing her in some favourite piece, Mrs. Charles Kemble, accompanied by Talma, went round to her dressing-room to compliment her on her performance. When the door opened, Mars was sitting before the looking-glass, half undressed, with her bosom almost quite bare; and Mrs. Charles Kemble hesitated about going in. But Talma saw no reason why they should retreat; and, as they entered the room, he said to Mars, *"Ah Mademoiselle, votre miroir est bien traître!"*

CHARLES MATHEWS THE ELDER [*ff. 121–22ʳ*]

Though his acting was always respectable, and in some characters rose much above mediocrity, he was far better on the whole as a mimic than as a regular comedian. The "entertainments" which, during several seasons, he gave, night after night, without any one to assist him, justly obtained great popularity: if they were not free from indifferent puns, these were overlooked amid the rich humour which predominated; for instance, if when he quoted Shakespeare's song, "Tell me where is fancy bred," the audience were not particularly amused by the exclamation of the little girl, "O, pa, our baker sells fancy bread," they could not fail to be highly gratified by his admirable personation (in a cap and shawl) of the Old Scotch Lady, who tells a long story about nothing.[87]

I have already mentioned his imitations of Coleridge;[88] and I may add that I have been present when in a private room he has imitated to the very life the manner and language of O'Connell and Sheil while speaking before the House of Commons.

During one of the last visits I ever paid him at Highgate, he complained of feeling far from well: "but," he said, "I have to act tonight at Drury-lane Theatre, along with Liston, in Colman's *Who Wants a Guinea?,* and, no doubt, as soon as I step upon the stage, I shall forget my illness."

That he was nervous and over-sensitive to a painful degree, I had a striking proof. When manager of the Adelphi Theatre in conjunction with Yates, he had frequently asked Harness and myself to meet him there before the play began, that he might put us into a private box. Accordingly, one evening we walked to the Adelphi, and entered it by the back-door: but Mathews had not yet arrived from Highgate; and we were requested by poor old Pope (who in his declining fortunes had become stage-manager of the Adelphi) to seat ourselves in the Green-room, which was then quite empty. On Mathews's arrival, we accompanied him up-stairs to his dressing-room, where he proceeded to array himself for the part of Monsieur Mallet in [the play of that name by Moncrieff]; during which operation Pope came in, and poured into his ear sundry flattering speeches—"No wonder that people preferred the Adelphi to all other theatres—the Adelphi was the only place in London where really good acting was to be seen," &c, &c. Just before the rising of the curtain, Harness and I were shown into the stage-box. The performance commenced; and Mathews and Mrs. Yates played very pleasingly as the father and daughter. At the end of the first act Mathews surprised us by suddenly bouncing into our box, and sitting down at the back of it, out of the view of the audience: he was in a state of great excitement, and declared that a party in the box next above us had come expressly to annoy and insult him, for they not only kept up a constant chattering, but they laughed at all those portions of his acting which he intended to be pathetic. We tried to convince him how unlikely it was that the party in question should bear him any ill-will; and we urged that in all probability they were persons (of whom there are not a few) with such an itch for talking that they could not be silent even during the most interesting scenes of a play. But he left the box, very little soothed by our arguments : and Mrs. Yates afterwards told me that she had felt very uncomfortable the whole evening, expecting every moment that Mathews would formally address the supposed offenders.

Mathews was the devoted admirer of John Kemble and Mrs. Siddons, and ever ready to deny the merits of any performers who were cried up in opposition to his two idols. Hence he could not endure the elder Kean, saying that in the iii^d act of *Othello,* when Kean exclaimed "O, blood, blood, blood," crossing the stage and clutching with his hands, he realized the idea, not of a noble Moorish warrior, but of a brutal Indian savage. Hence, too, Madame Pasta in Medea appeared to Mathews only "a little woman, bustling about, with her arms akimbo, and with the gait of a cookmaid."

[J O S E P H S.] M U N D E N [*f. 139*]

His performance of Cockletop in O'Keeffe's farce of *Modern Antiques* is immortalized by Lamb in *Elia* ["On the Acting of Munden"] ; and, among many other characters in which he was equally happy, were Autolycus in Shakespeare's *Winter's Tale,* Marrall in Massinger's *New Way to Pay Old Debts,* Old Dornton in Holcroft's *Road to Ruin,* Adam Winterton in Colman's *Iron Chest,* and Scrub in Farquhar's *Beaux' Stratagem.* His acting in the last-mentioned comedy has been pronounced by a competent judge to be on a par with that of Garrick :[89] and I have here to notice the gross buffoonery which I have seen him engraft on the part of Scrub while playing it in the country, but which, I suppose, he never ventured to introduce at a London theatre.

In the fourth act of *The Beaux' Stratagem,* Aimwell, pretending to have a fit, is carried in a chair into the house of Lady Bountiful; and presently, feigning to recover his senses, he breaks out into a rant,—

> "Where am I ?
> Sure, I have pass'd the gulf of silent death,
> And now am landed on th'Elysian shore.

> Behold the goddess of those happy plains!—
> Fair Proserpine, let me adore thy bright divinity.
> [*Kneels to Dorinda, and kisses her hand."*

Now, as soon as the scene was over, Munden re-entered and went through a parody of the above lines: he threw himself into the chair which Aimwell had occupied, and then starting up from it, exclaimed—

> "Where am I?
> Sure, I have pass'd the gulf of silent death,
> And now am landed on th'*Egyptian* shore.
> Behold the goddess of those happy plains!—
> Fair *Porcupine*, let me adore thy bright *virginity,"*—

and all this gag[90] he uttered with a prodigious deal of face-making and extravagant gesticulation; drawing down thunders of applause from an audience, who, doubtless, were quite unconscious that it did not form a portion of the original play.

MRS. PIOZZI AND CONWAY THE ACTOR [*ff. 143–45ʳ*]

In 1843 was published a thin pamphlet entitled *Love Letters of Mrs. Piozzi, Written when She was Eighty, to William Augustus Conway,*—who was then in his twenty-seventh year;[91] and though the language of those Letters may be thought insufficient to justify such a title, it is certain that they exhibit an ardour of romantic affection which has little of a maternal character.— That their genuineness should ever have been doubted[92] appears to me surprising, for they are marked throughout by the peculiarities of the writer,—her elasticity of spirit, her playful fancy, and her slip-slop style; nor have I forgotten, that when they first were published, a gentleman, who was a native of Bath and had resided there during the whole period embraced by the Letters, declared to me that the various private individuals and the trifling events incidentally noticed in them were all so perfectly familiar to him, that "he could not for a moment entertain a suspicion of forgery in the case." Besides, is it likely that the idea of forging such Letters would ever have occurred to any one either in America (where, it is stated, and with minute detail, the originals were sold among Conway's other effects which were found on shipboard after his unfortunate death)[93] or in our own country? What could have been the object of such a forgery?— Whether they are to be considered as "love-letters," or merely as the effusions of a "warm friendship that is of every-day occurrence between youth and age that is not crabbed,"[94] I do not pretend to determine: but I conceive that those who have hitherto been disposed to regard them in the former light, will see additional grounds for so regarding them, if they read for the first time the following remarkable statement, which comes from a source too respectable to be slighted. "We ourselves heard the late Charles Mathews say—and no one who knew him will question his veracity—that Conway had himself shown him Mrs. Piozzi's offer of marriage, and asked his opinion and advice. Mathews told him at once that he could not honourably take advantage of it. 'That,' said Conway, 'is what I myself felt; but in a matter so important to one so poor as I am, I also felt that my own decision should be confirmed by the opinion of a friend. I now know what to do.' This, we repeat, we heard from Mathews himself, at the time the circumstance occurred, and we therefore believe it."[95] I dismiss the subject by mentioning, that, to my certain knowledge, Mrs. Piozzi once said to Mrs. Siddons, "The two happiest days of my life were those on which I was introduced to you and to Mr. Conway,"—a speech which was far from pleasing to the great actress.

The writer of the Preface to the *Letters* is quite ignorant of Conway's parentage, merely observing that he "was of *[a] respectable family" [p. 10]. The fact is, he was a natural son of Lord George Seymour; and his baptismal name was William Augustus Rudd. He began life as an apprentice to a jeweller in Bristol;[96] and though he had always felt an inclination to become an actor (which perhaps was strengthened by the consciousness of his personal beauty), he nevertheless would have endeavoured, on the expiration of his apprenticeship, to better his condition by other means than the theatre if his father would have lent him a helping hand; but, as he informed Macready, Lord G. S. turned a deaf ear to his repeated applications "to do something for him," and he took to the stage as his only resource. In 1813 he made his first appearance in London, at Covent-Garden Theatre, in the part of Alexander the Great [in Lee's *The Rival Queens*] and was very favourably received: he soon afterwards played, and with applause, the chief characters in several of Shakespeare's dramas; and perhaps some of my readers will remember him as the Romeo, the Jaffeir [in *Venice Preserved*], and the Polydore [in Otway's *The Orphan*], to Miss O'Neill's Juliet, Belvidera, and Monimia. His success in those his earlier days may no doubt be attributed partly to the impression made on the audience by his incomparable face and figure, which realised one's idea of an Antinous of six feet high: but he was a much better actor than is assumed by the editor of the *Letters,* whose low and unjust estimate of Conway's histrionic powers [pp. 11–12] is echoed by Mr. Hayward in his *Autobiography, &c of Mrs. Piozzi* [I, 357–58]. My own opinion is, that in tragedy he was not inferior to any performer at present (1867)[97] belonging to the metropolitan theatres; and what is more to the purpose, I have heard Macready allow that he possessed "considerable talent." It was not, however, considerable enough to render him an object of permanent attraction; and, with the lapse of time, his popularity gradually declined. Having been five years absent from the London boards, he appeared at the Haymarket Theatre in 1821,[98] and though there was rather an improvement than a falling-off in his acting, he had then ceased to interest the public: unfortunately, too, his unusual height made him look almost gigantic in so confined an area. (Indeed, he had himself always complained of being "too tall"; and once, while he and Charles Kemble were standing on the Covent-Garden stage during the performance of *The Orphan,* he kept stooping so excessively in order to conceal his height, that C. K. could not help whispering to him, "For heaven's sake hold up your head: the audience are not thinking about your tallness.") After all, how did this once-admired representative of heroes and lovers end his London career? *By serving as prompter at the Haymarket Theatre!* a change which he felt acutely; for, along with a noble form, nature had given him a woman's sensitiveness: and now, when a guest at the table of Macready, or of any other old friend or acquaintance who kindly invited him to their house, he was *"so humble"* (not affectedly like Dickens's [Uriah Heep] but in all sincerity), that it was painful to witness the effect produced by his altered circum-

stances on one whose conduct had been always strictly honourable,
and whose manners were those of a perfect gentleman.

The rest of Conway's story is well known. In hopes of retrieving his
fortune, he went to America on a theatrical speculation : but there utter
disappointment awaited him, mainly in consequence of the persevering
hostility of the public press; and he determined to abandon the stage for
the pulpit. Accordingly with a view of taking orders, he applied himself
to the study of Hebrew, in which he is said to have made considerable
progress, and to which probably his attention had been directed at a
much earlier period by Mrs. Piozzi, who was a constant dabbler in the
Hebrew Scriptures. But the low spirits to which he had long been
subject increased more and more; and during a voyage from New York
to Charleston, just as the vessel was crossing the bar of the latter place,
he, in a fit of deep despondency, threw himself overboard and was
drowned, on the 24ᵗʰ of January 1828.

MRS. [ELIZABETH] POPE (MISS YOUNG);
HOLCROFT'S FOLLIES OF A DAY OR THE
MARRIAGE OF FIGARO; [CHARLES] BONNOR
[*f. 146ʳ*]

"I saw Mrs. Pope (Garrick's Miss Young)⁹⁹ play Susanna in *The
Marriage of Figaro:* I have a perfect recollection of her acting; and it
was violent and exaggerated in the extreme." *Mrs. C. Kemble.*

The drama in question, *The Follies of a Day or the Marriage of
Figaro,* founded by Holcroft on *La Folle Journée ou Le Mariage de
Figaro* of Beaumarchais, was produced under very remarkable circumstances. In his "Advertisement" to the printed copy Holcroft says; "To
enumerate all the obstacles encountered and overcome in bringing this
comedy on the English stage would be to indulge this vanity *[of self-
love] ; which it is every wise man's pride and every prudent man's
interest to resist. It may, however, afford some pleasure to be informed
*[*sic*], that, finding *[*sic*] it impossible to procure a copy of the original French, though a journey to Paris was undertaken expressly for
that purpose, the copy made use of in the composing [*sic*] *The Follies*

of a Day was taken by memory only during eight or nine representations; that I furnished the plot, incidents, entrances, and exits, and gave some other occasional hints; that the remainder was the work of a young Frenchman *[Bonneville], whose talents and whose heart are an ornament and an honour to his country; and that, after it was brought to England and received by Mr. Harris, it was translated, cast, copied, recopied, studied, and, in one of its longest parts, restudied, and played in little more than a month *[in 1784]."[100]

The part of Figaro was acted by "Mr. Bonnor":[101] wh[o] during his latest years resided at Aberdeen, where he died very old and greatly respected. There I knew him well,—a little, slightly built man, with an unceasing flow of lively conversation, somewhat theatrical, but without a shadow of vulgarity. And I remember that when John Kemble passed through Aberdeen on his way home from a visit to Lord Aberdeen at Haddo House, he expressed his regret that he had not time "to see his old friend Bonnor."

MISS [JANE] POPE [*f. 147ʳ*]

This comic actress (whom Boaden terms "the paragon of chambermaids"[102]), was as respectable in private life as she was excellent on the stage. I never saw her: but I was well acquainted with her niece and the inheritrix of her handsome fortune, Mrs. Thomas; who told me the following facts.— George the Third was so smitten by the youthful charms of Miss Pope, that, through the medium of a nobleman, he offered her any sum she might choose to name, if she would receive him as a lover. Though her circumstances were far from independent, she firmly and at once rejected the tempting offer. A few years before her death at an advanced age, Miss Pope and Mrs. Thomas were in a private box at one of the theatres; when the late Duke of Cambridge came into it, and talked to them for some time; saying, in the course of conversation, "You, Miss Pope, are the only woman in the world that ever made my mother jealous."

Miss Pope had carefully preserved a large bundle of letters addressed to her by the friend and patroness of her early days, the celebrated Kitty

Clive. I have seen them in the possession of Mrs. Thomas, and they probably still exist.[103]

GEORGE RAYMOND [ff. 153–55]

Was educated at Eton (where he had Shelley, Milman, &c for his schoolfellows) and at Trinity College, Cambridge, and became a member of the [bar]; but, though in his earlier years he once or twice went the northern circuit, he did so chiefly for amusement's sake, having succeeded to a considerable patrimony which rendered him independent of a profession.

Being very fond of the stage, he was much in the society of dramatists and players: George Colman and Elliston were among his most intimate associates; and I have passed many a pleasant hour at his house in company with one whom we both equally esteemed,—Charles Kemble.

In his youth Raymond was remarkably handsome; and used to set off his person to the best advantage by means of the most fashionable attire. During portions of the years 1819, 1820, he resided at Edinburgh, where he was known by the name of "the English dandy"; and such was the jealousy his good looks and elegant parure excited among the beaux of Prince's-street, that, according to his own account, they formed a regular conspiracy to mortify him, and damned a harmless comedy of his composition, which was brought out at the Edinburgh theatre, May, 1820, merely because they had traced it to his pen. It was called *More Plots Than One,* and was acted for the benefit of William Murray, the brother of Mrs. Henry Siddons. For the failure of this comedy he was consoled several years after by the success of his *Lone Hut,* a tremendously sensational melodrama which was produced in London at the Lyceum [1842].— He not only attempted dramatic writing, but on several occasions trod the stage as an amateur actor. I have heard him mention that he once played Jaffeir,—I forget where; and I know that at the Leamington Theatre, while it was under the management of his friend Elliston, he performed Charles Surface, the female part of the audience unanimously pronouncing him to be "charming."

Raymond made sundry happy puns (a minor kind of wit which has frequently been practised even by very celebrated persons who have condemned it as barbarous).[104] One day, while on the northern circuit, he was dining at Bury with Justice Holroyd, Crabb Robinson, and others of the bar. A couple of roast ducks were on the table before Holroyd; and when Robinson said to Raymond "Shall I help you to mutton?" the answer was "No, thank you, I'll take some of *adhuc sub judice.*"[105]— Among the proprietors of Covent-Garden Theatre was a Mr. Moore, a hatter in a great way of business, who kept a shop at the Piccadilly-end of Bond Street, and kept moreover a *chère amie* whom he used to drive about in a phaeton. Raymond happened to be walking with Beazley, when this theatrical hatter appeared at a short distance in his chariot, the lady, as usual, being with him. "Who's that?" said Beazley. "O," replied Raymond (quoting a line of *Othello* with the addition of a single letter),—

"It is the Moor: I know him by his *s*trumpet."

Though a man of pleasure, Raymond at times applied himself to literature with considerable diligence. He had perseverance enough to torture the whole history of England into rhyme: but nobody, I presume, has ever had the perseverance to read his metrical *Chronicles* through. He shows some research, too, in his *Memoirs of* [*R. W.*] *Elliston,* which reached a second edition [1857], and is entertaining to those who are interested in the biography of players, though a suspicion attaches to it, as to most books of the same description, that some of the anecdotes, if not apocryphal, are at least greatly exaggerated. His latest and, on the whole, his best publication is entitled *Drafts for Acceptance;* a small volume, consisting of essays and tales with a sprinkling of verse, which proves that nature had not denied him a portion either of fancy or humour. This volume is so little known, that I now extract from it the following stanzas on a fascinating contra-alto singer, whom perhaps some of my readers may remember as Pippo in *La Gazza Ladra* and as Arsace in *Semiramide.* . . .[106]

In the same miscellany is a *jeu d'esprit* entitled *A Model Prologue,*— not a bad specimen of verses which (like Swift's celebrated song,

"Fluttering, spread thy purple pinions," &c) seem, if read hastily, to convey a sense, while in fact they are entirely destitute of meaning: indeed Hood thought so well of it, that he printed it (for the first time) in one of his *Comic Annuals*.[107] It opens thus;

> "When Grecian splendour, unadorn'd by art,
> Confirm'd the Theban oracle—in part,—
> When Genius walk'd digestive o'er the scene.
> In meagre mystery of unletter'd mien,—
> When man first saw, with an inverted eye,
> The tearful breath of purple panoply,
> 'Twas then the Muse, with adamantine grace,
> Replied prophetic from her Pythian base,
> And Roscius bent his Macedonian knee
> Before the squadrons of Melpomene," &c.

As Raymond has not mentioned the ridiculous circumstances which suggested this tissue of nonsense, it may be noticed here. The Drurylane company, when under the management of Stephen Price, included a comedian named Gattie, who was far from contemptible in the common run of elderly characters, and was even excellent in the part of Monsieur Tonson.[108] The manager and some of his friends, wishing to amuse themselves with Gattie's simplicity, put into his hands a long and absurd Epilogue, to be spoken by him after a play which, they pretended, had been sent to the licenser, and was daily expected at the theatre. Gattie forthwith began to study the Epilogue; during the delivery of which he had to appear in three different dresses;—having pulled off first one garment, and then another, he was to be discovered in his favourite part of Monsieur Tonson. All this necessitated sundry rehearsings. At last, Gattie, having mastered the difficulties of the Epilogue, declared himself ready to speak it; when Harley suddenly entered the Green-Room, and announced the melancholy tidings, that Colman had positively refused to license the play, in consequence of which, the Epilogue would not be wanted. On hearing this, Gattie was wild with vexation; for not only had he had a great deal of trouble with the Epilogue, but Mrs. Gattie had been at much pains so to adjust the requisite dresses that he might slip them off quickly and easily. Raymond, being, in those days, very frequently behind the scenes of Drurylane Theatre, witnessed the progress and the finale of this rather cruel joke; and was present when somebody started the idea that a Prologue should be composed as a counterpart to the Epilogue just described, and that, by means of it, a certain actor, who had laughed exceedingly at the trick played on Gattie, should, in his turn and in a similar manner, be made an object of ridicule. Such was the origin of the *Model Prologue:* the first line of which is by Poole, who struck, as it were, the key-note; the rest was written by Raymond *currente calamo*. The actor whom it was intended to hoax, remarked that "it seemed very obscure"; but, in his case, the jest was carried no further.— I may add, that Gattie, the victim of the Epilogue, terminated his career rather oddly: for some reason or other, having altogether abandoned the stage, he retired to Oxford,—not to study the Classics, but to set up a snuff-shop; and there he died in the odour of— tobacco.

Though so handsome a man, and so greatly admired by the other sex, Raymond was never married.— After an illness of several years, which commenced with paralysis, and which, rendering him gradually weaker and weaker (but without affecting his intellect), confined him at last to bed, he expired May 13, 1867, in his 71st year.

---

1. Almeria faints *twice* in *The Mourning Bride* (act i. sc. 2, and act iv. sc. 1); but on neither occasion is Zara present. Mrs. Siddons, therefore, must have seen this premature fainting from the wing, where she very often used to sit, instead of retiring to the green-room.

2. He is generally supposed to have been the son of an Edmund Kean and a *Miss* Carey. [The *DNB* concurs. See also Hillebrand, *Kean*, pp. 2 ff.]

3. See it minutely related in [Bryan W.] Procter's *Life of [Edmund] Kean* [London, 1835], vol. ii. p. 194 sqq. [In Hillebrand's account, Kean watched over Cooke's reinterment in New York and erected a monument to the actor; "in his pocket he carried away a bone of the forefinger of his saint" (*Kean*, pp. 222–23).]

4. [Howard's first appearance on the stage was at Exeter, 26 March 1813, in *The Savages* (Hillebrand, *Kean*, p. 75).]

5. ["Here, mark a poor desolate maid."]

6. [They show 21 roles on 18 dates; a fuller list is in Hillebrand, *Kean*, pp. 73–75. Dyce scribbled at the bottom of the leaf, "K. first appeared in London Jany 26th, 1814." Hillebrand relates this famous event (Kean in Shylock at Drury Lane) on pp. 108 ff.]

7. [Cf. *King Richard III with the Descriptive Notes Recording Edmund Kean's Performance made by James H. Hackett*, ed. Alan S. Downer (London, 1959), pp. xxx–xxxii, 98.]

8.   "O, now, for ever
               Farewell the tranquil mind! farewell content," &c

                                                        Act iii. sc. 3

9.   "*Iago.* She did deceive her father, marrying you;
              And when she seem'd to shake and fear your looks,
              She lov'd them most.
              Othello.   *And so she did."*

                                                        Act iii. sc. 3

10. [See n. 24 below.]

11. [This information is duplicated, in much the same language, by "a conversation preserved by John Forster" (Forster Collection, Victoria and Albert Museum, MS. 48 E 3, No. 315); printed in Hackett's *Descriptive Notes,* ed. Downer, p. xvii.]

12. [See *Macready's Reminiscences,* ed. Sir Frederick Pollock (New York, 1875), pp. 102–3.]

13. [This scrap of a leaf, so numbered in the MS, was inserted after f. 62. Hawkins's "Preface" is dated 1 March 1869; thus this cranky note may have been Dyce's last addition to the MS.]

14. They had already acted together in one or two plays at Glasgow,—where [they were applauded in J. H. Payne's *Brutus,* Sept. 1828. See Hillebrand, *Kean,* p. 298.]

15. A small property with a house on it, near Horndean in Hampshire, which Charles Kean had recently purchased, and which was the residence of his mother during the last years of her life.

16. [These characteristically Romantic comments refer to one of the earliest attempts to restore Shakespeare. On 20 February 1845 Samuel Phelps "produced for the first time Richard III., and from the text of Shakespeare in lieu of the Colley Cibber edition, which had so long held possession of the stage" (W. May Phelps and John Forbes-Robertson, *The Life and Life-Work of Samuel Phelps* [London, 1886], p. 69). This marvel ran for twenty-four nights. A favorable review describing it may be found in the above memoir, pp. 74–75.]

17. Forrest failed in London because his acting, powerful as it undoubtedly was, had such an admixture of coarseness and extravagance as a British audience could not tolerate. But, under the erroneous impression that he owed his failure to the partizans of Macready, he did not scruple to outrage all decency by going into the pit of the Edinburgh Theatre and openly hissing Macready in Hamlet! And the persecution which Macready afterwards underwent in America on account of his alleged enmity to Forrest is hardly yet forgotten.

18. A letter written by me to Charles Kean, at the request of Macready, to ask if he would play Othello to Macready's Iago,—the proceeds of which performance were to be applied to defraying the cost of the statue of Mrs. Siddons now placed in Westminster Abbey.

19. [Dyce's note to this sentence in *The Album,* p. 265, mentions Kemble's asthma and adds, ". . . we have frequently observed him reduced to the indecorous necessity of spitting on the stage."]

20. ["The Pleasures of Imagination," I, 492–500.]

21. [James Boaden, *Memoirs of the Life of John Philip Kemble* (London, 1825), I, 91–104.]

22. [In *The Album,* p. 271, Dyce continues: "Perhaps, towards the end of the tragedy, he was somewhat deficient in that martial ardour which burns in the bosom of the usurping tyrant."]

23. [A word here is illegible.]

24. [Two scribbled paragraphs remain on f. 77^r. They relate to Edmund Kean's acting of Sir Giles Overreach and his effect upon Mrs. Renaud, the anecdote on f. 63^r given above in the article on Kean. The original is in *The Album,* p. 255.]

25. [6th ed. (London, 1800), pp. 33–36.]

26. [A few words are missing in this and the following lacuna owing to a tear in the leaf.]

27. [Alexander Barclay's *Myrrour*] *of gode manners*. [The leaf is torn.]

28. [Dyce is perhaps referring to Michael Kelly.]

29. [The unique MS is in the Larpent Collection at the Huntington Library. See Baker, *Kemble,* p. 43 n.]

30. [On f. 75ᵛ Dyce transcribed from *The Album,* p. 263 n., a brief account of Kemble's last performance, the basis of what follows (ff. 81–82).]

31. [These words follow a deleted sentence corresponding to the next paragraph.]

32. On that night Abbot (as a substitute for C. Kemble) read the part of Young Woodville; which tended still further to render the whole performance heavy.

33. [This leaf, which follows f. 85 in the MS, has no number.]

34. [I have mentioned the first paragraph on this side of the leaf in n. 30. The present paragraph is to be found in *The Album,* p. 264 n.]

35. [P. iv in the Dublin, 1801, edition.]

36. [Things are shuffled here, and the actual letters have been numbered as part of the MS. The original of the first is ff. 93–94, of the second ff. 91–92. Dyce's transcript is on ff. 95, 90ʳ. I print the originals, with Dyce's notes.]

37. Alluding to the D[eepdene], Mr. Hope's mansion near Dorking.

38. Where C. Kemble at that time had a house.

39. [Probably *The Foscari* (Covent Garden, 4 Nov. 1826).]

40. The wife of John Phil[ip] Kemble.

41. A clever and very gentlemanly youth, who took orders, and has been long dead. He had lived chiefly at Bath; and an article by him entitled "The Bath Man," which appeared in *The Album* [IV (1824–25), 173–89, 413–34; it is unsigned], made the good folks of that city extremely angry.

42. Her son, afterwards so eminent as an Anglo-Saxon scholar.

43. [Dyce omits the address in his transcript.]

44. [Dyce omits this much of the sentence.]

45. Elizabeth Kemble, wife of C. E. Whitlock, manager of the Theatre at Newcastle-upon-Tyne. Before her marriage she played for some time at Drurylane Theatre. Having accompanied her husband to America in a professional expedition, she acted there for many years with such success as to realize a handsome fortune.

46. *Hamlet,* act i. sc. i.

47. [A.] Hayward's [edition of] *Autobiography, &c, of Mrs. Piozzi* [*Autobiography Letters and Literary Remains of Mrs. Piozzi (Thrale)*], vol. i. p. 352, sec. ed. [London, 1861].

48. [Thomas Campbell, *Life of Mrs. Siddons* (London, 1834), I, 62.]

49. "Mr. Garrick would also flatter me by sending me into one of the boxes when he acted any of his great characters." Campbell's *Life of Mrs. Siddons,* vol. i. p. 61.

50. [They show 11 roles on 11 dates in 1776–77, 1779.]

51. [William] Forbes's *Life of Dr. Beattie* [*An Account of the Life and Writings of James Beattie*], vol. ii. p.p. 138–9, ed. 1806, 4ᵗᵒ.

52. "Zara's surprising Almeria and Osmyn in conference, produces an incident, which, from situation and circumstance, is rather of the comic than the tragic strain. One princess jealous of another's superior charms may indeed be made a serious subject, as in The Distressed Mother; but the expressions of anger and resentment in this captive queen seldom fail to excite laughter. Mrs. Porter, who was deservedly admired in Zara, and Mrs. Pritchard her successor in that part, could not, with all their skill, prevent the risibility of the audience in this interview. Mrs. Siddons alone preserves the dignity and truth of character, unmixed with any incitement to mirth from countenance, expression, or action." [Thomas] Davies's *Dram. Miscell.* [*Dra-*

matic Miscellanies: Consisting of Critical Observations on Several Plays of Shake-speare (London, 1785)] vol. iii. p[p]. 373[-74].

53. *Critical Essays on the Performers of the London Theatres,* &c, 1807, p[p]. 20[-21].

54. *Observations on Tamerlane* [p. 5],—*British Theatre* [(London, 1808), X].— Hazlitt, whose admiration of Mrs. Siddons knew no bounds, writes as follows; "The very sight of her *[Mrs. Siddons's] name in the play-bills, in *'Tamerlane'* or 'Alex-ander the Great,' threw a light upon the day, and drew after it a long trail of eastern glory, a joy and felicity unutterable, that has since vanished in the mists of criticism and the glitter of idle distinctions." *Memoirs of W[illiam] Hazlitt* [London, 1867] by W. Carew Hazlitt, vol. i. p. 202.— On one occasion, in the dying scene of Arpasia, Mrs. Siddons was so overcome by her feelings that she actually fainted. Of this the audience were immediately aware by the violence with which her head struck the stage and by the disorder of her dress; and for some time great alarm and excitement prevailed in the theatre.

55. "Mrs. Siddons very lately in the third act of the Fair Penitent was so far affected with assuming the mingled passions of pride, fear, anger, and conscious guilt, that I might appeal to the spectators whether, in spite of the rouge which the actress is obliged to put on, some paleness did not shew itself in her countenance." *Dram. Miscell.* vol. iii. p. 58.

56. The late Mr. Adair Hawkins, who had practised as a surgeon, told me, that, in company with a friend, also a medical man, he saw Mrs. Siddons act Rosalind, and that her swoon at sight of the bloody handkerchief was so true to nature that they could hardly believe it to be feigned.

57. For a benefit.

58. See a Letter of Miss Seward to Whalley [6 Aug. 1795],—*Journals and Correspondence of [Thomas S.] Whalley* [edited] by [Rev. Hill] Wickham [London, 1863], vol. ii. p. 98.

59. [The leaf is torn, making illegible a note on Dr. John Thomson, professor of general pathology in the University of Edinburgh, who apparently had something to say about Mrs. Siddons's acting and Dugald Stewart's oratory.]

60. In Whalley's *Journals and Correspondence,* edited by Mr. Wickham, is a blunder connected with the above-mentioned Address, *so strange and unparalleled that I cannot even invent an hypothesis to account for it.* He informs us that in 1781 *[1782] Mrs. Siddons took leave of the Bath-audience . . . . "when she led forward on the stage her three children, most becomingly dressed, and repeated:—

> 'These are the moles that heave me from your side,
> Where I was rooted, where I could have died. . . .' "

> vol. i. p. 7

[I have spared the reader Twiss's section.] Now, the first two lines just cited are really from the Address, written by herself, which Mrs. Siddons delivered at Bath in 1781: *but the eight remaining lines,* "Perhaps your hearts," &c, *form the conclusion of the Address composed for her by her nephew Horace Twiss, and spoken by her at Covent-Garden Theatre in 1812!* Both Addresses may be read in Campbell's *Life of Mrs. Siddons,* vol. i. p[p]. 90[-92], vol. ii. p[p]. 338[-39]. And is it not surprising that Mr. Wickham was not struck by the utter absurdity of making Mrs. Siddons declare in 1782, that "her lips had poured *so long* the charmed sorrows of your Shakespeare's song"? [F. 205ʳ comprises what is apparently a rough draft of a letter containing most of this information.]

61. She was the daughter of Tate Wilkinson, the York manager, and author of those queer productions, *Memoirs of His Own Life* and *The Wandering Patentee.* In 1798, at the request of Mrs. Siddons, who had long felt a deep regard for her, Miss Wilkinson became a permanent inmate in the Siddons family, not as a humble companion, for she was in easy circumstances, but as a cherished friend; and there she remained till the death of the great actress. She was a very worthy person, and not devoid of talent. That the gods had not made her sentimental and romantic she

could not help. On a day following one of Mrs. Siddons's benefits when she had been playing a highly tragic part, Miss R—— said to Miss Wilkinson, "Surely Mrs. Siddons must have been dreadfully exhausted by the wear and tear of her feelings last night." "Yes, indeed," replied Miss Wilkinson; "and you can't think what a quantity of cold mutton and cold apple-tart she ate for supper."

62. In the "Supplement" to his *Memoirs of Mrs. Siddons* [2d ed. (London, 1831)] Boaden says; "*[Her son] Mr. George John Siddons, a few months before the death of his father, married, in India, Miss *Fonhill*, daughter of Judge *Fonhill*, by whom he has a numerous family." [II,] p. 412,—where *"Fonhill"* is a mistake for *"Fombell."*

63. Concerning that work see the close of the article "Thomas Campbell." [It will not be found there.]

64. Vol. ii. p.p. 364–5. [The anecdote about Mrs. Glover at the end of this paragraph has been printed from an MS in the Forster Collection (No. 315) by Alan S. Downer, *The Eminent Tragedian: William Charles Macready* (Cambridge, Mass., 1966), p. 77.]

65. I may notice that when she selected Shakespeare's *Measure for Measure* for one of her public readings, she retained a portion of the comic dialogue, but without laying much stress on it.

66. "L'actrice la plus noble dans ses manières, Madame Siddons, ne perd rien de sa dignité quand elle se prosterne contre terre." *Corinne* par Mad. De Staël Holstein, t. iii. p. 202, ed. 1807.

67. The second son of Charles Kemble. He afterwards went into the army; and died shortly before his father.

68. Mrs. Faucit.

69. In Congreve's *Way of the World*.

70. I have doubts about this name; but I can answer for the correctness of the anecdote in other respects. [Compare the version in *Diary, Reminiscences, and Correspondence of Henry Crabb Robinson,* ed. Thomas Sadler, 3d ed. (London and New York, 1872), I, 217.]

71. He probably had seen one of her sisters in the part.

72. [Cf. Dyce's *Recollections of the Table-Talk of Samuel Rogers. To Which is Added Porsoniana*, 3d ed. (London, 1856), p. 190. In 1833, Crabb Robinson witnessed the "entertainment" in the anecdote which follows (*Diary*, ed. Sadler, II, 135).]

73. In a sale-catalogue of books I find,—

> Marlborough (Duke of) Life, Death and Burial of Cock Robin,
> set to Music for four Voices, *coloured engraving*
> LARGE PAPER (*unique*), *red morocco super extra, g. e.*
> *with arms of the Duke of Marlborough stamped in*
> *gold on sides*   n.d.

How honoured is Cock Robin—to have had his story read and wept-over by Mrs. Siddons, and set to music by a duke!

74. [See *Piozzi*, ed. Hayward, I, 116.]

75. Be it remembered that in those days the reputation of Sir Thomas Lawrence was undeservedly great.

76. In my *Recollections of the Table-Talk of Samuel Rogers*, &c, p. 190, third ed., where this anecdote of Mrs. Siddons is given, I have, by an oversight, described Miss Brunton as being afterwards *Lady Craven*. But the Miss Brunton alluded to by Mrs. Siddons was a rather clever tragic actress who married the Della-Cruscan poet Merry: the Miss Brunton, whose great beauty and faultless conduct in private life raised her to the rank of Lady Craven, was a comic actress of moderate ability, and the sister of Mrs. Merry.

77. But Boaden thought very differently of King's acting in those two parts: see *Life of Kemble,* vol. i. p[p]. 60[–61].

78. On being appointed Licenser and Examiner of plays, Colman quitted that locality. He died at his house in Brompton Square.

79. Latterly she had a much better Orlando—indeed, most probably the very best ever seen—Charles Kemble.

80. In the song, "When daisies pied," &c, which belongs to *Love's Labour's Lost*, and which is generally introduced by all Rosalinds who are able to sing.

81. It was in the part of Nell that Mrs. Clive (then Miss Raftor) first convinced the public of her great comic powers.

82. Qy. in Act v. sc. 3?— A reader of the play will be at a loss to know how Mrs. Jordan contrived to engraft on that scene, or, indeed, on any other scene, the extravagance here complained of: but that she did something extremely *outré* is beyond a doubt; and it must be remembered that any liberty taken by such a darling actress would be readily enough forgiven by the public, though not by Charles Kemble. "Saturday, January 9th *[1808]. In the evening went to Drurylane. 'The Wonder.' Elliston very poor in Felix, and Mrs. Jordan bringing out too often her oysterwoman notes in Violante, which destroys all the effect of her otherwise captivating voice." *Miss Berry's Journals* [*Extracts of the Journals and Correspondence of Miss Berry from the Year 1783 to 1852*, ed. Lady Theresa Lewis (London, 1865)], vol. ii. p. 338.

83. [The original of this letter comprises both sides of leaves 86 and 87. I follow the original instead of the transcript by Dyce, who corrects the spelling and regularizes capitalization and punctuation. He leaves gaps for the readings that I have indicated as doubtful, excepting "any," for which he reads "my." According to Nicoll (*English Drama*, IV, 338; V, 443), Kenney's last production was either (appropriately) *Up the Flue* (1846), written in collaboration with Dion Boucicault, or *London Pride* (1859), performed ten years after his death. However, the *DNB* concurs with Dyce that *Infatuation* was his last play.]

84. ["What was practically his first appearance in London took place 31 Oct. 1801 as Richard III" (*DNB*).]

85. In Macklin's *Man of the World*.

86. In Macklin's farce, *Marriage* [i.e., *Love*] *à la Mode*.

87. Years before these entertainments, Bannister used to give (at theatres) a medley somewhat similar to them, though immeasurably inferior, entitled *Bannister's Budget* (in which I remember two lines of a song,—

> "I am a wild and wandering boy,
> And I come from *the isle of Troy*"!!).

This *Budget* was not his own composition, but written expressly for him. Mathews's entertainments were concocted by himself. [This note clearly belongs to the first paragraph, though Dyce has not so indicated.]

88. See the article headed "Samuel Taylor Coleridge" in the present work.

89. "I saw Munden in Scrub, after Garrick, and perceived no inferiority." *Literary and Miscellaneous Memoirs* by [Joseph] Cradock [London, 1828], vol. iv [ed. J. B. Nichols]. p. 246. Cradock was considered to be a first-rate amateur actor: he was intimate with Garrick, whom he imitated very successfully.

90. *Gag* in theatrical language means the stuff introduced by an actor beyond what is "set down" for him.

91. [The *DNB* gives Mrs. Piozzi's birth-year as 1740/41 and Conway's as 1789. It claims that Conway's true name was Rugg. Dyce appears indebted to the "Preface" to the *Letters* for several details.]

92. "The genuineness of the letters is doubtful," &c. Hayward's *Autobiography, &c of Mrs. Piozzi*, vol. i. p. 359, sec. ed.

93. [See the "Preface" to the *Letters*, p. 14.]

94. *The Examiner*, Feb. 16, 1861 [No. 2768, p. 100],—cited by Mr. Hayward *ubi supra* [I, 359 n.].

95. *New Monthly Magazine* [ed. William Harrison Ainsworth] for April 1861 [N.S. CXXI], p. 447. [An unsigned review of Hayward.]

96. So I learned from Mrs. Clarke, the wife of the manager of the Liverpool Theatre: the jeweller was her father; and she was well acquainted with Conway his apprentice.— Mr. and Mrs. Clarke were a very worthy couple and much esteemed by the members of the theatrical profession: they both died nearly about the same time, not long after he had retired from the management at Liverpool; where he used to play in comedy and she in tragedy.— Mrs. Clarke, while a young married woman, came out as Euphrasia in *The Grecian Daughter* at Covent-Garden Theatre during the O. P. Riots; when a debutante of far superior talent than she could boast would have had little or no chance of success, all being wild uproar.

97. At which date, it must be confessed, first-rate tragic acting is not to be seen.

98. "New Theatre Royal, Haymarket, This evening The Provoked Husband, Lord Townly, Mr. Conway (his first appearance in London these five years)." *The Times* for July 5, 1821 [p. 2b]. On the 6ᵗʰ of the following Septʳ he played Jaffeir (his last part) and repeated it several times at intervals.

99. Miss Young had reached a "pretty age" when she bestowed her hand on the stripling Pope, who will be recollected as a veteran actor by some readers of the present work. (And see the article "Charles Mathews" [. . .])—In a letter to Dr. Whalley, dated Septʳ 28, 1785, Mrs. Siddons writes, "Miss Young is married to a Mr. Pope, a very boy, and the only child she will have by her marriage." Whalley's *Journals and Correspondence*, &c, vol. i. p. 446.

100. [P. v in the London, 1785, edition.]

101. "Mr. Holcroft himself played the part of Figaro the first night, in the absence of Mr. Bonner [*sic*], for whom it was designed, and who afterwards took it." *Holcroft's Memoirs* [*Memoirs of the Late Thomas Holcroft, Written by Himself*, ed. William Hazlitt (London, 1816)], vol. ii. p[p]. 58[-59].

102. *Life of Kemble,* vol. i. p. 82.

103. [One exchange between Mrs. Clive and Miss Pope is printed by Percy Fitzgerald, *The Life of Mrs. Catherine Clive* (London, 1888), pp. 97-99.]

104. [As evidence, Dyce quotes from two works by Cousin D'Avalon: *Voltairiana* and *Diderotiana.*]

105. "Et adhuc sub judice lis est." Horace,—*Ars Poetica,* 78.

106. ["Brambilla."]

107. [VI (1835), 123-24. It is there entitled "An Occasional Prologue."]

108. [In the play by Moncrieff, not to be confused with the earlier-mentioned verse-tale of the same title by John Taylor.]

PREFACE
TO CHAPTER THREE

T HESE MEMOIRS OF DYCE's scholarly and clerical brethren contain
some of his best writing. I have given the place of honor to
Thomas Taylor the Platonist (1758–1835). Unlike the others,
he has exerted direct influence even in this century, and some of his
work has recently enjoyed a splendid reissue in *Thomas Taylor the
Platonist: Selected Writings,* ed. Kathleen Raine and George M. Harper (Princeton, N. J., 1969). This volume provides the "basic" Taylor
and an exhaustive bibliography; also, in two prefatory essays it illus-
trates his importance to English Romantics from Coleridge to Yeats
and his influence as well on the American idealists. The three early
biographical essays that it reprints duplicate very little of Dyce's article.
One of these (pp. 105–21) is autobiographical and was apparently unknown to Dyce, though he repeats the anecdote of Mary Wollstonecraft's
affectation about wine and teacups (p. 113). Dyce's vignette of Taylor
and "Blake the artist," the man with whom the Platonist is most often
associated, is unique, and it rings true for both eccentrics. Indeed, it is
the first solid bit of evidence that the two men knew each other personally. Especially vital for an understanding of Taylor's stature are
Frank B. Evans III, "Thomas Taylor, Platonist of the Romantic Period," *PMLA* LV (1940), 1060–79; and George M. Harper, *The Neo-*

platonism of William Blake (Chapel Hill, N. C., 1961), passim. Dyce's article sheds much new light on the last years of a man whom Harper calls "the most important disseminator of ancient philosophy in the history of English and American literature" (p. [v]).

The remaining articles appear in their manuscript order. All of the principals have been enrolled in the *DNB,* with the exception of Dr. John Shaw, who has no claim to be there. Dyce has told us virtually all that will be of interest today, and I will not greatly expand his accounts here. Fortunately, he has chosen to point up the "freaks and vagaries" of men like Edmund H. Barker (1788–1839), George Burges (1786?–1864), and Dr. Samuel Parr (1747–1825), a pedagogue and controversialist termed "the whig Johnson." Among the many original stories is that of George Steevens (1736–1800) and Dr. Johnson; it is not in Boswell, though it resembles a remark Johnson made to Beauclerk on 13 April 1778. (Dyce's source, "J. Nicol," is no doubt John Nichols. I do not find the story in the latter's *Literary Anecdotes* or *Illustrations of the Literary History of the Eighteenth Century.*) The "unknown tongues" exploited by Edward Irving (1792–1834), the renowned preacher, began to wag in 1830.

Happily, Victorian biographies of scholars are generally not so infested with hackwork as are the stage reminiscences of the time. Still, the former genre shares with the latter the disadvantage of being largely derivative. The better accounts give us an idea of the scholarly occupations, critical wars, and learned jests that interested the audience Dyce had in mind, and a fair specimen of this kind of writing is Henry J. Nicoll's *Great Scholars* (Edinburgh, 1880). Like Dyce he writes on Bentley, Porson, Parr, Sir William Jones, and Bishop Blomfield. His report of Blomfield's skirmishes with Barker (pp. 242–45) is worth summarizing, since it is one of the longest-lived anecdotes outlined by Dyce. The trouble began with the rivalry between the *Museum Criticum,* a periodical started by Blomfield, and the *Classical Journal* of Barker's printer friend Abraham Valpy. (In the *Journal,* incidentally, Barker at times criticized his own work and then replied to this criticism with triumphant refutations—all done anonymously, of course.) When Barker and Valpy began editing Stephens's *Greek Thesaurus* in 1816, they had 1,100 subscribers, a number that understandably diminished after Blomfield's article in the *Quarterly Review*. By Blomfield's reckoning, Barker had added so much verbiage that page 688 of his edition corresponded to page 53 of the original. It must, he concluded, reach fifty folio volumes in about seventy years, forming a periodical that the subscribers might bequeath to their heirs. Barker's reply in *Aristarchus Anti-Blomfieldianus* is incoherent with rage; but he and Valpy did at last hold the *Thesaurus* down to ten volumes. A "Memoir" is prefixed to the first volume of Barker's *Literary Anecdotes and Contemporary Reminiscences* (London, 1852).

Most such bellicosity in the age of Bentley, an era that his disciple Richard Porson (1759–1808) had extended into the nineteenth century, was involved with verbal criticism. Textual scholarship became a discipline and emendation an art; not until the more modern forms of "the higher criticism" was much attention paid to interpretation. Dyce's prophecy that Thomas Tyrwhitt's reputation would outlive Porson's has come true, but both men have been superseded by giants like Skeat. Nonetheless, the scholarly continuum that begins in the late seventeenth century is intimately bound to the more purely "literary" tradition that produced both Pope and Wordsworth. One can marvel at Dyce's seeming acquaintance with everyone south of the Tweed, yet it is not surprising that he moved so easily in so many circles: in this he was not exceptional. As this chapter shows, men of letters in Dyce's time seldom confined themselves to one specialized aspect of their literary culture.

CHAPTER THREE ❖ THE CLERISY

THOMAS TAYLOR, THE PLATONIST [*ff. 207–12, 212a*^{r}]

He very frequently visited me in Gray's Inn; and I occasionally saw him in Manor-Place, Walworth, where, during the last forty-five years of his life, he occupied one of the smallest houses possible. When I knew him he was a widower for the second time, with two children by his first wife, a daughter and a son. He and his daughter, who was married and taught music, had quarrelled and were not on speaking terms. His son, who was baptized Proclus and lived with him, was an eccentric empty-headed stripling, bred to no profession, and amused himself by writing nonsensical dramas for the lowest of the minor theatres.

Taylor told me that, on account of his persisting in the study of the Platonic philosophy, he was turned out of his father's house when a very young man.

He had taught himself Greek, with the niceties of which language he was most imperfectly acquainted; hence the errors in his various translations: but his knowledge of the *matter* of Plato, of Aristotle, of the multitudinous commentators on Aristotle, of Proclus, of Plotinus, &c., was probably never equalled by that of any of his countrymen.[1] His acquaintance with Latin was also comparatively imperfect: when Creuzer and Boissonade wrote to him in that language, he used to answer their letters in English. I have heard him make gross false quantities both in Greek and Latin, while "spouting" passages of the ancient poets; which he was fond of doing, for he had a very powerful memory, and could repeat whole pages of obscure classics, such as Dionysius Periegetes, &c. The consciousness of his own deficiencies in critical scholarship prompted him to undervalue it: accordingly, having gone down to Oxford to transcribe a manuscript of Olympiodorus in the Bodleian Library, and having been invited by Coplestone to dine at Oriel College, he made himself very ridiculous after dinner by declaiming against verbal critics.

He did not conceal his contempt for Christianity: but what his religious belief really was, I never distinctly understood. It is at least certain that he had a horror of atheists; and it was even suspected by some that he believed in a plurality of deities,—a suspicion which certain passages in his writings would seem somewhat to favour. The walls of the little study, in which he had executed the greater portion of his immense literary labours, were ornamented with many very small pieces of plate-glass, a few inches in breadth and length, set in gilt frames; and when I asked him what these tiny mirrors meant, he evaded the question by replying that "he was fond of light." I have heard it asserted that they were votive offerings.[2]

He firmly believed in ghosts and in supernatural warnings. Among his acquaintances was John Hinckley, the translator of *The History of Rinaldo Rinaldini,* a German novel, who died in his Chambers at Gray's Inn, and was partly eaten up by blue-flies before it was known that he was dead,[3]—a catastrophe which was supernaturally communicated to Taylor!

He also firmly believed in astrology. Having received a letter from an adept in that science who resided at Birmingham, announcing that the stars portended him a disaster before the expiration of a certain time, Taylor kept close at home, and refused all invitations to visit abroad till the evil hour had passed. He was compelled, however, to go into the city on business while the danger was yet impending; "and," said he to me, "as I was crossing Blackfriars-Bridge on my way homewards, I very narrowly escaped being run over by a hackney-coach."

He firmly believed, too, in alchemy. "Whence," he would exclaim, "could the Egyptians, who had no mines, have possibly obtained the quantity of gold they possessed, except by alchemy?"

One day he said to me, "A French astronomer has lately seen a planet through the moon; I always knew that she was transparent." On my observing that I had always been led to understand she was an opaque body, and asking of what he supposed her to consist, he replied, "I believe her to be a portion of that vivific fire which burns in man."

He was fluent in talk and expressed himself well. While discussing any subject, he evidently thought that he adduced an unanswerable argument by declaring that such and such was the opinion of Plato, or of Plotinus, &c, &c. Once in my Chambers in Gray's Inn, when the conversation turned on suicide, he astonished the company by gravely quoting some ancient worthy to prove that there are circumstances under which a man is quite justified in killing himself,—for instance, "if he should happen to fall desperately and incurably in love with his grandmother."

On my asking him if he really believed the assertion of Iamblichus, that the river Nessus, while Pythagoras was crossing it, said in a distinct voice, "Hail, Pythagoras (Χαιρε, Πυθαγόρα) !"[4] he replied, "Certainly I do."

The two persons among the moderns, who, in Taylor's estimation, had done the most injury to philosophy and science, were Lord Bacon and Sir Isaac Newton.

His taste in prose-fiction may be conceived from his decidedly preferring *Parismus Prince of Bohemia* to the novels of Sir Walter Scott.

In the *Bibliotheca Parriana* (the Catalogue of Dr. Parr's Library [by H. G. Bohn (London, 1827)]), p. 388, we are informed that on a copy of Taylor's *Dissertation on the Eleusinian and Bacchic Mysteries* [1790], Parr had written, "By Mr. Taylor, the learned mystic, whom Porson and his tribe most injustly derided." Now, I know that the original manuscript of that note contained an epithet which the editor thought proper to omit—"Porson and his *odious* tribe."

An entry in Holcroft's Diary, dated Nov' 14th, 1798, stands thus: "Dined on Monday with P——; Platonist Taylor, and D—— present. Taylor intolerant and abusive to all who do not pretend to understand and put faith in his Platonic jargon. Had he the power, according to

P——, he would bring every man of us to the stake. From my own experience, P——'s description is scarcely exaggerated; but though a bigot, Taylor is an honest one."[5] Of his meeting Holcroft on another occasion Taylor gave me the following account: "I once dined at Northmore's[6] when Godwin, Holcroft, and Wolcot (Peter Pindar) were there. The French revolution having been mentioned, I observed, that the atrocities which attended it were not to be wondered at, as those who brought it about were a set of atheists. 'Sir,' cried Holcroft, 'do you mean to say that all atheists are villains? If so, I think it right to tell you that *I am an atheist.*' My answer was, 'I am sorry, Mr. Holcroft, to hear you make such a confession.' On this, Holcroft grew warm, and replied to me very rudely; when Northmore said, 'Gentlemen, I cannot suffer such language at my table, and request that you will change the subject of conversation.' "

Taylor used frequently to meet Mrs. Carter at Bennet Langton's. He described her as a very agreeable, unaffected, and vulgar-looking woman. Of her translation of Epictetus he thought highly; though he objected to her rendering the Greek word προαιρεσις by the English "*choice*,"—instead of "*deliberate choice.*"

Mary Wollstonecraft, before her marriage, lodged and boarded several months at Taylor's house (during the life of his first wife, and previous to his removal to Manor-Place, where he died). At that time, he said, she was very modest and unassuming. But after she became acquainted with literary persons at Johnson's (the bookseller in Paul's Churchyard), and set up for an authoress, her affectation was intolerable: she would make her servant feed her, while she continued reading or writing, and declared that she was so absorbed in study as not to know whether she was eating beef or mutton; for the sake of singularity, she would drink wine out of a tea-cup, &c, &c.

Taylor, so absurd himself in many respects, was ready enough to laugh at the strange fancies of others,—for instance, at those of that half-crazed man of real [?] genius, Blake the artist. "Pray, Mr. Taylor," said Blake one day, "did you ever find yourself, as it were, standing close beside the vast and luminous orb of the moon?"— "Not that I remember, Mr. Blake: did you ever?"— "Yes, frequently; and I have felt an almost irresistible desire to throw myself into it headlong."— "I think, Mr. Blake, you had better not; for if you were to do so, you most probably would never come out of it again."

Taylor's two great patrons were Mr. William Meredith of Harley Place and the Duke of Norfolk:[7] his translation of Aristotle was printed at the expense of the former; his translation of Plato at the expense of the latter. He used to call them his *two tyrants,* and said that he had suffered as much from their overbearing insolence and caprice as his master Plato had endured from the elder and the younger Dionysius.

Meredith settled on him an annuity of a hundred pounds,—"which was less than he left his valet," said Taylor somewhat ungratefully, and forgetting that the valet had been much more serviceable to Meredith than himself. It was for this *tyrant* that Lawrence painted a full-length portrait of Taylor, in which the coarse features of the original were very skilfully softened.

The Duke of Norfolk, though a professed admirer of the philosophy of the ancients, was a gross sensualist. Taylor—whose stories of his amours will not bear repetition here—said that "his eating was wonderful," and that he had seen him gobble up at dinner the whole of the kidney-fat of a large loin of veal. Among the longest excursions Taylor ever made from London was a journey to Arundel Castle, whither he accompanied the Duke in his carriage; and his grace happening to be in an ill humour during the journey, did not exchange a word with his companion, but sat reading Payne Knight's *Essay on the Worship of Priapus.* Taylor remained a week at Arundel Castle; and while there, one night (as he informed several of his friends) he saw the ghost of Queen Mawd.

The good-natured Duke of Sussex, who had some learning (especially in Hebrew), and enjoyed the society of literary men, occasionally invited Taylor to Kensington Palace; where, doubtless, he, as well as Dr. Parr, were not the less welcome because they were "oddities." Of the following letter I kept a copy by Taylor's particular desire:

"Dear Sir,

During some conversation which I had the honour to have last Wednesday with his Royal Highness the Duke of Sussex, I happened to mention that according to Simplicius, who was one of the most acute of Aristotle's Interpreters, the fall of man as narrated by Moses is a fable, originally derived from the Egyptians; and being myself persuaded that it is so, it has since occurred to me that the narration, in conformity to the most ancient theology, may be developed as follows.

In the first place, the fable obscurely indicates the pre-existence of the soul, in the regions of perfect bliss, i.e., in Platonic language, in the intelligible world, and its lapse from thence into the regions of mortality. This intelligible world is signified by Paradise. In the second place, Adam denotes the rational, and Eve the irrational part of the soul; the latter of which perfectly corresponds to the Pandora of the Greeks; and the Serpent is matter. The irrational part therefore, by inclining to matter, becomes vitiated, and the rational part is also defiled by listening to the suggestions of the irrational soul thus corrupted. This leads to the eating of the forbidden fruit, through which they are no longer conversant with good only, but become acquainted with evil. Hence they are no longer naked, or divested of material garments, but are covered with fig-leaves, i.e. with corporeal and mortal vestments. And in the third place, they are afterwards expelled from Paradise, i.e. they fall into the realms of mortality and matter.

Such is my explanation of the fable. You will oblige me by showing it to his Royal Highness, who appears to me to be one of the most learned and intelligent princes in Europe. I need not add that I shall be extremely gratified to find that he approves of my solution of this enigma.

I remain, Dear Sir,
with great esteem,
Yours sincerely,
Tho. Taylor.

Manor Place,
    August 27th 1824.
        To T. J. Pettigrew Esqre,
            Saville Row,
                Burlington Gardens."

Among Taylor's friends was Kelsall, a very fair scholar, who published several works on classical subjects.[8] He possessed considerable property; and was not a little eccentric,—so much so, indeed, that, if Taylor was to be believed, Kelsall had made a will directing the bulk of his fortune to be laid out in building a temple to the Sun on the shores of the Caspian;[9] which extraordinary bequest Taylor mentioned to me with something like anger, insinuating that Kelsall ought rather to have left the money in question to *him*. (Be it observed that Kelsall was younger than Taylor by a good many years, and, as will afterwards be seen, was one of the few persons invited to his funeral.)

Cory, the author of *Ancient Fragments,*[10] &c,—a solicitor in Boswell's Court, and as pure and amiable a young man as ever existed,—requested me to introduce him to Taylor, whose writings had made a strong impression on him. I did so, by taking him to breakfast at Manor Place; and he speedily formed the strictest intimacy with the master of the house, looking up to him with a veneration akin to that which the philosophers of Greece excited in their disciples.

Breakfasts were the only entertainments Taylor attempted to give. They took place in a very small parlour containing a piano-forte which had been procured for the use of his daughter before her marriage; and I remember that one forenoon, Dr. Kitchiner, who was occasionally a guest at those breakfasts, played and sung "God Save the King" with an energy so tremendous that half-a-dozen ragged urchins came crowding round the window.

Taylor and George Burges seldom were together without disputing. Taylor despised (or affected to despise) a critical knowledge of Greek, which was Burges's forte; and Burges had a contempt for Taylor's want of that knowledge and ignorance of metre. Besides, Burges annoyed Taylor by talking in a disparaging way (and, no doubt, often very much at random) of certain ancient worthies whom Taylor regarded with great respect. Taylor once said to me, "Yesterday I met Burges in the street, and had some conversation with him; and what do you think, sir, he said?" I could not possibly guess. "Sir," continued Taylor, his lips quivering with indignation, "he said that *Hermogenes was an ass!*"

Some years before his death, I suggested to Taylor the writing of his autobiography; and he was so pleased with the idea that he begged me to treat about its publication with Pickering, who agreed to purchase it on terms with which Taylor was well satisfied. But though he began the work, and indeed made some progress in it, he presently gave it up entirely, feeling perhaps that at his period of life it was too laborious a task. This I have always regretted, for he had much to tell that was curious, and he would have told it faithfully and without exaggeration.

As age crept upon him, his health began to break; and finding himself unequal to the long walks which he used formerly to take, his visits to me at Gray's Inn became less frequent. But I occasionally went to see him at Manor-Place; and now and then I received from him short letters like the following:—

"Manor Place, Walworth, Jan. 14, 1835.

My dear Sir,

Many thanks for your transcript from Elmsley's edition of the *Œdip. Col.* of Sophocles. As my studies have been principally confined to the writings of the ancient philosophers, I was not aware that the sentence alluded to in your letter is to be found in Theognis, Valerius Maximus, Solinus, &c; but it is strange that such verbalists as Burton and Brunck should have been ignorant that Plutarch in his work entitled *Consolation to Apollonius* has inserted an extract from a lost treatise of Aristotle, in which this passage is given.

Hoping that I shall soon have the pleasure of seeing you in Manor Place, I remain,

Very sincerely Yours,

Thomas Taylor.

P.S. Suffer me to remind you of the following passage in one of the Letters of Apollonius Tyaneus: . . . *[I have a friendship with philosophers: but with sophists, grammarians, or any other such set of wretched creatures, I have neither at present a friendship, nor ever hereafter shall have]."[11]

"My dear Sir,

Many thanks for your exceeding kindness.

I am glad to find that you speak favourably of the exposition which I sent you.

Hoping that I shall soon see you after your return from Scotland, and wishing you in the mean time perfect health and success in all your undertakings, I remain, with great esteem,

Yours most sincerely,

Thomas Taylor.

Manor Place,
    April 8ᵗʰ 1835."

The words "exceeding kindness" in the above letter allude to small presents of wine, &c, by which I feel a satisfaction in thinking that I added somewhat to his comforts.

To the end of his existence Taylor endeavoured to carry into practice the precepts of the Grecian philosophers; and encountered "the inevitable hour" with all the resolution of an ancient stoic. I went to see him the day before he died; and when I inquired "how he was," he answered, "I have passed a dreadful night of pain; *but you remember what Posidonius said to Pompey*" (that pain was not an evil).[12]

The only attendants at his funeral were his brother (whom I had never before met or even heard of), his son Proclus, Cory, Kelsall, and myself; and "on a raw and gusty day," November 6ᵗʰ, 1835, we saw him—a half-heathen philosopher—consigned to the grave in the Christian burial-ground of Newington Church. On that occasion, poor Proclus startled us by hysteric bursts of grief; for he felt his father's death acutely. But he was a silly youth, and soon after wasted in theatrical speculations at minor theatres the scanty patrimony to which he succeeded.

EDMUND HENRY BARKER [*ff. 19–21ʳ*]

Was educated at Trinity College, Cambridge, where, in 1809, he gained the medals for the Greek and Latin Epigrams;[13] and having afterwards devoted himself to literature,—chiefly to classical literature,—he published a vast variety of volumes, in which his industry was more conspicuous than his learning, though the latter was by no means contemptible. Of his indomitable perseverance he has left a monument in his edition of [Henry] Stephens's *Greek Thesaurus* [1816–26], which was printed by Valpy, and which he strove to render as complete as possible by means of rare books and the MS. Notes of scholars foreign as well as English, purchased, from all quarters, at extravagant prices. In constructing and printing the Index to that work,—an Index vying, I believe, in completeness with any of the Indices ever made by the united efforts of individuals,—Barker was occupied fully three years; and such was his positive love of drudgery, that, as he himself informed me, the years so spent "were among the happiest of his life." Unfortunately, however, as editor of the *Thesaurus* he showed extreme want of judgment, more particularly in swelling it with whole pages of superfluous matter, strangely jumbled together; and while as yet only a small portion of the work had been published, it drew forth from the pen of Blomfield (subsequently the bishop) a very clever and severe critique in *The Quarterly Review* [XXII (1820), 302–48]. To that attack Barker replied in *Aristarchus Anti-Blomfieldianus*,[14]—a rambling pamphlet of such intolerable dullness that few persons, I presume, have been able to read it through. All this brought poor Barker into bad odour with the public, and rendered it adviseable that (to his great mortification) his name should not appear on the title-page of the *Thesaurus*.

Barker was a bibliomaniac after Dr. Dibdin's own heart; and for several years he was an excellent customer to Thorpe and other London booksellers, whose tempting catalogues were regularly sent down to Thetford, where he had fixed his residence. But his income (arising partly from money settled upon his wife) was comparatively limited; and his extensive purchases of books (quite independent of those, which, as already mentioned, he had made for the *Thesaurus*), his having printed sundry unsaleable volumes at his own expense, and other acts of imprudence, combined to throw him into serious difficulties. From these, however, he confidently expected to be freed on the issue of a law-suit, by which he laid claim to a property of £4000 per annum. This hope proved utterly abortive: he lost the law-suit, which he had carried on for ten years; he was reduced to poverty, and obliged to sell his beloved library to satisfy his creditors; and having left his wife and family at Thetford, he—a first-rate "architect of fine chateaux in air" —migrated to London, with many a scheme floating in his brain for the bettering of his circumstances. That his home was none of the happiest I conclude from his once having said to me in Gray's Inn, "Really your Chambers seem very comfortable: *if Mrs. Barker were dead,* I should like to have a set myself."

Months and months passed away, during which he was busily engaged in literary labour, printing at his own risk (with his usual indiscretion) volumes for which he had no immediate means of payment. During that period, too, he bestowed more of his company upon his friends than suited with their necessary avocations, preparing "copy" and correcting his proof-sheets for hours together at their houses; the late Basil Montagu, Dr. Giles, and myself being especial sufferers from his volunteer visits, though we forebore showing any impatience at this intrusiveness on the part of an amiable man in such a condition. He still cherished visions of his future prosperity, and felt assured that "he should eventually possess a library not inferior to the one which he had been compelled to part with."

But from such dreams he was rudely awakened by being arrested for debt. He was conveyed to a sponging-house in Chancery-Lane; whence he was removed to the Queen's Bench, and afterwards to the Fleet. While in confinement, he wrote to me as follows:

> "The Fleet-Prison, 15 in Fair,
> March 16, 1838.

Dear Sir,

I am a candidate for the Registrarship of the University of London (Somerset-House), £600 a year. The candidates will be very numerous; but my Testimonials, of which I have already sent in 80, will decidedly place me at the head of the candidates, and I have more Testimonials to send in: I muster 7 Bishops, 1 Dean, 2 Archdeacons, 10 Doctors of Divinity, 1 Royal Duke, and 1 Duke of Royal descent. On *two* public occasions already (viz. for the Latin Professorship at the first starting of the London University, now University-College, and for the Head-Mastership of Stamford School) my Testimonials were allowed to be the *best;* and I failed in *both* instances on the same ground, that I was *not* a schoolmaster by profession. Will you have the goodness to send a Testimonial of learning, candor, morals, manners,

activity, zeal, punctuality, and the 1001 virtues and graces which shine
out in my character! Make no allusion to my being here, as I shall be
out before the election. Mitford sent a *long* Letter to the Mayor of
Stamford, which I use on this occasion. I remain,

Dear Sir,

Very truly Yours,

E. H. Barker.

The Rev. Alexander Dyce,
    Gray's Inn."

I need hardly observe that he was not appointed to the Registrarship
about which he wrote me the above letter.

Barker was liberated from the Fleet after a detention of ten months;
during which he received from individuals high in the church and
from others (to whom he had applied for aid as a distressed man
of letters) not less than several hundred pounds; and if he had only
possessed an atom of prudence, it was just possible that he might yet
have recovered his old position in society. But, alas! in evil hour, at
Jackson's Coffee-house in Bow Street, he had formed an acquaintance
with certain sharpers, who, taking advantage of his extreme simplicity,
and easily persuading him that they were the destined repairers of his
fortunes, had involved him in a multiplicity of bill-transactions, by
which, while they reaped all the benefit, his liabilities amounted at last
to an incredible sum. He was now utterly ruined: he gave up all literary
pursuits; he very seldom came near his friends, but was almost constantly in the train of the above-mentioned sharpers, following them to
theatres and other haunts of gaiety,—a mode of life strangely opposed
to the habits of his earlier days, and, I may add, strangely at variance
with his personal appearance, which was exactly that of a grave and
dignified clergyman.

I had not seen him for weeks, when one evening I met him in Great
Newport Street looking so haggard and emaciated that I could not
doubt he spoke the truth in telling me that he felt extremely unwell.
About a fortnight after this, Dr. Giles received information that he was
lying dead in the second floor of an obscure lodging-house in Tavistock-
Court,[15] Covent-Garden, where he had been living, under a false name,

with a middle-aged female who passed as his wife. He had become acquainted with her at one of the theatres; and such was her devotion to him, that, when he was in the last extremity, she sold the few trinkets she possessed to procure him medicines and necessaries. He died of a sort of rapid atrophy.

Barker was interred March 26ᵗʰ, 1839, in the burial-ground of Saint Andrew's, Holborn; but no tomb-stone marks his grave. Dr. Giles, who on many occasions had shown great kindness to the deceased, generously defrayed the charges of the funeral; which, at his invitation, was attended by Basil Montagu, George Burges, another gentleman [Maxon] (Barker's solicitor), and myself.

BISHOP [JAMES H.] MONK'S LIFE OF BENTLEY; MY EDITION OF BENTLEY'S WORKS, &c. [*ff. 23–27ᵛ*]

In the range of English Biography there are, I believe, very few books superior in some respects to Monk's *Life of Bentley*. The author, indeed, was not an eloquent and brilliant writer: but he was thoroughly conversant with his subject, and took unwearied pains to attain correctness in all his statements; and I once heard an eminent lawyer express surprise that Monk should have been able without legal assistance to give so clear and lucid a narrative of Bentley's confused and interminable quarrels about the mastership of Trinity College, &c.— Monk was a sound scholar of the Porsonian school: but though acute and sensible, he was not gifted with those talents which enable their possessor to command the attention of society; hence, when I was one day deservedly praising to Mr. Rogers *The Life of Bentley,* the poet exclaimed, "You astonish me: *we* look upon Monk as a dull commonplace man,"—*we* meaning the persons eminent for fashion, rank, and literature, with whom, after his elevation to the Bench, Monk not unfrequently associated.

In *The Life of* [*Richard*] *Bentley* [London, 1833], vol. i. p. 271 sqq., sec. ed., the Bishop gives an account of the publication of the great critic's *Emendationes in Menandrum et Philemona,* wherein he exposed the gross errors of Le Clerc in his edition of the fragments of those poets. The *Emendationes* were conveyed to the bitter enemy of Le Clerc, Peter Burman of Utrecht, without the author's name, but with a permission to print them and to usher them into the world with a preface of his own,—a permission of which Burman eagerly availed himself. "The secret of this production," says Monk, "was not duly kept even till its birth: a report was circulated that Burman was about to publish something written by Bentley against the editor of Menander. This was owing to the indiscretion of his friend Dr. Francis Hare, who was then in Holland as Chaplain General to the army of the Duke of Marlborough, and to whom the conveyance of the parcel was committed. He put it into the hands of Johnson, a Scotch bookseller at the Hague, to be forwarded to Utrecht; but forgetting or disregarding the caution of secrecy, declared that he had received it from Dr. Bentley. Alexander Cunningham, the future antagonist of our critic, who also resided at the Hague, having learnt these tidings from the bookseller, apprised Le Clerc, with whom he was intimate, and propagated the news with much industry," &c [I, 273–74]. To the Bishop's account of this transaction I may add the following letter from Dr. Hare to Dr. Sike, which years ago I transcribed from the original, then in the possession of Rodd the bookseller :—

"Flines, May 15, 1710.

Rev⁴ Sir,

I received the favour of yours of the 20ᵗʰ past, a few hours after the last letters went away, or else I had sent an answer with them. The packet, which Dr. Bentley was pleased to recommend to my care for Mr. Burmannus, was immediately sent to Mr. Cardennel [*sic*] at the Hague, who had acknowledged the receipt of it before I left England, as I remember I told Dr. Bentley myself: but it may very well be that it might not be come to Mr. B*[urman]'s hands when his letter of the 9ᵗʰ was written to you, for it was about that time, not above a day or two before, entrusted to the care of one Johnston [*sic*], a bookseller at the Hague, to send it to Mr. B*[urman] with some books that he was then getting ready for him; so that I don't at all doubt but that it is long since come safe to his hands. If you have any other commands for

me on this side, I shall be very glad of the honour to serve you, being
with great respect,

Rev^d S^r,

Y^r most obedient humble servant,

Fr. Hare.

My most humble service
to Dr. Bentley, &c.
To the Reverend
Dr. Syke, Professor
of Hebrew, at Trinity
College in Cambridge."

Bentley, when a young man, was tutor to the son of the very
learned Dr. Edward Stillingfleet, Dean of St. Paul's, and afterwards
Bishop of Worcester. "Bentley," observes Monk, "was proud of expressing the veneration with which he regarded his patron *[Bishop
Stillingfleet]" xxxx and when he was interred in Worcester Cathedral,
and a monument erected to him by his son, Bentley wrote the inscription on it, which "continues to be admired for its eloquence and propriety among the ornaments of that venerable structure." *The Life of
Bentley,* vol. i. p. 134, sec. ed.— Now, in his various notices of
Stillingfleet, no allusion is made by Monk to the small biographical
essay, entitled *The Life and Character of . . . Dr. Edw. Stillingfleet
. . . London, . . . MDCCX. . . .*[16] It is written in a plain, bold,
manly style by one who had the highest reverence and admiration for
the deceased prelate, and was perfectly conversant with the particulars
of his career: and I presume that it was not known to Monk; for I
firmly believe that, if he had ever seen it, he must have felt as certain as
I do that it proceeded from the pen of Bentley.

In 1836–38, I published three volumes of Bentley's *Works,* and
originally intended to have greatly increased the collection both from
printed and from MS sources: but the indifference of general readers
to classical literature prevented my carrying-out the design.

The following letters addressed to me—the two first by Bishop
Monk, the four last by the Rev. John Wordsworth, son of the Master

of Trinity College, Cambridge—require little or no explanation. . . .[17]

Subsequently to the date of the immediately preceding letter, I had become personally acquainted with John Wordsworth, who occasionally called upon me during his visits to London; and most deeply and favourably was I impressed by his modesty, ingenuousness, and passionate love of Greek and Latin literature, in which he had made extraordinary progress.

It was now arranged by Bishop Monk that Bentley's Correspondence should be edited by John Wordsworth. The documents necessary for that purpose were accordingly transferred to his hands by the Bishop; and I sent him the few unprinted letters of the great critic which I happened to possess.

"Trin. Coll. November 14th, 1838.

My dear Sir,

I know not how to thank you sufficiently for your great kindness in sending me the Bentleian letters, which I found lying here on my return to college, and for your very friendly offer of further assistance. Since I came back to Cambridge I have been completely laid up with a severe attack of fever, from which I am now slowly recovering. I am still so weak and helpless that I can only leave my bed for three or four hours in the course of the day. I am, therefore, quite unable to write a long letter, and I hope you will kindly allow me to communicate with you further at some future time, when I am better able to do so, respecting the papers placed in my hands and the sources to which I should refer for further information.

Believe me, my dear sir,

Very truly and gratefully yours,

John Wordsworth."

But an early death put an end to the labours of John Wordsworth not only on Bentley's Correspondence, but on other works which he had in preparation,—the most important of these being an edition of Æschylus.[18] He died at Trinity Lodge, Decr 31st, 1839; and the task of editing Bentley's Correspondence devolved on his brother Christopher (now Bishop [of Lincoln]), who published it in two volumes, 1842.

[EDWARD] IRVING AND THE UNKNOWN TONGUES [*ff. 55–56ʳ*]

When "the Unknown Tongues" were attracting crowds to Irving's Church in Regent Square, I went to hear them, accompanied by Mitford and Willmott.[19] It was originally intended that Harness should be of our party: but as he was then Irving's neighbour, serving as minister of St. Pancras' Parochial Chapel in Regent Square, he fancied that there might be something indecorous in his going;[20] and it was agreed that, after "the performance," which was a very early one, we should breakfast at his house, and give him an account of the marvels we had heard and seen.

Accordingly, somewhat before 7 o'clock in the morning of a week-day, we proceeded to the Scotch Church in Regent Square, where we got "good places" without much difficulty. Irving was already seated at his desk; and, with the lamp-light falling on his fine but haggard features and on his long straggling locks of "sable-silvered" hair, he certainly presented a very striking appearance. The service, consisting of prayers and portions of the Bible read and expounded by Irving, was ever and anon interrupted by bursts of the Unknown Tongues (which, be it observed, on the occasion now described, were, without exception, *English Tongues!*) from various parts of the church. The speakers were both men and women, all of them in a state of the greatest excitement; the men howling, or rather shrieking out, their sentences; the women pouring out theirs with less violence and less rapidity, but with voices sustained (and seemingly without effort) at a wonderfully high pitch. That they thought themselves inspired, I make do doubt; and that Irving thought them so too, was manifest; for as soon as any one of them began to hold forth, Irving left off praying or (as it might be) reading, put his hand behind his ear to catch more fully the blessed sounds, and when they had ceased, addressed the congregation with "My brethren, he (or she) says so and so,"—repeating as closely as he could what the man or woman had just uttered. And *what* did they utter? Words strung together with very little meaning; fragments of Scripture unconnected with each other; the whole rendered absurd by endless repetitions; e.g. a very lady-like young person, who spoke at considerable length, kept exclaiming I know not how often, "for he cometh, for he cometh to judge the earth."

———

What follows is from a letter addressed by Dean Milman, while [incumbent] of Reading, to my above-mentioned friend Harness: it relates to the earlier part of Irving's London career before the breaking-out of the unknown tongues :—

"What else but clanship *[and] the most inveterate party-spirit can raise all this hubbub about Mr. Irving? I have got his work, I have read, laboured to read *[it] ; but such turgid nonsense, such pompous nothing! Where he argues, he argues ill; where he declaims, he declaims in vulgarisms, which uttered by Liston at the Haymarket, would be catchwords and jokes in the street: his very Scotch is bad Scotch. And is this what Lord Liverpool, Canning, Brougham are all thronging to hear? ** Murray gave me the book, with some understanding that it might enter into my scheme of an article on Pulpit Eloquence *[for *The Quarterly Review*] :[21] but my article is meant to be very calm and dispassionate; and I shall be in a passion, and be tempted to turn a man, who is doing much good with all his absurdity, into ridicule. Ask Murray from me whether any one has undertaken the review: at all events I will go quietly on in my own path; and perhaps, if no one else is inclined, ride over this king of shreds and patches. **** The difficulty of the article is, that if I set directly at our present system of preaching, I shall do no good, and, not that I mind it, frighten the big-wigs out of all their powder: and I want to show both why and how the alteration should be made, going to the bottom of the business. Besides, I am quite sure that our Church Discipline *[and] our long service is at the bottom of it all: and the B^{ttt} Bs^{ttts} are certainly right, that where you will find one eloquent man who preaches

with Bossuet's strength and Massillon's eloquence, you will have twenty
charlatans, Irvings, &c, who will vitiate the taste, and corrupt the style
of all the youth : preaching will become, like the writings in the magazines, a tissue of unmeaning flowers and figures. You shall see the
article, if it escapes the fire.****

Reading, July 13th"

[WILLIAM] JONES OF NAYLAND [f. 57^r]

For some time I served the curacy of Nayland in Suffolk; and
there I learned from the oldest inhabitants various anecdotes of this
eminent divine and excellent man.

He was passionately fond of music and a proficient in it.[22] Yet—
as he informed his curate Mr. Sims,[23] who related the circumstance to
me—he was about thirty years of age before he felt any fondness for,
or paid any attention to, that science. One summer evening, while
walking in a woody lane near Nayland, and listening to the singing of
the birds, he all at once found that he had "music in his soul." From
that hour, it became the chief amusement of his life.

Pegler, the organist of Nayland, told me that he has frequently
seen Jones come running in from the garden where he had been working, and, though his hands were all covered with mould, seat himself
at the organ in order to preserve some musical idea which had suddenly
occurred to him.

GEORGE BURGES [ff. 96, 97a, 97–103^r]

George Burges was born in Bengal, where his father carried on
the business of a watchmaker, and with such success that he was enabled to leave him a sum amounting to four thousand pounds. On the
strength of that money, and by the advice of his guardian, seconded
by his own wishes, the young "Bengalensis,"[24] already remarkable for
precocity of talent, was entered a member of Trinity College, Cambridge. There he devoted himself to the study of Greek with enthusias-

tic ardour; and while yet an undergraduate, gave a striking proof of his proficiency in that language by publishing, in 1807, an edition of *The Troades* of Euripides, with a Preface and critical Notes in Latin. Hence the expectation that he was destined to perform great achievements as a scholar, was doubtless entertained by others as well as by [Peter] Elmsley; who has mentioned him as follows in his Preface to *The Bacchæ* of Euripides; "Editionem hujus fabulae promiserat vir ingenio, doctrina, et Græcarum literarum amore, vix cuiquam secundus, Georgius Burgesius, qui in Troadum editione, quam pæne puer instituit, talem de se spem excitavit, qualem, mea sententia, nemo ante eum huic studiorum generi addictus adolescentulus."[25] Unfortunately, however, Burges failed to realize the hopes which his first work had excited. While its readers wondered how the stripling-editor should have attained such skill in verbal criticism, they were willing to attribute the over-boldness of his emendations to the inconsiderateness of youth, and to believe that, in his maturer years, he would show himself more guarded in conjecture: but, on the contrary, as he grew older, he grew more and more daring as a critic, and in his later publications he either altered, or proposed to alter, the text with an inexcusable wantonness. There was, indeed, no end to the surprising ingenuity of his alterations; and one can only regret that it was unaccompanied by judgment; for, if nature had not denied him that invaluable gift, he might possibly have deserved to rank with those whom Burney has characterized as "heroes."[26] At last the name of George Burges became among the learned all over Europe, synonymous with "slashing editor"; and when I have pointed out to him in the writings of sundry German scholars allusions to his intolerable "audacia," he would exclaim, "Well, damn it, let them call me audacious if they please,—they cannot tax me with ignorance of Greek."

A copy of *The Troades* was, of course, presented by Burges to Porson, who earnestly advised him to adopt some profession, and to make classical literature the amusement, not the main business, of his life.

While a student at Cambridge, Burges was thrown from horseback, broke his leg, and limped ever after: by which accident, he used to declare, "he had sustained a loss of ten thousand pounds"; for being rather good-looking, though far from the Adonis he fancied himself to be, he had quite made up his mind that he was to carry off an heiress who possessed that sum.

After leaving college, he resided for a considerable time at Eton in the capacity of a private tutor; and subsequently he took up his abode in London, where gradually, by a succession of absurd speculations, he got rid of the whole of his patrimony, and not seldom found it difficult how to procure food for himself and his family,—he being now a husband and a father. My readers will hardly credit the subjoined details.

1. He used to drive about London in a two-horsed ugly vehicle, the pannels of which were ornamented with hieroglyphics in oil-colours, emblematic of his peculiar views on the origin of language; and I have been often amused by the astonishment he excited in the frequenters of the Park, as he swept past them with a careless rapidity and a complacent smile. He also had two coaches plying up and down the New Road, with his name on them at full length; and during this period, when he called at the houses of his friends, he used to leave a card inscribed "Mr. George Burges αρματοποιος *[chariot-maker or coach-builder]."

2. He spent a largish sum on the construction of a whale-shaped machine, which was to convey passengers through the air from Dover to Calais.

3. He invented a coat which was to fit better and prove more convenient to the wearer than coats of the common make, and which had a single button in the centre of the back: but I never heard of its being worn by anyone except himself.

4. He set up as a stay-maker, and distributed the following handbill very neatly lithographed:

"Corsets à la Vénus.

Burges and Co. respectfully beg leave to invite Ladies of Title, Taste, and Fashion, to inspect their Corsets à la Vénus recently invented by a scientific Foreigner *[Burges himself], who, after devoting many years to effect an improvement, so much desired in that part of female dress, has happily succeeded in discovering a Corset that, uniting ease with elegance, not only improves the figure, but prevents likewise the numer-ous evils arising from the undue compression of the Chest.

As the fewest number of bones, compatible with the support of the body, are to be found in the Corsets à la Vénus, they are particu-larly recommended to the attention of Ladies of a delicate constitution, and are especially adapted for young persons, as they neither interfere with the action of the muscles, nor impede the growth of the limbs. 78, Charlotte St.

Fitzroy Sq^{r."}"

As Burges could not, of course, take the measure of ladies himself, he sent his wife to do so. But the scheme proved wholly abortive; for the very few fair ones who patronized it soon found that they were not a whit liker the Cyprian goddess than they had been before.

5. That he once had a printing-office appears from the words "Printed by G. Burges, Kenton Street," on the reverse of the title-page and on the last leaf of *The Son of Erin, or The Cause of the Greeks, a Play in Five Acts, by a Native of Bengal, George Burges A. M. of Trin. Coll. Cambridge, 1823*. This enormously long and unreadable jumble of (bad) blank-verse, prose, and songs (several of them marked "Air by G. Burges"), was intended to bring about a reform in modern dramatic writing by showing what it really ought to be. The Dedication runs thus: "To George Byron, who, blending the brilliant tints of poetic fancy with the sober shades of philosophic truth, has with a mighty mind and masterly hand depicted the spirit of monarchy, this drama is inscribed by an Asiatic liberal, George Burges."— "Byron came to see us to-day, and appeared extremely discomposed; after half-an-hour's conversation on indifferent subjects, he at length broke forth with, 'Only fancy my receiving to-day a tragedy dedicated as follows —"From George ―― to George Byron!" This is being cool with a vengeance. I never was more provoked. How stupid, how ignorant, to pass over my rank! I am determined not to read the tragedy; for a man capable of committing such a solecism in good breeding and com-mon decency, can write nothing worthy of being read.' We were

astonished at witnessing the annoyance this circumstance gave him.xxx We endeavoured to console him by telling him that we knew Mr. George —— a little, and that he was clever and agreeable, as also that his passing over the title of Byron was meant as a compliment; it was a delicate preference shown to the renown accorded to George Byron the poet over the rank and title which were adventitious advantages ennobled by the possessor, but that could add nothing to his fame. All our arguments were vain; he said, 'this could not be the man's feelings, as he reduced him (Lord Byron) to the same level as himself.' " *Conversations of Lord Byron with the Countess of Blessington* [2d ed. (London, 1850)], p[p]. 93[-94, 94-95].

6. He had persuaded himself that in a knowledge of architecture he equalled, if not exceeded, all his contemporaries; and ever and anon he used to draw designs for various edifices, which, I need hardly add, were never erected. Yet they looked very pretty on paper,—especially a sketch for the new frontage to the British Museum, which he sent in to the committee appointed to determine on the choice of a design.

It must be understood that the freaks & vagaries just described, though I have enumerated them in an uninterrupted series, extended over a space of many years, during which Burges occasionally obtained trifling sums by editing and translating classical works, and now and then received pecuniary assistance from various friends.

I do not mean to tax Burges with impudence when I mention, that he was the reverse of shy,—that he would not scruple to address perfect strangers, and would enter into conversation with them, sometimes showing a strange want of tact in what he said. So, one day at the British Museum, seeing Cramer busy with a MS. of Homer, and having inquired who he was, Burges went up to him, introduced himself, and presently (by way of making an agreeable remark!) observed, "I think, sir, that when you published your recent volume of *Anecdota,* you could not have been fresh from the reading of Euripides, else you would have recollected that a passage which you do not trace to its source comes from that poet."

In 1834 Burges endeavoured to bring himself conspicuously before the public by delivering a course of Lectures, which he announced in the following elaborate prospectus. . . .[27]

"LECTURE III. January 21.

Ancient Lyric Poetry—Pindar—His Beauties and Defects—First recorded Eruption of Mount Ætna—First recorded Eclipse of the Sun —The Origin of Rhyme—Traces of it in Homer—Female Poets— Their Inferiority to Male, and why—Sappho a fictitious name—The Odes of Anacreon not genuine—Latin Lyric Poetry—Catullus and Horace—Their Inferiority to the Greek in Fancy, but superiority in Precision of Language—English Lyrics—Cowley—Gray—Collins— Southey's Thalaba—Shelley's Queen Mab—Byron's Manfred—Form of the seven-stringed Lyre, and why so—Apollo said to be the God of Light and Music; and why so; why said to be beardless. . . .

LECTURE VII. February 19.

Ancient Philosophers superior to the Moderns in Physics, Metaphysics and Morals, and why—Dutens on the Origin of Discoveries attributed to the Moderns—The Properties of Matter better described then than now—Their Application of Physical Science, if not more extensive, more wise—In Arts they effected much by simple means; the Moderns effect little by means not simple—Air-Balloons and locomotive Vehicles known Centuries ago—Salverte on the Occult Sciences of the Ancients—Brewster on their Magical Knowledge—The Newtonian Theory untenable—Whewell and the Quarterly Reviewer—The Form of the Sun an Optical Illusion—Its Power the Effect of Matter in Motion.

LECTURE VIII. February 26.

Ancient Metaphysics, what—Their Connexion with Physics—The Soul, what—Its Form, as shown by the Ancients—Its Immortality can and cannot be proved Metaphysically—The Inference drawn by Plato from its supposed Immortality—The Properties of Mind and Matter compared—Physiognomy, Phrenology and Palmistry all partially true—Their Utility in a System of Education—The Moral Philosophy of the Ancients and Moderns Compared—Paley's Definition of Virtue defective—That of Socrates superior—The Duty of Morality a misnomer—Byron's Picture of Socrates in Prison—Why Socrates requested his Friends to sacrifice a Cock to Æsculapius—His Death —The real Cause of it—The Effects of it compared with the Effects of similar Persecutions—Conclusion. . . ."

In connection with these Lectures he sent out this hand-bill :—

"GOOD AND CHEAP BREAD,
WITHOUT RUIN TO THE FARMER.

The Nobility and Gentry, in or out of Parliament, and now nearly ruined by the awful depression of the Landed Interest, are respectfully informed that MR. GEORGE BURGES, M. A. of Trinity College, Cambridge, will, in his Seventh Lecture, detail an easy plan by which His Majesty's Ministers may, if they will, increase the Revenue a Million sterling annually; and so improve the soil of England, as to enable it to feed Sixty Millions of mouths on cheaper and better bread-corn than can be grown upon, or imported from, any other part of the Globe.

The Lecture will commence at half-past Eight precisely, P.M., at No. 30, Bedford Street, Covent Garden."

In spite of what Burges thought a tempting prospectus, these Lectures drew together only a very small audience, consisting chiefly of a few of his old friends, Kenyon, Merivale (the translator of *The Greek Anthology*), Mitford, myself, &c, with a sprinkling of booksellers, who looked up to Burges as a prodigy of learning, and who, though they comprehended little or nothing of his discourse, listened to it with an exemplary patience. For my own part, I sat on thorns while he was stating as facts some of the most extravagant fancies that ever were begotten in a human brain: e.g. he boldly asserted that the Pyramids had a foundation corresponding exactly with the portion of them above ground,—that they tapered down under the earth in the same manner and with the same dimensions as they rose into the air above its surface.— In one of the Lectures he sung (and with a rather sweet voice) the Ode of the pseudo-Anacreon, Θελω λεγειν Ατρειδας, to the tune of "Malbrook."

All honour to Charles James Blomfield, Bishop of London, for his noble behaviour to George Burges!— They had been on terms of intimacy while fellow-students at Trinity College, Cambridge: but Blomfield (long before he was raised to the Bench) having attacked, in an excellent article in *The Quarterly Review*, Barker's edition of Stephens's *Thesaurus*, which was issued by Valpy, who was Burges's publisher and friend; and having also sneered in *The Museum Criticum* (as he well might do) at Burges's *re-writing* of the text of Æschylus [II (1826), no. 7, 488–509],—the latter assailed Blomfield in sundry publications with a disgusting intemperance of language, perhaps exceeding that which Scioppius and the most foul-mouthed of the early critics poured out upon their adversaries. Years had elapsed, and Burges was still cherishing his wrath against the Bishop, when one day they happened to meet in Great Russel Street, Bloomsbury. No sooner had they passed each other than the Bishop turned round and called out "Burges!"; who also immediately turned round and limped up to the Bishop. "Burges," continued the latter, "I hope that all which formerly took place between us is as entirely forgotten by you as it is by me." To such an appeal Burges could not be insensible, and returned a becoming answer to the Bishop, who from that time till the time of his (the Bishop's) death showed him great kindness, occasionally visiting him at his lodgings and making him presents of money.

But the person to whom Burges was the most deeply indebted was his old college-friend John Kenyon, author of *A Rhymed Plea for Tolerance* and various other poems, which rise considerably above mediocrity, and to which the public have hardly done justice. Kenyon not only aided him frequently with handsome sums, but informed him that he had bequeathed him a thousand pounds,—an announcement which relieved Burges from much anxiety about the future, and which assuredly—for he was the most unselfish of human beings—did not awaken in him any longing for the testator's death.— Kenyon having died Decʳ 3, 1856, Burges received the promised legacy, which his wife took care not to allow him to "make ducks and drakes of," as he had done with his patrimony. After some debate, it having been resolved that the whole family should remove to Ramsgate, thither they went: and there Burges, or rather, Mrs. Burges, having purchased two very small houses, they occupied part of one of them, and let the rest of it and [the] whole of the other house to lodgers during the gay season,—a plan which proved successful.

At Ramsgate, in his diminutive but neatly fitted-up dwelling, Burges quietly pursued for a considerable time his Greek studies with all the ardour of youth, till he was forced to abandon them from a failure in the sight of both eyes, which ended in confirmed cataract. He wrote to consult me about getting it removed; and, in consequence of an application on my part, that eminent oculist Mr. White Cooper consented to operate on him gratis, if he would pro tempore become an inmate of St. Mary's Hospital. Burges readily consented, and came up to London; when calling on me one forenoon, he gave proof that, though he was unable to see a single letter of Greek, it still was uppermost in his thoughts; for, almost immediately after entering the room, he begged me to read to him an article in Hesychius (as connected with a passage of Euripides) which had recently been running in his head.

But I had to deal with an untractable man: he all at once determined (why I never could discover) that he would not become a patient in St. Mary's Hospital; and he threw himself, as it were, at random, into the Ophthalmic Hospital in Moorfields, where he quite charmed the younger surgeons by his clever and facetious talk, was operated upon, and returned to Ramsgate in perfect possession of his sight.

He was now in the highest spirits, resumed his Greek, and prophesied to his friends that, old as he was, he had yet many years to live. But, alas! ere long the insanity, which hitherto had only displayed itself in the wildest eccentricities, burst forth in all its fury: he was bent on attempting the life of his respectable wife (of whom he had grown violently jealous!), and on drowning himself by a leap from the pier; and had he not been carefully watched by his family, he most probably would have committed one or both of these tragic desperate deeds.

Luckily this miserable state of existence lasted comparatively but a short time: he suddenly had a stroke of paralysis, from which he never rallied, and expired in Hardress Street, Ramsgate, [11 January 1864], aged [78].

On his tomb might have been engraved with strict propriety the words by which he sometimes described himself,—"Honest George Burges"; for he was utterly free from the slightest taint of guile or deceit, and would not for worlds have deviated from truth even in matters of the smallest importance.

I possess a huge mass of his letters, papers on different subjects, &c; from which I select these extracts. . . .[28]

"My dear Dyce,

Ever since I first met you in Pickering's shop your conduct towards a broken down scholar has been so uniformly kind that I needed not your recent proof of regard to make me feel myself no less a debtor in deeds than in words. But as you forbid my saying anything upon what you are pleased to consider a trifle though to me in my present uncertain state it is a matter of some importance I will drop all further allusion to the subject, & fill the remainder of the sheet with what I hope will be more to your taste.

When I left Town for Cambridge I went with some though not very sanguine hopes of success. I did however rather better than I expected —not in the way of Lectures, for three guineas was the whole amount of my receipts, but in the way of pupilising [?], by which I pocketed £13 in 6 weeks, & by translating two orations of Demosthenes into English for which I hope to receive by the end of next week £7, so that my trip ought unless fortune is determined to keep me down to yield me £23. This however is not all. For I am given to understand that I may fairly look forward to the chance of obtaining four pupils in the next term at [. . .] price of £14 each, & should I be lucky enough to get a pup[il] to do himself credit as a Classical scholar, I may anticipate the certainty of having more than I shall know what to do with. But this you will say is talking of chickens &c. You will be pleased however to hear that one of my Cambridge pupils has thought it good for him, & Heaven knows it is not less so for my self, to take some lessons during the long vacation; & what is better still feels that I can forward him in his pursuits especially in Greek & Latin Composition in verse; a specimen of which I have sent you. Both the translations were knocked off in about two hours & [a] half; & unless I deceive myself, you will think them not bad.

No sooner had I finished them than I sent them to the Examiner with a note in which I stated that Dobree had put the Greek into my hands as a hitherto but little known fragment of Philemon, & that I had found the Latin amongst the papers of Valckenaer, by whom they were attributed to Hugo Grotius. Mr. Steel however smelt a rat, I suppose, having heard of my *Bacchic* madness, & would not deign to even thank me for the trouble I had taken in sending him such *exquisite* morceaus of Greek & Latin versification. By the bye, can you tell me, who is the Author of the English Sonnet—& can you make enquiries at Aberdeen whether there is any demand for a Greek & Latin Professor. I have been told by a friend of mine, that there is an opening for a scholar such as your humble servant in Scotland. I confess I am disposed to doubt the fact. But you will perhaps be able to decide the question either from your own personal knowledge or that of your northern friends.

I am sorry to hear that your eyes are still bad, & not the less so as I fear that my scrawl will put them to the test of deciphering what will scarcely repay the pain of doing so.

I found Wilmot very kind at Cambridge & feel indebted to him for my second pupil, who I trust will turn out a good scholar. He has some capital points about him, especially a delicate taste, & can construe Greek prose with spirit & fidelity united. Wilmot's work is rapidly proceeding to a reprint when he means to rewrite it. So you had better wait till it appears, for otherwise you will read a book aliusque et idem. When do you come to Town? I have still much to say, but can at present only add the name of your much obliged

George Burges

I am still in the old place & shall probably remain there during the vacation.

The Revd Alexander Dyce
  Rosebank
    Aberdeen
      N. B.
[Postmark: July 6, 1834 (?).]"

RICHARD PAYNE KNIGHT [*ff. 104–7*^r]

In my *Recollections of the Table-talk of Samuel Rogers* is this statement :—

"Payne Knight was seized with an utter loathing of life, and destroyed himself. He had complaints which were very painful, and his nerves were completely shattered. Shortly before his death, he would come to me of an evening, and tell me how sick he was of existence. He had recourse to the strongest prussic acid; and, I understand, he was dead before it touched his lips."[29]

No sooner had this statement been published than Payne Knight's niece, the late Mrs. Francis Walpole, dictated to an old servant of her uncle the following declaration, which appeared in *The Times* and in other newspapers :—

"To the Editor of 'The Table-talk of the late Samuel Rogers.'
Sir,— With another member of my family, I was in the service of the late Mr. Payne Knight at the period of his decease (April 29th, 1824); and I beg most unequivocally to contradict the statement of the late Mr. Samuel Rogers, that Mr. Payne Knight committed suicide by prussic acid. No such suspicion existed at the time; no such traces were found in his room; and no coroner's inquest was held on the body. Respect for the family of Mr. Payne Knight, and interest in his surviving relatives (to one of the nearest of whom I commit this statement), induce me to take the liberty of addressing you, and entreating you to give publicity to the fact that Mr. Payne Knight's death was caused by apoplexy, according to the predictions and reports of his medical attendants.

I remain, Sir, your obedient servant,

John Jackson.

The Royal Oak Hotel, Leominster, Herefordshire,
    March 15th, 1856."

I must confess, that, in spite of this flat contradiction to Rogers's statement, I continue far from convinced that Payne Knight did not destroy himself. Nor was Rogers singular in attributing his death to poison: it was well known to several persons alive when Rogers's statement was published (the late Dr. Alexander Henderson and others), that the late Mr. Roger Wilbraham, who had been on the most intimate terms with Payne Knight, used to speak of his suicide as a fact not to be questioned.[30] Be it remembered too that, as Rogers observed, he was suffering great pain from complaints brought on by a long course of dissoluteness; and, moreover, that (as we may gather from his writings) he was not troubled with those religious scruples which would have restrained many men from attempting self-destruction.

In consequence of John Jackson's declaration, a correspondence—a friendly one—took place between Mrs. Francis Walpole and myself; and, among other letters which I received from her was that now subjoined, detailing what she believed to be the real circumstances of her uncle's death, and giving an interesting account of the habits of a remarkable man, who, though a mean poet (vide his *Landscape,* his *Progress of Civil Society,* and his *Alfred*), was undoubtedly a profound Greek scholar (see his *Carmina Homerica, Ilias et Odyssea,* his *Analytical Essay on the Greek Alphabet,* his *Discourse on the Worship of Priapus,* and his *Inquiry into the Symbolical Language of Ancient Art and Mythology*), as well as a metaphysician of no ordinary acuteness (witness his *Analytical Inquiry into the Principles of Taste*).

"65 Eaton Square,
March 22ᵈ, 1856.

Sir,

At his death Mr. Payne Knight was nearly seventy-six years of age. During the two preceding years his bodily strength had obviously failed; and I had frequently heard him lament that his means of occupation were so limited, Homer being the only author who afforded him pleasure. When threatened with apoplexy, all application was strictly prohibited; while lighter studies failed to excite interest. His nerves had long been affected, and his hand had become unsteady, from the habit of drinking twice per day the most intensely strong coffee, while the indulgence of his unexampled appetite for animal food was unlimited. When he was latterly urged by his medical men to abandon these practices, and to confine himself to a simple and early dinner, he rarely failed to make a second ample, varied, and luxurious meal at a late hour. He refused to be cupped, bled, or blistered; and, after one experiment, he discontinued the use of the cold shower-bath. In compliance with my uncle's cordial invitation, and according to my father's annual custom, he arrived in London on the eve of the 1st Horticultural Meeting, of which Society he was President, on the 29th of April 1824, and found his brother a corpse. I was in town soon after, and obtained the following particulars from Dr. Wilson Phillip, Sir Antony Carlisle, and my uncle's old servants :—

Mr. Payne Knight had appeared confused and disposed to doze during the greater part of the preceding day; but expressed anxiety about his brother's arrival. He retired to rest at 8 o'clock, leaving a box of invaluable gems in his library. This box was about 8 inches in height; and it was his invariable custom to place it under his pillow. On his valet Thomas Sharpe's asking if he should fetch it, Mr. Payne Knight replied, 'No, I am too ill:—do not leave me until I sleep.' In a short time he appeared to sleep and to snore (which was the stertorous breathing preceding death). Thomas Sharpe left him, and found that all was over in the morning.

I omitted to state that Dr. Wilson Phillip considered that my uncle's death was accelerated by the altered position of his head, which was of course so many inches lower than usual.

> I am, Sir,
> Your ob^t Servant,
> Elizabeth Walpole."

When I read this letter to my friend the late Dr. Alexander Henderson (see above), he professed himself still unconvinced that Payne Knight did not commit suicide; a circumstance which in all probability would be concealed from Mrs. Francis Walpole, who was not in her uncle's house at the time of his death,—not even in London.

DR. [SAMUEL] PARR [*ff. 141–42ʳ*]

While reading the service in his church at Hatton, Parr would here and there interlard it with brief glosses: for instance, after pronouncing the name "Debŏrah" in [*Judges* IV], he would pause, turn round to the congregation, and add, "More properly, '*Debō-rah*'"; and on the words of the Creed, "descended into hell," he would, in like manner, remark, "More properly, 'descended into *Hades*.'"

He would frequently declare, "I will have no bastards in *my* parish."— "But how, Doctor, can you help it?"— "Why, sir, when I find any unmarried woman in the family way, I ascertain who is her paramour, summon him before me, and say, 'You must marry this woman immediately, for I will have no bastards in *my* parish.' I turn a deaf ear to any excuses he may make; and if he be very poor, I generally give him a small sum to enable him to commence house-keeping; for I will have no bastards in *my* parish."

Parr was a latitudinarian in religion, and a radical in politics: yet he long indulged the hope of being raised to the episcopal bench; and one evening at Lady Augusta Murray's, he said, with perfect gravity, "My dear Lady Augusta, when I am a bishop, I intend to wear a rim of purple velvet round each cuff of my coat." (Parr's aspirations after a bishoprick are thus alluded to in [Ralph Broome's] *Letters from Simpkin the Second to his Dear Brother in Wales; Containing an Humble Description of the Trial of Warren Hastings, Esq.,* &c;

"This same Managers' Box I've observ'd to be lin'd
With hungry expectants of every kind;
And Parr, as a regency bishop elect,
Has a claim to a seat among those who expect;
For finding his Latin, his wig, and his birch,
All too weak to secure his ascent in the church,
He dashingly join'd Opposition in form,
Determin'd to carry a mitre by storm."

p. 93, ed. 1789.)

Though a very kind-hearted man, he was (like Dr. Johnson, whom he greatly admired, and perhaps imitated) a downright tyrant in conversation, and often made use of such language as would hardly be tolerated in society now-adays. At a dinner-party given by Lady Augusta Murray, Mr. (afterwards so notorious as Sir Lumley) Skeffington asked Parr some question about the religion of the Chaldæans; when Parr, fancying that Skeffington meant to *quizz* him, exclaimed, with a tremendous scowl, "Wait, sir, wait till the ladies are gone, and then I'll pounce upon you."— He treated still more rudely my friend Harness, who, having become intimate with Betty (the Young Roscius) while they were students together at Cambridge, once ventured, in opposition to Parr, to say a few words in praise of his friend's acting. This elicited from Parr a violent tirade against Betty, which concluded with "As for you, Mr. Harness, I look upon you, sir, as a young theatrical puppy."

To Jones of Nayland, who was himself a man of very simple manners, Parr's pomposity and grandiloquence could not fail to be offensive. Jones had long wished to be introduced to Parr; and, after their meeting, characterized him as being "all smoke and smother" (which was not true:—Parr was only partly so).

Beloe, it is well known, drew a most unjust portrait of Parr in *The Sexagenarian,* under the name of Orbilius: but it is not so well known that, after the death of Beloe, who left his family in great distress, the generous Parr sent his widow a present of fifty pounds.

[RICHARD] PORSON [ff. 148–52]

Among the *Porsoniana,* which I appended to my *Recollections of the Table-talk of Samuel Rogers* (and which a Mr. Watson, in a wretched *Life of Porson* [1861], has made great use of, with very inadequate acknowledgement) a paragraph runs thus :—

"It is not known who wrote *Six more Letters to Granville Sharp,*[31] which, according to the title-page, are by *Gregory Blunt.* They were very generally attributed to Porson; and I *[Mr. William Maltby *loquitur*] have been in a bookseller's shop with him, when a person has come in, and asked for 'Mr. Porson's Remarks on Sharp.' I do not believe that he was the author of them; but I have little doubt that he gave some assistance to the author, particularly in the notes. He always praised the work, and recommended it to his friends." p[p]. 335[-36], third ed.

I am now enabled to speak positively concerning the authorship of the *Six more Letters,* through the kindness of the late Dr. David Irving of Edinburgh, who favoured me with the following communication:—

"6 Meadow Place,
27ᵗʰ August, 1858.

Sir,
    I have perused with much pleasure the *Table-Talk of Rogers* and the *Porsoniana;* for which, I think, the editor has not yet received due commendation. As to the authorship of *Blunt's Letters to Sharp,* I can supply you with authentic information; I know from unquestionable authority that they were written by John Mason Good, M.D. To this remarkable man I was introduced by my ingenious and estimable friend, the Rev. Thomas Jervis, the successor of Dr. Kippis in the chapel at Westminster. At his chambers in Gray's Inn I met Dr. Good at breakfast, and after he withdrew, Mr. Jervis presented me with a copy of the *Letters,* mentioning the name of the author without reserve or hesitation. I do not think it very probable that he derived any assistance from Porson; but, as the work is apparently formed on the model of the admirable *Letters to Travis,* and breathes a portion of the same spirit, it might more readily obtain the approbation of Porson, who was not much inclined to be lavish of his commendation. After a long interval, I had the pleasure of seeing Dr. Gregory[32] in Edinburgh; and when I ventured to express some degree of surprise that he had not made the slightest allusion to so conspicuous a publication, he replied that any notice of it would have been very painful to the family of his friend. When this work made its appearance, he was in the fervour of Unitarian zeal, and he has occasionally discussed sacred

topics in a tone of levity; but towards the close of his life, he renounced the opinions which he had long and eagerly maintained, and died in the communion of the established church."[33]

Porson[34] used generally *in the morning* to wear black-satin breeches and silk-stockings, and *in the evening* trousers and boots! John Mitford told me that the only time he ever saw him was in Sotheby's saleroom, whither he had come to purchase a copy of Serranus's Plato; and that his face was then covered with long stripes of black sticking-plaster, which he had put on in consequence, it was supposed, of a fall, and which gave him a very bravo-like appearance.

His own books were, for the most part, engrained with dirt, inside and outside; and on those which he borrowed from his friends he often left indelible stains. "Look," Richard Heber would say in a melancholy tone, "only look at this volume which Porson has just returned to me! When I lent it to him, it was quite spotless, and now it is perfectly beastly."

His chambers in the Temple were covered with dust, and contained an atmosphere by no means agreeable to persons of delicate nerves. Coplestone (afterwards Bishop of Llandaff) and Dr. Sheppard [. . .] once paid him a morning-visit there; and Shep[. . .],[35] observing how uncomfortable his companion was made by the odour of the room, took an opportunity of opening the window under the pretext of admiring the view. As they came down stairs, Coplestone exclaimed, "Shepp[. . .], you deserve a civic crown, for saving the life of a citizen!"

Dr. Routh, the learned and venerable President of Magdalen-College, Oxford, used often to relate what follows.— Porson, Parr, and Burney were his guests. The wine had circulated very freely, the President alone keeping his head cool, while the others, more or less, had lost their better reason. Porson, however, had not lost his memory, but spouted Greek verses in praise of drinking very fluently. Parr even ventured on a Bacchanalian song, "which alarmed me," said Routh, "for the sake of the college; but nothing could stop him, and I was much amused, though fearing he must be overheard." After the song, the President retired, with Parr and Burney, to tea, Porson remaining in the dining-room, and requesting porter and ale, which were brought to him, as he usually drank them after swallowing [an] abundance of wine. About two o'clock in the morning, as Routh was going to bed, he took a parting peep at Porson; and seeing him grovelling on the floor,—in plain terms, dead-drunk,—ordered a servant to sit up and watch him. About six o'clock, the servant went into the dining-room, and found Porson, calm and collected, seated at a table, with three or four volumes of Æschylus before him, reading and writing with as much zeal as he had the night before manifested in consuming the President's port.

When George Burges was at Trinity-College, Cambridge, Porson advised him to secure a fellowship before devoting himself to philological studies. "By such pursuits," said Porson, "you must not expect to make anything: all I ever made by my Euripides, was four-pence on each copy of the *Hecuba*."

A coldness arose between Porson and Elmsley in consequence of the critique on Schweighaeuser's edition of Athenæus which the latter wrote for the *Edinburgh Review* [III (1803–4), 181–94]. In that article some emendations were given, which Porson said he had thrown out in the course of conversation, not imagining that Elmsley would ever propose them as his own.

There is little doubt that Elmsley derived a good many of his corrections of *The Acharnians* of Aristophanes from manuscript notes on Porson's books; which he carefully examined the day before they were sold, though Doctors Raine and Burney had given strict orders to Payne and Mackinley that Elmsley should not see them. This was told by Raine to Burges, who told it to me.

When Gaisford informed Porson that he contemplated publishing an edition of Hephæstion, but that he feared his scholarship was not sufficient for the undertaking, Porson encouraged him to proceed with it, saying that he considered him quite equal to the task. (That he was so, he has shown: his Hephæstion is excellently edited.)

In those days Gaisford, with all his respect for Porson, used to say, "If Porson were to die tomorrow, he will not leave behind him a greater name than Tyrwhitt." (A prediction which has not been fulfilled; for Porson's reputation is now much greater than Tyrwhitt's:

yet, in variety of learning, Porson was far inferior to Tyrwhitt, who possessed not only a truly critical knowledge of Greek, but also an intimate acquaintance with the early English writers, and with the literature of Italy and France.)

[JOSEPH] RITSON [*f. 156ʳ*][36]

Every body knows that Ritson strictly abstained from animal food. One night he was supping with Douce, when a girl (a niece of Mrs. D.) exclaimed, "Only look at Mr. Ritson! I thought he never tasted animal food; and yet he's now devouring hundreds of living things in that piece of old cheese!" Ritson, who chose to fancy that Douce had incited her to make the observation, was vehemently angry, and quarrelled with him in consequence; and, I believe, a perfect reconciliation never took place between them.

Sir Walter Scott used to say that Ritson's temper bore a strong resemblance to that of Rousseau.

DR. [JOHN] SHAW OF MAGDALEN COLLEGE [*f. 186ʳ*]

I used to see him constantly walking about Oxford,—a little, bleareyed old man. It is well-known that Brunck's Apollonius Rhodius destroyed the reputation of Shaw's edition of that poet [2d ed., 1779]. When Shaw read Brunck's contemptuous remarks[37] on his labours, he said, "I shall henceforth keep my eyes for the woodcocks" (alluding to his love of field-sports); and, accordingly, from that time he gave up the study of Greek literature.

He was a notorious punster. When Dr. Routh, the President of Magdalen College, married at a very advanced period of life, and soon after he had finished the publication of his *Reliquiæ Sacræ,*—Shaw, congratulating him on his nuptials, said, "Now, Mr. President, instead of thy *fathers,* thou shalt have **children.**"

GEORGE STEEVENS [*f. 206ʳ*]

"One day, as Sir John Hawkins was going upstairs to visit Johnson, he met Steevens coming down. 'Really, doctor,' said the knight on entering the room, 'I am surprised that you allow such a malicious person as Steevens to frequent your house.' 'Pooh, sir,' replied Johnson, 'Steevens is not malicious,—he is only uniformly mischievous.'"
J. Nicol.

Some one asked Isaac Reed when he last saw Steevens. The answer was, "I have not seen him for about a year, but I have spoken to him every morning during that period before I have got out of bed." Now, Steevens was in the daily habit of walking from his house at Hampstead, at a very early hour, to Reed's chambers in [Staple's Inn], where he used to correct the proof-sheets of his *Shakespeare, 1793,* and talk to Isaac through the key-hole of his bedroom. Hence the lines in [Thomas J.] Mathias's *Pursuits of Literature;*

> "Come then, I'll breathe at large etherial air,
> Far from the bar, the senate, and the court,
> And in Avonian fields with Steevens sport,
> (Whom late, from Hampstead journeying to his book,
> Aurora oft for Cephalus mistook,
> What time he brush'd her dews with hasty pace,
> To meet the printer's dev'let face to face :)," &c.
> p[p]. 134[-35], [7th] ed. 1798.

Dibdin has greatly exaggerated the horrors of Steevens's death-bed in the account he gives of it in [. . .];[38] but Dibdin was not solicitous about accuracy in his statements.

A FRENCHMAN'S IDEA OF TRANSLATION [*f. 225ʳ*]

When my old college friend, the Rev. Arthur Johnson Daniel, was residing at Paris, he became acquainted with a literary Frenchman, who understood English pretty well, and who asked my friend to recommend to him some popular English work, that he might translate it into French. A volume by Miss Jane Taylor of Ongar (whose writings were then in considerable estimation) happened to be lying on the table; and Daniel, taking it up, said, "Here is a clever tale: but I fear it would not suit the French taste, for it turns more or less on religious principle."— "Pooh," replied the Parisian, "dat is no objection. Religious principle! pooh, I vill easily substitute another principle,—*la gloire.*"

LOST TO SHAME [*f. 227ʳ*]

During my residence at Oxford after I had taken my degree, there was, among the undergraduates of my college (Exeter) a youth named Tomlin,—handsome, gentlemanly, and always extremely well dressed; who went through his academical course respectably enough, his conduct neither giving offence nor exciting praise.

His tutor was my intimate friend, the Rev. Josiah Forshall, then Fellow of Exeter college, and at a later period tolerably well known in London as Keeper of the MSS. in the British Museum. With that establishment Forshall had been connected many years, when one morning he was told by his servant that a poor man was very anxious to see him. He accordingly came down stairs, and found waiting for him at the door a dirty ragged fellow, with a beard of several weeks' growth, and carrying a basket of crockery on his head. "What do you want? and who are you?" asked Forshall. "Sir," replied the man, "I should be obliged if you could spare me some old clothes and a trifle of money: my name, sir, is Tomlin: you, sir, were my tutor at Exeter College." Greatly, of course, was Forshall surprised at this discovery, and not a little shocked to find, on further talk with him, that Tomlin felt no shame at his metamorphosis, and had evidently no wish to rise above the wretched condition to which (in consequence of some gross misconduct) he had sunk. Having received from Forshall an old coat, a little money, and a loaf, away he marched, quite contented, with the crockery on his head.

LORD TEIGNMOUTH'S LIFE OF SIR WILLIAM
JONES [*f. 229ʳ*]

I one day happened to mention this work to my venerable friend,
Mr. William Maltby (of the London Institution), when he stated what
follows:—

"Lady Jones consulted me about the choice of a person to write the
Life of Sir William. Four persons had been suggested to her,—Parr,
Howley (afterwards Archbishop of Canterbury), Roscoe, and Hayley.
I advised her to fix on Parr; but, for some reason or other, she at last
chose Sir J[ohn]. Shore (Lord Teignmouth).

"When I told Parr that Shore was to write the Life, he exclaimed
with great vehemence, 'Then, Maltby, it will be truncated and disfigured!' It was so certainly in the case of a letter from Jones to Price[39]
(which I furnished for it), a passage about the French Revolution
having been omitted: and I much more than suspect that Sir William's
religious opinions are in some degree misrepresented by his biographer."

Lord Teignmouth informs us that "it was a favourite opinion of
Sir William Jones, that all men are born with an equal capacity for
improvement":[40] and Maltby assured me that Porson agreed with
Jones in this opinion,—doubtless a most erroneous one.

---

1. [Cf. Dyce's *Recollections of the Table-Talk of Samuel Rogers. To Which is
Added Porsoniana,* 3d ed. (London, 1856), p. 327 n.] I possess his copies of *Proclus on
the Timæus and Republic of Plato,* and of *Proclus on the Theology of Plato,* with a
vast number of MS. emendations, which his knowledge of the subjects (notwithstanding his comparative want of scholarship) enabled him to make.

2. My old friend certainly appears to have had some semi-pagan tendencies; but
they have been absurdly exaggerated by sundry writers: e.g. "It is traditionally related of Taylor, the translator of Plato, that he was found in the act of sacrificing an
ox to Jupiter—or rather, that the ox, proving recalcitrant, was about to sacrifice
Taylor." *The Saturday Review* for July 11, 1868 [XXVI], p. 61.

He was dreadfully indignant at the following passage of Southey's [. . .], and pronounced it to have no foundation in truth. [Southey called Taylor a "pagan Methodist"
and "le grand payen." See Taylor's *Selected Writings,* ed. Raine and Harper, p. 34;
Selections from the Letters of Robert Southey, ed. John W. Warter (London, 1856), I,
192.]

3. The Obituary of *The Gentleman's Magazine* for Dec[r] 1814 [LXXXIV, N.S. 7, 609] records his death as follows. " . . . A Coroner's Inquest sat on the body: verdict —*Died by the Visitation of God.*" [I have omitted most of the quotation.]

4. [*De Vita Pythagorica*, XXVIII, 134.]

5. *Memoirs of [the Late Thomas] Holcroft* [ed. William Hazlitt (London, 1816)], vol. iii. p[p]. 63[-64]. The "P——" mentioned above is, I believe, *Perry*, editor of *The Morning Chronicle.*— By the by, Holcroft's *Memoirs* was a favourite book with Rogers, who often cited it as affording a striking instance of talents and perseverance overcoming the disadvantages of low birth and poverty.

6. Northmore was a pupil of Gilbert Wakefield, and by no means a contemptible scholar, as his two editions of Tryphiodorus show. He also published some other things, —*Washington or Liberty Restored, a Poem in Ten Books,* &c.

7. The eleventh Duke of Norfolk: he died in 1815.

8. *A Letter from Athens to a Friend in England; The Two Last Pleadings of Cicero Against Verres, with Notes,* &c.

9. What truth there might have been in this I cannot say: but it is a fact that my friend John Mitford had a brother who had been a civil servant in India, and who bequeathed money for the erection of a temple to Vishnoo,—a bequest which the law very properly set aside.

10. *Ancient Fragments of the Phœnician, Chaldæan, Egyptian, Tyrian, Carthaginian, Indian, Persian, and other Writers . . . ,* sec. ed. 1832. Of the several volumes he published, this is the most valuable. But, like Taylor, he was deficient in critical scholarship.

11. [I have omitted the Greek.] *Epist.* i.— The same consciousness of his own deficiency as a verbal critic which made Taylor always ready to sneer at "grammarians," probably induced Piron to write the following verses. . . . [There ensues "Epitaphe d'un Grammarien." This and the following note are on f. 212a[r]. The above letter and the next were printed, with minor variations, in "Tayloriana," *Platonist*, II, no. 4 (Orange, N. J., 1884), 61. They were supplied by R. F. Sketchley of the South Kensington Museum, who found them in a copy of Taylor's translation of the *Phaidros.* Many numbers of the *Platonist* contain material on Taylor.]

12. See Cicero, *Tusc. Disp.* ii. 25. [Cf. *Table-Talk*, pp. 327–28 n.]

13. In these early productions Barker showed more talent than he ever exhibited at any later period of his life. I subjoin them, believing that scholars will acknowledge their merit. . . . [There follow "ΑΡΧΗ ῾ΗΜΙΣΥ ΠΑΝΤΟΣ" and "STRENUA INERTIA," the latter having to do with a squirrel in a treadmill cage.]

14. [I omit the long, macaronic title (1820).] . . . No Second Part of this pamphlet was ever published. The mysterious letters O.T.N. which Barker chose to append to his name on title-pages were meant to signify *Of Thetford, Norfolk.*

15. On the south side of Covent-Garden: it has since been pulled down.

16. [The omissions are mine.]

17. [Nor do they all merit publication. Monk's first letter (9 Feb. 1836) deals with editorial matters and wishes Dyce well in the Bentley project; the second (6 Oct.) acknowledges receipt of the first two volumes. John Wordsworth writes (Nov. 1837) concerning Dyce's request to examine the Bentley letters in the possession of Trinity College. He relates (17 Dec.) the nature of the MS holdings, the stipulations concerning their examination, the publication of some by Monk, and the fact that some are missing. On 25 Dec. he tells Dyce that the Bishop has the missing letters and, intending to publish them, will not give them up. These transcriptions occupy ff. 24[v]–26[v].]

18. "But the work which, as a scholar, he most desired to execute, was an edition of Æschylus. During a period of several years he had directed his attention to that object; and if his life had been prolonged to the present time, some of the results of his industry would now, in all probability, have been before the world; for, at his death, his Observations upon the Works of that Tragedian had reached such a state of maturity, that one of the Plays, illustrated by him, will, it is hoped, ere long appear, to be fol-

lowed, at short intervals, by others in succession." C. Wordsworth's Preface to Bentley's *Correspondence* [(London, 1842), I], p. xviii. No portion of the Æschylus has hitherto appeared.

19. i.e. Robert Aris Willmott, who afterwards took orders, and was for some time incumbent of Bear Wood, Berks. He published poems and several things in prose; all very pretty, but (like his conduct in life) not free from weakness. [Above this article's title Dyce has scribbled "abt 1832."]

20. In Nov. 1831 Harness had preached a sermon in Regent Square Chapel against the Unknown Tongues; which he printed with the title *Modern Claims to Miraculous Gifts of the Spirit Considered*, &c.

21. [XXIX (1823), 283–313: among other things, a review of Irving's *For the Oracles of God . . . For Judgment to Come* (1823).]

22. "He understood both theory and practice. His Treatise on the Art of Music is reckoned to display a profound knowledge of the subject; and his compositions, a morning and evening Cathedral Service, ten Church Pieces for the organ, with four Anthems in score for the use of the Church of Nayland, are greatly admired, as of the old school, in the true classical style." [William] Stevens's *Life of W. Jones* [in Jones's *Works* (London, 1801), I], p. xxix.

23. He succeeded Jones in the perpetual curacy of Nayland. While I was Mr. Sims's substitute at that place, he had the rectory of West Bergholt, Essex, where I was always received with more than kindness by him and his family; some of whom perhaps may yet survive, and retain, as I do, a pleasing recollection of our intercourse.

24. An epithet which Burges more than once applied to himself in print, and which, to his great amusement, completely puzzled the continental scholars.

25. [Oxon., 1821] P. 10.

26. See his [. . .] [Perhaps a reference to any in the series of articles on classical subjects which Charles Burney published in the *Monthly Review*. The Dyce Collection has a number of them.]

27. [I have selected three lectures from this astonishing document (f. 100). The course of eight must have been a bargain at its price of 12s.]

28. [The article thus far comprises ff. 98–102^v. Dyce next transcribes (ff. 102^v–103^r) Burges's translation of William Drummond of Hawthornden's sonnet, "I Know That All Beneath the Moon Decays," into Greek iambics, together with "Little Bo-Peep" done into both Greek and Latin; the originals of these efforts are ff. 96^r, 97a. Dyce has not transcribed "Carmen Lyricum Euripidis in Iph. T. 1058 et Sqq. Latine vertit G. Burges" (f. 96^v) or a message from Burges (f. 97). I print only the last item (which is torn at one point).]

29. P. 206, third ed. [The letter that follows is printed on p. xiii. The *DNB* quotes the *Gentleman's Magazine* to the effect that Knight died of "an apoplectic affection."]

30. [Cf. *Table-Talk*, p. xiii n.]

31. "These *Six more Letters* form a sort of supplement to a publication by the late Dr. Christopher Wordsworth, entitled *Six Letters to Granville Sharp, Esq., respecting his Remarks on the Uses of the Definitive Article in the Greek Text of the New Testament*, 1802. In the 'Advertisement' to *Who wrote* ΕΙΚΩΝ ΒΑΣΙΛΙΚΗ, *&c*, 1824, Dr. Wordsworth states that *Six more Letters* 'assured him privately' that the *Six more Letters* were not from his pen" [p. 336 n].

32. i.e. Dr. Olinthus Gregory, who wrote the *Life* of Mason Good.

33. Though not in any way relating to Porson, the remainder of Dr. Irving's letter to me is worth quoting. . . . [Not unless one is interested in the evidence that Dr. Good wrote "a suppressed work bearing the unusual and outlandish title of *Tackwims*." The note is on ff. 148^v and 151^r.]

34. [I have omitted ff. 149–50, an interleaved version of n. 31, which includes an extensive transcript from Dr. Wordsworth's "Advertisement."]

35. [I find more than one "Sheppard" or "Shepherd" who might fit the occasion.]

36. [There is a canceled draft of this article on f. 236ʳ. As Professor Schoenbaum points out (*TLS*, 22 Jan. 1971, p. 102), another version of this story appears in Bertrand H. Bronson, *Joseph Ritson: Scholar-at-Arms* (Berkeley, Calif., 1938), I, 267.]

37. Richard Heber told me as a positive fact, that, when he was abroad, *he saw* a proof-sheet of a Preface to Brunck's Apollonius which was suppressed; wherein, with inconceivable grossness and bad taste, Brunck observed that "though Shaw might be *magister artium* and *magister caccandi et mingendi*, &c, he was nevertheless a mere tyro in Greek."

I possess the text of Apollonius beautifully written on vellum by Brunck.

38. [Thomas F. Dibdin, *Bibliomania; or Book Madness: A Bibliographical Romance*, 2d ed. (London, 1811), pp. 589–90.]

39. [*Memoirs of the Life, Writings, and Correspondence of Sir William Jones*] P. 422, ed. 1807, 8vo.

40. P. 489.

PREFACE
TO CHAPTER FOUR

HE "PARTS" OF THIS CHAPTER are editorial and quasi-logical, and I have included Robert Owen for want of a better place. These are the persons whose society Dyce most coveted, or whose names he most wished to be somehow linked with. His gossip is characteristic; he stretches his recollection to include Jamesian encounters of little moment, and he does not hesitate to draw upon the memory of others. But such gems as Coleridge on the history of Brazil atone for any reaching.

His taste is most often typical, as for instance in his regret over Coleridge's metaphysics. Nor does he substantially revise our understanding of Lewis's *Monk,* criticism of which was fathered by the same STC ("We stare and tremble"). But we see traces of independence on such occasions as his defense of Southey and his offering of samples from the forgotten work of lady poets.

Some of the gossip has been published from other sources, as my notes are meant to suggest. Dyce himself was fairly scrupulous in indicating what he knew was not original. Indeed, it seems at times that he was obsessed with the idea of correcting all past errors in regard to his subjects. Where subsequent publication has duplicated his material, he is nearly always shown to be fair and accurate.

It is unfortunate that he held so strictly to his practice of not giving detailed notice to persons yet living (ca. 1867–69). Thus we miss Dickens, Forster, John Payne Collier, Tennyson, Harness, and many others of his acquaintance. But his diary may yet be found.

Only one of the articles needs attention here, that on Mary Russell Mitford, who is now remembered for *Our Village* and for letters like those to Harness herein. They have escaped Caroline M. Duncan-Jones's *Miss Mitford and Mr. Harness: Records of a Friendship* (London, 1955), a book that does nothing to explain "that foolish letter" alluded to in the first missive, presumably written in May 1828. The letters selected by Dyce have mostly to do with *Rienzi* and its attendant woes. But her career as a playwright began some years before. Talfourd had introduced her to Macready, who acted in *Julian* (1823); and Charles Kemble played the leading role in *Foscari* (1826). *Inez de Castro,* the cause of so much trouble, was never finally staged, by Kemble or anyone else. *Rienzi,* her greatest success, was presented on 9 October 1828, starring Charles M. Young. The very long delay after its composition was owed, it would seem, to Macready's fussiness and procrastination. The reference to Dyce in the last letter concerns one of his methods of ingratiation: he had presented her with a copy of his edition of Peele.

CHAPTER FOUR ❖
THE ARTS

PART I: THE LAKE POETS

SAMUEL TAYLOR COLERIDGE [*ff. 37–41*]

Of Coleridge I saw little: but I have heard much about him from those who knew him well, and who all agreed in regretting that he should have bewildered himself and others in the mazes of metaphysics, instead of writing verse. Surely, as a picture-poet he has been excelled by few: he paints objects with a vividness which would seem to show that they must have been before his eyes with almost the strength of realities.[1] In this respect what can be more striking than portions of *Christabel?* e.g. . . .[2] Or than the description of the sea-snakes in *The Ancient Mariner?* . . .

Byron, Hodgson, and Harness used to rave about *The Ancient Mariner,*[3] and were constantly quoting it: whenever they were guilty of any unfortunate piece of awkwardness,—such as breaking a wineglass, or spilling a cup of coffee,—they would exclaim, in allusion to their favourite poem, "Dear me, I have shot an albatross!"

I have repeatedly heard my friend, the late John Kenyon, cite the following instance of Coleridge's fatal passion for opium.[4] One night, after a dinner at Kenyon's house in London, Coleridge proceeded to walk home to his lodgings; and, as the weather was very fine, Kenyon, for the sake of exercise, accompanied him part of the way. It was nearly twelve o'clock, and the shops were all shut. When they came to a chemist's shop (in what street I forget), Coleridge suddenly stopped, and knocked at the door. No attention being paid to his knocking, he continued it more and more violently, till he had wrought himself up to a state of great excitement. At last the chemist appeared at a window, and asked rather angrily, "What was the matter?" On learning who had knocked, he said in a milder tone of voice, "O, Mr. Coleridge? very well"; and, shutting the window, presently came down stairs, and opened the door to serve his old customer. The fact was, Coleridge happened to be "out of opium," and consequently felt so miserable, that he could not return home till he had procured a fresh supply.

Southey was a somewhat impatient listener to Coleridge's metaphysical and long-winded talk. When Southey was engaged on his *History of Brazil,* Coleridge said to him, "My dear Southey, I wish to know how you intend to treat of man in that important work. Do you mean, like Herodotus, to treat of man as man in general? or do you mean, like Thucydides, to treat of man as man political? or do you mean, like Polybius, to treat of man as man military? or do you mean—" "Coleridge," cried Southey, *"I mean to write the History of Brazil."*

Coleridge had a mortal antipathy to Scotchmen, produced perhaps, or at any rate strengthened, by the remarks of the Edinburgh reviewers on the Lake poets. Speaking of a certain North-Briton *[Sir James Mackintosh?], he said, "Sir, he is a Scotchman and a rascal, and I do not lay the emphasis on *rascal."*[5]

Coleridge, *when thinking aloud,* would address any one he met: and I have heard the elder Charles Mathews act, with matchless humour, a scene (founded, he said, on fact), of which the following is a fragment,—mimicking to the life the solemn tones of Coleridge, and the surprise and squeaking voice of the urchin whom he addressed:—

"Coleridge, walking near Highgate, meets an apothecary's boy.

Coleridge. I have been considering, boy, that though I have known several persons good because they were religious, I have seldom known persons religious because they were good—

Boy. Sir?

. . . .

Coleridge. Boy, did you never reflect on the magnificence and beauty of the external universe?

Boy. No, sir, never," &c, &c.

Mathews was a very frequent visitor to Coleridge, who had a great regard for him.

James Wallack was present among the other actors in the Green-room of Drurylane Theatre when Coleridge read to them his tragedy of *Remorse,* and gave them particular directions how certain passages were to be delivered. His reading was a sort of high musical chant; and his ideas of stage-effect were so exquisitely ridiculous, that the actors had great difficulty in listening to him without bursting out into laughter. Wallack used to describe this scene and to imitate Coleridge very amusingly. (In that tragedy Wallack played the trifling part of Naomi, having not yet risen to the position which he afterwards held in the theatre. He indeed never became a first-rate actor except in melodrame; and he had received little education, having been on the stage from his childhood: but nature had endowed him with talents which, if they had been properly cultivated, would have ensured him success in any profession.)

I add here three poems by Coleridge which have not been inserted in any edition of his Works.

i.

From *The Gentleman's Magazine* for Decr 1793, vol. LXIII. p. 1133. . . .[6]

ii.

Mrs. Robinson—the Perdita of George the Fourth when Prince of Wales—towards the close of her life was entirely deprived of the use of her limbs by a torturing and incurable rheumatism. She, how-ever, bore this affliction with great fortitude and patience; and still took pleasure in the society of various literary men, who were drawn to her by the fascination of her manners and the charms of her con-versation, and were anxious to soothe her sufferings to the utmost of their power. It does not appear that Coleridge frequented the reunions of the brilliant Perdita: but we find him paying his court to her in verse a short time previous to her decease; for, among the "Tributary lines addressed to Mrs. Robinson, during her life-time, by different friends, with her answers," in vol. iv. p[p]. 141[-44] of her *Memoirs* [London, 1801], is included. . . .[7]

The preceding poem is followed by lines headed *Mrs. Robinson to the Poet Coleridge,*[8] dated Oct[r] 1800; which lines show that she was then familiar with his *Kubla Khan,* though that remarkable composition was not printed till 1816.[9]

iii.

Mrs. Robinson died Dec[r] 26, 1800 (see *Gent. Mag.:*—the date of her death is wrongly given in Chalmers's *Biog. Dict.* and in the French *Biog. Univ.*),[10] leaving an only child, Maria Elizabeth Robinson, to whom she was deeply attached, and by whom her affection was fully returned. In 1804 was published a small volume entitled *The Wild Wreath. Dedicated (by Permission) to H. R. H. the Duchess of York, by M. E. Robinson.* It contains various poems by Mrs. Robinson, Merry, M. G. Lewis, Southey, Darwin, &c; and, among others. . . .[11]

WILLIAM WORDSWORTH [*ff. 213–23[r]*]

With this great man, whose genius has been slowly but at last fully acknowledged by the multitude, and now exercises such a powerful influence on the more recent poetic literature of his country, I was on very intimate terms, the admiration I had expressed for his *Excursion* having led to our acquaintance; and several letters, which at various times he addressed to me, are printed in his *Memoirs* [London, 1851] by his nephew [Christopher Wordsworth]; see vol. ii. p.p. 214, 219, 220, 225, 274, 275, 278, 281, 284, 350. Though he invited me over and over again to pass some days with him at Rydal Mount, I unfortunately could not make it convenient to do so; for at that period it was my duty, not my choice, to spend a large portion of the year in the north of Scotland: but whenever Wordsworth visited London, which latterly he occasionally did, we used to meet very frequently both at my Chambers in Gray's Inn and at the houses of our mutual friends.

His wife generally accompanied him to London, and sometimes their daughter Dora.— Mrs. Wordsworth was the exemplar of all that is amiable in woman; and moreover is shown to have been endowed with true poetic genius by the fact, that, while Wordsworth was composing his verses on the Daffodils ("I wander'd lonely as a cloud," &c), and had left a blank after the lines,

> "For oft, when on my couch I lie
>   In vacant or in pensive mood,"

uncertain how to complete the stanza,—Mrs. Wordsworth filled up the lacuna thus,

> "They flash upon that inward eye
>   Which is the bliss of solitude":

yet such was her modesty, that she positively forbade any mention being made, in any edition of her husband's Works, that these two lines (perhaps the best in the poem) were supplied by her.—[12] Dora, the darling of her parents, married the late Mr. Edward Quillinan, a gentleman who published sundry clever things both in verse[13] and prose. In spite of his high esteem for Quillinan, who looked up to him with all the reverence of a votary, Wordsworth had long objected to this marriage with great earnestness, 1[stly] because Quillinan was a widower with two daughters, 2[dly] because he was a Roman Catholic, and 3[dly] because he was poor and had incurred the most serious liabilities in consequence of his connection with the Brydges family, his first wife having been a daughter of Sir Egerton Brydges. Wordsworth, however, at last ceased to oppose the marriage, which took place in 1841; nor could there possibly have been a happier union till it was dissolved in 1847, when Dora, whose constitution was always delicate, died in her father's house, to the inexpressible grief of her husband, her parents, and all her family. Her talents were much above the common order; she inherited a love of literature, and wrote prose with grace and spirit: see her *Journal of a Few Months' Residence in Portugal, and Glimpses of the South of Spain,*[14] whither, in the hope that a more genial climate might improve her health, she had gone in 1845, along with her husband and one of her step-daughters.

But to return to Wordsworth's London life. Being now an acknowledged "lion," his society was eagerly courted by the fashionable world: "To-day," he would say, "I dine with Miss Coutts, who takes me in the evening to a party at Sir Francis Burdett's; tomorrow I dine with Lady," &c, &c. "And can it be," I asked Mrs. Wordsworth (who kept quite aloof from these festivities), "can it be that he really finds pleasure in such a whirl round of gaiety?" "Yes," she replied, "he really does, because it is something new to him; but he will soon tire of it, and gladly return to our quiet home."

While poet-laureate (in which office he succeeded Southey), and resident at Rydal Mount, Wordsworth received an invitation to a state-ball to be given by Queen Victoria; and, as such an invitation was not to be slighted, he rather unwillingly came to London. For this important occasion he borrowed Rogers's court-suit (which, by the by, must have possessed a marvellous power of adapting itself to the varieties of the human frame, since another celebrated poet had figured in it at Buckingham-Palace); and he brought to town a dress-sword, lent to him by the late Dr. John Davy of Ambleside (the brother of Sir Humphry); as also a soiled pair of white kid-gloves, which poor Moxon[15] laboured so hard to purify by means of Indian rubber that he threw himself into a violent perspiration.— That our poet laureate went to the ball not without some flutter of spirits and some degree of uneasiness is certain: but his interview with royalty proved highly satisfactory; and he told me soon after, that "the Queen talked to him very kindly and at considerable length both about his own poetry and on other subjects."

I subjoin some miscellaneous fragments of Wordsworth's conversation: whatever may be thought of them, I can vouch for their accuracy.[16]

"It was very wrong in me to say in the earlier editions of my *Poems,* that Pope *pilfered* from the older English poets; for it was not the fashion of his day to acknowledge in notes any borrowed expressions. I have the highest admiration of Pope; still I think he had little poetic feeling."

"Dryden's *Juvenal*[17] is in many parts excellent,—even superior to the original." . . .

"Gray's *Installation Ode* is certainly, on the whole, a fine one."

"*Yardley Oak,* which Hayley found among Cowper's papers, differs remarkably both in boldness of style and in versification from his acknowledged works: but I don't mean to say that it is not Cowper's."

"When I was very young I read a novel called *The Sisters of Ashton,* which affected me so much that I absolutely washed it with my tears:—I met with it lately, and found that it was a wretched piece of stuff."

"The pleasure I derive from architecture, sculpture, and painting (which I have perhaps vainly endeavoured to express in parts of my poetry) is only second to the pleasure which I derive from nature."

"I should like very well to reside in London during several months of the year: but I cannot say that I relish the short visits I pay to it, during which I live in a constant bustle, breakfasting and dining out every day, and keeping much later hours than suit my habits. I delight in the walks about London, to which no one, no poet at least, has done justice: how charming is the walk along the Serpentine! There is no nobler view in London than that of Cheapside and the rise of Ludgate Hill. To me the streets present objects of great picturesqueness: even a butcher's shop by candle-light, with its varieties of colour, light, and shade is very striking." . . .

"When I first saw the Rialto at Venice I was greatly disappointed: it had so many associations in my mind! and I expected something very different from a mean-looking bridge."

"The scenery of Switzerland, with its sharp peaks and precipices, its dark fir-trees and pure white snow, is not well adapted for pictures; the forms and combination of colour are bad."

"I have given up my intention of publishing *a selection* from Thomson's *Works* (poems and plays), because I think I ought not to treat in that manner so distinguished a poet. I have the most ardent admiration and profound respect for Thomson. I doubt if any writer since Milton has shown so much poetic feeling. Parts of *The Castle of Indolence* are divine. I say nothing of his taste; and Burns had more passion."

"Dyer is another writer full of poetic feeling, and a great favourite of mine. The subject of *The Fleece* is an unfortunate one; but what fine and minute observation of external nature it exhibits! Dyer was originally a painter, and is exquisitely picturesque as well as imaginative in his writings. Recollect the passage in his *Ruins of Rome;*

> 'The pilgrim oft
> At dead of night, 'mid his oraison hears
> Aghast the voice of Time disparting towers,
> Tumbling all precipitate down-dash'd,
> Rattling around, loud thundering to the moon.'
> [ll. 38–42]

Now, common descriptive poets—Sir Walter Scott, for instance—if they had been describing the fall of a ruin, would have entered into a detail of its appearance,—they would have told us of the clouds of dust that consequently arose, of the birds that were startled from their nests, &c; but they never could have hit on that most striking thought,—

> '*The voice of Time* disparting towers.' "[18] . . .

"Lady Winchelsea is really a charming writer."[19]

"In Logan's *Ode to the Cuckoo*[20] is one beautiful stanza;

> 'Sweet bird, thy bower is ever green,
> Thy sky is ever clear;
> Thou hast no sorrow in thy song,
> No winter in thy year.'
> [st. vi]

His *Braes of Yarrow* is very good. In this passage the repetition of the word 'promis'd' has a fine effect;

> 'He promis'd me a milk-white steed
> To bear me to his father's bowers;

He promis'd me a little page
To squire me to his father's towers.'
[ll. 9–12]

But the best stanza by far of that ballad is,

'They sought him east, they sought him west,
They sought him all the forest thorough;
They only saw the cloud of night,
They only heard the roar of Yarrow.' "
[ll. 29–32] . . .

"Joanna Baillie, with all her genius, does not understand *the art* of writing: she is strangely deficient in poetic diction."

"What is stated in some review or magazine,—that I said, Coleridge was the only person whose intellect ever astonished me,—is quite true. His talk was even finer in his youth than in his later days; for, as he advanced in life, it became a little dreamy and hyper-metaphysical.[21] The quantity of opium, too, which he took had an unfavourable effect on him: by the by, when he was travelling with me and my daughter, we both knew perfectly by his manner and conversation whether he had been taking much or little opium. He certainly wrote no more of *Christabel* than has appeared in print;[22] if he had, I must have known it. *The Ancient Mariner* was founded on a strange dream which one of Coleridge's friends had, who fancied he saw a skeleton ship with figures in it. Coleridge and I had both determined to write some poetry for a monthly magazine, the profits of which were to defray the expenses of a little excursion we proposed to make together. *The Ancient Mariner* was intended for this periodical, but was too long. I had a very small share in the composition of it; for I soon found that the style of Coleridge would not assimilate with mine. Besides [ll. 226–27] I supplied the verse, [ll. 13–16] and four or five lines more in different places of the poem. The idea of making the Mariner shoot an albatross was mine; for I had been reading in S[helvocke's *Voyages*] a description of albatrosses hovering over a vessel. I also suggested the re-animation of the dead bodies to work the ship. Coleridge did not excel in sonnet-writing; he had not given much thought to the construction of sonnets." . . .[23]

"Gifford's editions of the early dramatists are undoubtedly valuable: but he had no taste in poetry. His verses, 'I wish I was where Anna lies,' &c,[24] are not poetry,—no, sir, they are not poetry." . . .

" . . . After all, Sir Walter Scott's Poems are merely melodramas in rhyme." [Deleted:] I was on a visit at Abbotsford, just before Scott set out for the continent; and it was melancholy to witness how his mind was impaired. In my daughter's Album is an affecting memorial of it,—some lines (quatrains), which he wrote at her earnest request.

"Speaking to Scott about his edition of Dryden, I asked him if he had collated the text with the old copies. 'No,' he replied: 'do you suppose that I could spare time for such labour?' " . . .[25]

"Rogers's *Italy* has a very extensive sale on account of the illustrations: as a poem, there is really nothing in it."[26] . . .

"De Quincey, the opium-eater, is a person of great intellect and great attainments; I am sorry to add that he is a great liar and rascal: he has lately contributed to *Tait's Magazine* a series of papers on Coleridge, which are full of the grossest falsehoods. Hogg, the Ettrick Shepherd, is another liar of the first magnitude."[27]

"Thomas Moore is now in London, working (as I heard him say) against time[28] for *Lardner's Cyclopædia*. There is very great cleverness in all he does."

"There's old Sotheby walking about as brisk and active as ever! He has just sent me his translation of Homer. Quillinan read me a page or two of it; till he came to some expressions which I thought so faulty that I really was obliged to stop him,—I could not stand it."

"I remember nothing, throughout the whole range of poetry, in worse taste than the passage in Pollok's *Course of Time*,[29] where he describes a corpse beneath the dissector's knife rising to new life at the sound of the last trumpet;

'And as the anatomist, with all his band
Of rude disciples, o'er the subject hung,
And impolitely hew'd his way through bones

> And muscles of the sacred human form,
> Exposing barbarously to wanton gaze
> The mysteries of nature, joint embrac'd
> His kindred joint, the wounded flesh grew up,
> And suddenly the injur'd man awoke
> Among their hands, and stood array'd complete
> In immortality—forgiving scarce
> The insult offer'd to his clay in death.'
> > Book vii [191–201]." . . .

"In my lines on *St. Bees' Heads,* I adopted the unusual form of stanza from Charlotte Smith's *St. Monica,* a very pleasing poem which I had never read till I saw it in your *Specimens of British Poetesses.* Charlotte Smith was a personal friend of mine."

"When I compose a poem I generally begin with the most striking and prominent part; and if I feel pleased with my execution of that, I then proceed to fill up the other parts."

"In writing poetical descriptions of natural objects, it is better not to write them on the spot, because if you do, you will enter into a great deal of unnecessary detail : you should write just after the object is removed from your sight, and then its great features only will remain impressed upon your mind."

Wordsworth died April 23, 1850

SOUTHEY [*ff. 234–35*]

I had no intimacy with Southey; but I always found him friendly; and he took much interest in most of the books I edited, more particularly in my edition of that very original and remarkable writer, Skelton, though he did not live to see it published. He once recommended me to edit Marston, whom he praised, I think, somewhat beyond his merits.

The last time I saw Southey was not long before the commencement of that lamentable illness under which his mental powers completely gave way. It was in London,—at the lodgings of the Rev. Mr. Johnson, a gentleman who had formed an acquaintance with Southey and

Wordsworth, in consequence, I believe, of his having done clerical duty in their neighbourhood. One forenoon I met Wordsworth in the street, who said to me; "Southey is in town, and would like to see you; but he returns home tomorrow morning. He and I dine today at Mr. Johnson's; and there is no reason why you should not drop in there after dinner: your not knowing Mr. Johnson need not be any obstacle; he will be very glad to receive you." I accordingly went, in the evening, to the lodgings of Mr. Johnson (in The Quadrant, Regent Street), and was ushered into the dining-room, which the ladies—Mrs. Johnson and Mrs. Wordsworth—had just quitted. A handsome dessert was on the table, at which, besides the host, Wordsworth, and Southey, were seated four or five grave and rather odd-looking personages. My entrance caused a slight bustle; but after I had been introduced to Mr. Johnson and had shaken hands with Southey, the tranquillity of the party was restored, and I took a chair next to Wordsworth. What was my surprise, when the grave and rather odd-looking personages, one after the other, proceeded to speechify about education, schools, school-rooms, classes, &c, each speaker addressing himself exclusively to Southey, who listened with great attention, and kept nodding his head in token that he fully comprehended the various details. This curious performance, which my entrance had interrupted, was at last concluded; and I then learned who the grave and rather odd-looking personages were, and the reason of their haranguing:—Southey had undertaken to write the Life of Doctor Bell;[30] and, in order to furnish him with certain information necessary for the proper execution of the work, Mr. Johnson had invited a posse of Bell and Lancaster school-masters to meet him.— At that time there was nothing in Southey's appearance to indicate the dreadful calamity which was impending over him. His figure was well-made and slight; his countenance handsome, in spite of a rather too aquiline nose; his eyes were brilliant; and his snow-white curly hair gave, at first sight, the idea of his having just escaped from the tongs and powder-puff of a frisseur.— After we had taken tea in the drawing-room along with Mrs. Johnson and dear old Mrs. Wordsworth, Southey and I left the house together: he pressed me to pay him a visit at the Lakes; and we parted at the street-door in the Quadrant.

Southey, no doubt, had violent political prejudices, which sometimes led him to judge unfairly and uncharitably of others: but, on the whole, there could not well be a more amiable man. How fondly he was loved by all his relations and friends! Some time after his death, at a dinner-party given by John Kenyon, I sat beside that highly-gifted woman Mrs. Nelson Coleridge (who, though dying slowly of a cancer, was still extremely beautiful); and when I mentioned Southey to her, the tears came into her eyes, and she said in a low voice, "Ah, dear uncle Southey!"

What a *helluo librorum* he was, is shown by his *Common-place Book* published after his decease. The great business of his life was reading and writing. "Southey," said John Kenyon to me, "cares for nothing that does not come to him through the medium of a book. He once accompanied me and some other friends to the continent; and one day, at Paris, while the rest of the party sallied forth from the hotel 'to see sights,' Southey preferred remaining in his own room (which looked out on a dead-wall) and reading *Lucani Pharsalia*."

When a man with grown-up children marries a second time, the marriage seldom is a happy one; and in Southey's case it certainly produced much family discord. Of the talents of the second Mrs. Southey (Miss Caroline Bowles) the world has had proof in her writings; and I have heard those who knew her intimately declare that her virtues were equal to her talents: yet in the quarrels between her and her step-children, which reached their height after Southey's death, both Wordsworth and Mrs. Wordsworth (who were not likely to judge rashly) took the part of the children.

Like Sir Walter Scott and Moore, Southey was latterly in a state of idiotcy. "How is Southey?" I once asked Wordsworth; who replied, "Well enough in bodily health; but his intellect is utterly gone. He stares in his children's faces, and says, 'Who are you?'"

Though during his life his poetry was decidedly popular, it is now almost entirely neglected, very few of the younger readers of the present time having ever looked into it, "because," as one of them said to me, "they have been given to understand that Southey *was not a true poet*." Yet I know for certain that both Savage Landor and Byron pronounced his *Roderick* to be the greatest poem of the day; and if the opinion of the former was biassed by friendship for the author, that of the latter was at least unprejudiced. John Mitford always talked of his *Madoc* with admiration: and I must confess that for me his *Thalaba* has lost none of its charm.

PART 2: OTHER ROMANTICS

LORD AND LADY BYRON, &C. [*f. 31*]

Thomas Campbell, who, on the appearance of Moore's *Life of Byron,* came forward as the champion of Lady Byron, and made himself rather ridiculous (as in his later days he did in other instances) by "advertisements" on the subject and by talking of it in a state of over-excitement,—told me, as an undoubted fact, what follows: and Harness, who was ready enough on most occasions to defend Lord Byron, confessed that he feared it was true.— Some hours after Ada was born, Lord Byron came into his wife's room, and, seating himself on the bed, informed her that Lady Milbanke was in town. "My mother in town!" she replied; "good heavens, why, then, is she not with me?" "Nay," answered he, "you cannot see her." "For what reason," asked Lady Byron in great surprise. "Because," he rejoined in a bitter tone of voice, "because she is laid up at Mivart's Hotel with the erysipelas in her head; *and I hope in God that she will die.*"[31]

Campbell was the only one of Byron's friends who seemed to like Lady Byron. She was no favourite of Harness. Moore, in my presence, called her *"a disappointing person,"* adding that "when you entered the room, she advanced to receive you with a smile, but as soon as you began to talk to her, you were petrified by the coldness of her manners."

A want of sincerity pervades Moore's *Life of [Lord] Byron.* He there tells us (vol. i. p. 231, ed. duod. [London, 1832]) that the opinion of Rogers's genius expressed by the noble poet in 1809, remained ever after unchanged. Yet I heard Moore say, sometime before the publication of his book, that he had in his possession verses on Rogers by Byron which were so "furiously satirical" that they could never see the light,—alluding no doubt to those which were first printed in *Fraser's Magazine* [VII (1833), 81–84], and which will be found under the article "Samuel Rogers" in the present work.

Moore complained that he could learn few or no particulars concerning Byron from his faithful servant Fletcher, who always began to cry when his master's name was mentioned; "Fletcher gives me plenty of tears, but scarcely any information."

Byron ridiculed Sotheby in *Don Juan* [i.e., *Beppo*] under the name of Botherby from a mistaken idea that Sotheby was the author of an anonymous letter which he had received in Italy, and which contained severe strictures on his conduct and writings.[32]

Ada Byron (Lady Lovelace) died, as is well known, after a lingering illness from a torturing disease. From all accounts she appears to have had a slight taint of insanity; but she certainly was endowed with an intellect of a high order: indeed, I remember hearing Babbage say, that she was the only woman he ever was acquainted with who could "generalize."

THOMAS CAMPBELL [*ff. 33–35*]

To this celebrated man, whom I knew intimately for years, I was first introduced by the son of his sister-in-law, Dr. Wiss of Heidelberg, a person of some literary attainments, who died of consumption at about the age of thirty.

Besides the juvenile pieces which may be found in his *Works*, Campbell wrote a good deal in verse, while a student at the University of Glasgow. One of these early effusions, as he told me, was a satirical ballad on a certain preacher, whose conduct did not by any means accord with the doctrines he delivered from the pulpit; and it became so popular at Glasgow, that it was sung in the streets.

During his youth, in Edinburgh, he took part with Brougham and Horner in the composition of a burlesque novel; "which," he said, "we were obliged to leave unfinished, because our heroine got involved in adventures from which it was really impossible to rescue her."

His domestic felicity was not a little clouded. His wife (Miss Sinclair), a very handsome and pleasing woman, whom he loved extremely, used to say that "she believed the wives of poets were never happy." His son (and only surviving child) was subject to fits of insanity, and had been placed, for a while, in an asylum. I have frequently seen [?] him in society at his father's house; and a very affecting scene it was: Campbell, in anxiety lest he should comport himself improperly, kept his eye upon him constantly; and if, in the course of conversation, the young man ventured to throw out any remark, the father's face lighted up with pleasure.

When Lord Byron's severe character of Lady Holland appeared in Lady Blessington's Journal[33] Campbell remarked to me that he was not sorry to see it there, "for her ladyship deserved all the ill that could be spoken of her." Yet she and Campbell were once dear friends, and used to compare notes on the various cutting things Lord Byron had said to the one concerning the other: she used to tell Campbell how Byron had quizzed his wig and smart coat, &c; and Campbell, in return, would let her know what horror Byron had expressed of her "large fat feet," &c.

In [William] Beattie's *Life [and Letters]* of *[Thomas] Campbell* [London, 1849] (vol. ii. p. 303) is a letter from Campbell to Mrs. Fletcher, dated Dec' 24, 1815, wherein he complains that Richard Heber, the well-known bibliomaniac, had broken his promise of lending him certain books which were absolutely necessary for the completion of *The Specimens of the British Poets:* "I believe now, at the expiration of three years, and after a hundred delays, he will at last, thus late, give me the volumes; but he has kept me in suspense (had I not learnt a little philosophy, it would have been despairing vexation) respecting my publication, which could not come out without his aid. . . . Strange to say, though he has been to me 'more treacherous than Ney to Louis XVIII,' he is really a good-hearted fellow; and is— excepting practical penitence—quite as much hurt, surprised, and indignant at his own conduct, as I am myself." We learn, however, from a letter in an earlier portion of the same *Life* (vol. ii. p. 240) that Campbell had already profited not a little by occasional loans of Heber's literary treasures; for on Dec' 30, 1813, the great bookcollector wrote to him as follows; "I hope you received my second parcel safe, as I did the first, containing Greene's pieces, which you returned. I now forward a third to St. James's Place, composed entirely of Elizabethan poetry, most of which will, I hope, prove useful. By dint of rummaging, I think others, of the same era, may yet be furnished; but whether before I leave town, or not until my return in February, is uncertain." The fact is, that Campbell was under the greatest obligations to Heber; who (as I know by experience), unlike the generality of bibliomaniacs, was ever ready to afford to others the use of even his choicest rarities; and if he was somewhat slow in meeting the wants of Campbell, the delay must have arisen from the difficulty of finding the volumes required; for his matchless collection of English poetry was stowed away, without arrangement, in [eight houses]. Indeed, his continued liberality to the compiler of the *Specimens* was the more praise-worthy, inasmuch as the latter treated the books he borrowed from him with much the same carelessness as Johnson treated Garrick's early editions of Shakespeare's plays. This I was told by Heber himself: "Campbell," he said, "used to send back to me my precious little tomes, tumbled loose into a dirty bag, and when I took them out, I had to brush off the bits of straw that were sticking to them." As Campbell put forth his *Specimens* without a word of Preface, his obligations to Heber were never publicly acknowledged.

After the loss of his wife, which he felt the more acutely in consequence of the malady of his son, Campbell (though he ought not to be described as an habitual drunkard) was so often intoxicated that he greatly lowered himself in the estimation of the world. He would sometimes call on me in Gray's Inn during the forenoon on his way from Highgate, when he had lodgings there; and he seldom failed to ask for a glass of brandy and water. The last time I ever saw Thomas Hill (the prototype of Paul Pry), about three years be[fore] Campbell's death, he said to me, "I met our friend Campbell in the street this morning at eleven o'clock, and he was more than half drunk."

Another failing of Campbell,—which showed his lamentable want of self-respect, and how completely he slighted the precept in *The Minstrel,*

"Know thine own worth and reverence the lyre" [I, vii],—

was his indulging in language of extreme grossness. While dining with me in Gray's Inn he has touched on such subjects and used such expressions as made me and the rest of the company equally uncomfortable: and Serjeant Talfourd told me that he was present at a dinner-party given by Lord Jeffrey in Edinburgh when Campbell talked in a style which absolutely tortured his host. Those who met him for the first time were consequently often shocked and disappointed: Captain Sherer,[34] a great admirer of his poetry, was introduced to him at the table of one of the Messrs. Longman; and [. ˌ .] departure, said, "Yesterday, I would have given a hundred pounds to meet the author of *Gertrude;* today I would give a hundred that I had never seen him."

Campbell had been very handsome in his youth; and could not help feeling mortified at the change which was gradually wrought upon his outward man by the hand of time. One night in the back-drawing-room of Charles Kemble's house (in St. James's [at Park Place]), when he thought himself alone, he walked up to the mirror, and after carefully surveying the reflection of his features and giving his wig a pull, he muttered, in a tone of vexation, "Ugh! what it is to look like an auld cat!" He was not aware that Mrs. C. Kemble was close behind him.

He occasionally gave way to jokes which were little relished by those to whom they were addressed. He told me that Sheridan Knowles, while teaching elocution in Glasgow, invited him to hear his pupils recite. After the performance, Knowles asked him what he thought of it. Campbell replied, "I think you have done wonders, for you have engrafted your own Irish brogue on their native Scotch."

It would certainly seem that Campbell was in the habit of amusing his friends with anecdotes of himself which he did not scruple to alter *ad libitum,* relating them sometimes in one version and sometimes in another: at least I have heard him tell the following anecdote over and over again exactly as I now give it; and yet in his *Life* by Beattie (vol. iii. p[p]. 395[–97]) I find what is evidently the same anecdote strangely varied and enlarged:— Having bought some books at a stall in Holborn, he was asked by the bookseller, "Where shall I send them, sir?"— "To Mr. Campbell, Whitehall Place."— "Pray, sir, may I inquire if you are *the great* Mr. Campbell."— Here the purchaser thought it prudent to inquire, in his turn, "Whom do you mean by *the great*

Mr. Campbell?"— "Oh," answered the man without a moment's hesitation, "I, of course, mean the missionary who published the travels in Africa."[35]

Another story which he used to relate concerning himself (and which, as he once ventured to tell it to Mrs. Siddons, I may insert here) was this. When a young man, and during a journey from London to Edinburgh, he stopt for the night at (I believe) Dumfries. He had scarcely slipped into bed, when the door opened, and a pretty chambermaid, advancing towards him, said, "Hae ye ony objection, sir, to a bedfellow?"— "Not the least, my [de]ar," cried Campbell in considerable excitement.— "Eh, sir," rejoined the maiden, "I'm sae glad! for our Jock the driver has jist come hame, drunk; and as we dinna ken what to do wi' him, we'll pit him into the bed wi' you."

That Campbell was subject to fits of great depression [. . .][36] be believed. Horace Smith one day met him at Brigh[. . .] are you?" said Smith.— "Miserable! I am going to drown myself [. . .] can endure life no longer. I shall take a boat and when the [. . .] has rowed me out a sufficient distance, I shall throw myself into the sea."— "Pooh! you can drown yourself tomorrow: come and dine with me to-day." Campbell was prevailed on to do so without much difficulty; dined, had plenty of wine, and was happy enough.

In his *Life* by Beattie (vol. iii. p[p]. 66[–67]) a portion of a letter from Campbell to Sir Walter Scott, May 30th, 1830, runs thus: "When Napier of 'the Edinburgh' returns to you, he will probably tell in your city how heartily I laughed at the regrets of my Edinburgh friends, for my supposed intended marriage with a certain lady . . . The baseless fabric of a vision! . . . I thank you nevertheless for having been concerned about me." But in stating to Scott that his "supposed intended marriage was the baseless fabric of a vision," Campbell most certainly deviated from the truth. The "lady" in question was Miss Crumpe, an Irishwoman of considerable beauty, an accomplished musician, and authoress of some novels, *Geraldine of Desmond,* &c. Her mother, a clever and rather vulgar matron, had the highest admiration not only of her daughter's talents but of her personal charms; and was much vexed to find that an artist who happened to be painting a half-length of Miss Crumpe was necessarily precluded from giving a representation of the young lady's ancles, which were notoriously fine. "Dear me, sir," said Mrs. Crumpe, "what a pity! But could you not introduce my daughter's ancles, by themselves, in the corner of your picture, just as they introduce the Islands in the corner of the map of Scotland?"—Campbell had been carrying on for some time a flirtation with Miss Crumpe, resorting (as he informed me) to the rustic mode of love-making, *by treading on her toes under the table;* till, one fatal evening, he was so fascinated by her singing to the harp, her literary talk, and her "ancles," that he fairly "proposed" to her; and was accepted by the [lady] in due form. Next morning, like Macbeth, he was "afraid to think what he had done," and, in great tribulation, entreated Dr. Beattie to get him out of the scrape, if possible. His friend accordingly went on a very disagreeable embassy to Miss Crumpe, and with great difficulty, and much to the young lady's indignation, contrived at last to break off the engagement into which the poet had so rashly entered.

[BENJAMIN] HAYDON; LEIGH HUNT [ff. 45–46ʳ]

Haydon and Leigh Hunt having quarrelled, all intercourse ceased between them. Soon after this rupture, John Keats said to the former, "Haydon, as I was lately walking near Hampstead, I met Leigh Hunt and his family, some of whom were carrying baskets. I asked where they were going, and Hunt replied that 'they had set apart the day to hold a sort of festival in honour of you,—that they were to dine in the fields and drink your health.'" Haydon was much gratified by this account; for what a kindness Leigh Hunt must have for him, if even after their quarrel, he showed such respect for his character and talents! When some one told Hunt how delighted the painter was by this cir-cumstance, the author of *Rimini* exclaimed, with a hearty laugh, "Haydon!! why, we never thought of him: we were keeping the birth-day of Had*yn* [*sic*] the composer."[37]

Haydon was very anxious to become acquainted with Mrs. Siddons, and at last contrived to introduce himself to her. He regularly attended the same church as the great actress, and sat in a pew as near to hers as possible. He continued his devotions there for some time without suc-ceeding in his wish, till one Sunday after service, as Mrs. Siddons was walking down the aisle, he, in the most respectful manner, offered her his arm. She took it; probably knowing who he was, and pleased with the homage which he paid her.

When Haydon asked her to dine with him, he invited Hazlitt also. "I shall not come," said Hazlitt; "for I have been accustomed to see Mrs. Siddons only on the stage, and to regard her as something almost above humanity; and I do not choose to have the charm broken."

In order to mortify Northcote, Haydon called at his door with Mrs. Siddons hanging on his arm. Northcote could not bear him; and had told him one day, "Sir, if this gallery *[his painting-room] were crammed of gold, I would not give you a single coin."

To return to Leigh Hunt. His conversation was truly fascinating: if it evinced no great depth of thought, it was full of fancy and delicate playfulness, and proved him to be possessed of great variety of knowledge. He read both Greek and Latin with facility, though not critically; he was a good Italian and French scholar; and was familiar with all the more elegant literature of his own country. He had quite a passion for old forgotten novels: the last time I ever saw him, not long before his death, he was regretting that he had not been able to meet with a complete copy of *The Adventures of David Simple*,[38] written by Miss Fielding, sister to the author of *Tom Jones!* Admiring as he did—and as Hazlitt did also—many parts of Mrs. Radcliffe's works, he would have felt indignant at the mention of her by my friend Thackeray, who strangely and unjustly classes her—as well as the two Misses Porter— with Anne of Swansea,[39] the authoress of sundry volumes of unendurable nonsense in the shape of romances.

As a poet, though Leigh Hunt has not much vigour, he certainly shows considerable fancy, and a fine eye for the picturesque. He perhaps ventured on dangerous ground when he treated in *Rimini* an incident so marvellously sung by Dante; and the line in the English poem,—

"And kiss'd her, mouth to mouth, all in a tremble" [III, 604],—

sounds vulgar indeed when compared with the matchless Italian one from which it is imitated,—

"La bocca mi baciò tutto tremante" [*Inf.* V, 136].

But in the same portion of his tale Leigh Hunt has an original simile
of great beauty;

> "And Paulo by degrees gently embrac'd
> With one permitted arm her lovely waist;
> *And both their cheeks, like peaches on a tree,*
> *Lean'd with a touch together, thrillingly."*
> [III, 591–94]

Another passage very happily descriptive occurs in *Rimini;*

> "And in the midst, fresh whistling through the scene,
> A lightsome fountain starts from out the green,
> Clear and compact, till, *at its height o'er-run,*
> *It shakes its loosening silver in the sun."*
> [I, 81–84]

CHARLES LAMB AND HIS SISTER; A POEM BY LAMB [*ff. 108–9*]

Wordsworth related to me, as illustrative of the powerful influence
of *The Edinburgh Review,* the following fact. When Lamb had Chambers in The Temple, there lived on the same stair-case a gentleman with
whom he had no acquaintance, but who, when Lamb occasionally came
home late at night, obligingly used to furnish him with a light, hot
water for tea, &c. Now, the article on Lamb's *John Woodvil* in *The
Edinburgh Review* put an end to these civilities for ever; from the
moment of its appearance the candle and kettle of the gentleman were
no longer at the service of the unfortunate author.

Coleridge was talking once with great praise of Shakespeare's
Troilus and Cressida, when some one remarked that it contained
strange anachronisms, such as Hector quoting Aristotle. Upon this,
Coleridge proceeded to defend Shakespeare, maintaining that he had
introduced those anachronisms to show his contempt for chronology.
"I suppose, then," observed Lamb, "that Johnson must have alluded to
that, when, speaking of Shakespeare, he said,—

'And panting Time toil'd after him in vain.' "[40]

Lamb, who had such a serious and almost methodistical turn in his youth, was latterly indifferent about religion. He never indeed talked profanely,—for when he said that "Voltaire was a very good Jesus Christ for the French,"[41] he certainly did not intend to be profane;—but he seemed to have lost all religious feeling, and to hate all conversation concerning religion. When he was on his death-bed, Talfourd called to see him: "I hope," murmured Lamb, "you have not brought a parson with you."[42]

It is on record that several eminent men have had their favourite dainties: Pope could not resist the fascinations of stewed lampreys; Quin never missed an opportunity of feasting on John-Dories;[43] and Dr. Parr (whose digestive powers must have been astonishing) would eat up a quantity of lobster-sauce or shrimp-sauce without any of the fish which they were intended to accompany. Nor is Lamb's fondness for roast pig less notorious; see the "Dissertation" on that dish in his *Elia;* and compare the following letter—the original of which is in my possession—addressed by him to the mother of Mr. John Payne Collier. . . . [44]

Miss Lamb, it is well known, stabbed her mother to the heart in a fit of the periodical insanity to which she was always subject; and as during her sane hours she was perfectly aware of the dreadful deed she had committed during her madness, one would have supposed that the recollection of it would have rendered her very unhappy: but, strange to say, such was not the case. My friend and publisher, the late Edward Moxon (on whom, as the husband of Lamb's adopted daughter, the care of Miss Lamb had devolved after her brother's death) has repeatedly assured me that the murder of her mother had left no painful impression on her mind,—that she never by any chance alluded to it, and that it had become to her not unlike a half-forgotten dream.[45]

Shortly before Miss Lamb's death, I happened to call on Moxon in Dover-street, when he told me that she was then residing with him in a state of decided though calm insanity: "We do not allow her," he said. "to see strangers; but I am sure she would like to see you": and accordingly I was shown into the room where she was sitting. She looked very old and shrunken, and was begrimed with snuff, in which she indulged largely. At first there was nothing in her talk that betrayed a diseased intellect: at last our conversation took the following turn :—

"D. I suppose, Miss Lamb, you still continue to read novels."

"MISS L. Yes, a great many."

"D. Of course, you are fond of Charles Dickens's works."

"MISS L. I am indeed: and now, by the by, I'll tell you a curious anecdote of Dickens. The other forenoon he paid a visit to one of his friends; and while he was in the drawing-room, he inquired if they had pease for dinner that day. It appeared they had: so he desired the pease to be brought up to him; and putting on an apron, he good-naturedly shelled them for the benefit of the family."

When I had taken my leave of her, I said to Moxon, "Where could she have possibly picked up that nonsensical story about Dickens?" "O," he replied, "it was a sudden invention of her disordered brain: the name 'Dickens' suggested it; and she no doubt thought she was relating the truth."— Poor Miss Lamb! I afterwards learned that she was much gratified by having seen me on that occasion: "Didn't I," she said, "make myself agreeable to Mr. Dyce!"

While Moxon was meditating a new edition of Lamb's poetical works, he intended to include among them the following poem; but, ridiculously enough, he was unable to procure a copy, though it had been published by himself! Those who relish the author's peculiar humour (and it is Lamb "all over") cannot fail to be amused by it. As far as I recollect, it is not mentioned by any of his biographers. . . . [46]

MATTHEW GREGORY LEWIS [*ff. 116–18ᵛ*]

Not only in every bookseller's Catalogue which I happen to take up, but even in Lowndes's *Manual,* I find that the volume of poems entitled *Tales of Terror* is unhesitatingly assigned to Lewis;[47] though so far is it from warranting such an attribution, that in several places it contains positive evidence of his having had nothing to do with it. The mistake, I presume, was founded on the idea, that, because Lewis wrote *Tales of Wonder,* he must also have been the author of the *Tales of Terror.* I have been informed, with what truth I know not, that the latter, which is a very poor production, was composed by a set of young men, one of whom was the late Lord Aberdeen.

A melodrama, called [*Raymond and Agnes*] and taken from Lewis's *Monk,* is also wrongly printed as by him in Cumberland's *British Theatre.* It was written, I believe, by Farley the actor.[48]

In the *Reminiscences of Captain Gronow* is the following tissue of misstatements about Lewis. "The charges brought against him *[for writing *The Monk,* chiefly in Mathias's *Pursuits of Literature*[49]] cooled his friends, and heated his enemies; the young ladies were forbidden to speak to him, matrons even feared him . . . 'Monk' Lewis, unable to stand [against] the outcry thus raised against him, determined to try the effects of absence, and took his departure for the island in which his property was: but unfortunately for those who dissented from the ferocious judgment that was passed upon him, and for those who had discrimination enough to know that after all there was nothing very objectionable in his romance, and felt assured that posterity would do him justice, this amiable and kind-hearted man died on his passage out; leaving a blank in one variety of literature which has never been filled up." vol. i [London, 1862]. p[p]. 198 [,199].

1. Captain Gronow most ridiculously exaggerates the behaviour of "the young ladies" to Lewis and the "fear" he excited among the matrons. 2. Whatever outcry was occasioned by *The Monk* on its first appearance, that outcry had long ceased, and Lewis had been for many years a welcome guest and an especial favourite in the highest class of London society, when he visited Jamaica on two occasions (tearing himself away from his numerous noble and literary associates), with the sole object of ameliorating the condition of the negroes on his extensive estates; which, during his residence there, he spared no pains to effect (see his very interesting posthumous work, *The Journal of a West-India Proprietor,* &c) : and instead of "dying on his passage out," he died on his second voyage homewards in 1818. 3. As to Captain

Gronow's remark that "after all there was nothing very objectionable in his romance," we must charitably suppose that we have here only another instance of the Captain's downright ignorance; for the main plot of the book—the loves of Ambrosio and Matilda, and the rape of Antonia—is polluted by an indecency which is scarcely to be paralleled except in productions expressly intended for the brothel (and which was not to be done away by the omission of certain passages in the second [i.e., fourth] edition); besides, *The Monk* contains a gross attack on the Scriptures: and all this from the pen of a gentleman who, in the second edition, boldly put his name on the title-page, and proclaimed himself a member of the British Parliament!— The under-plot—the story of Raymond and Agnes and the Bleeding Nun—is harmless enough: for how much of it Lewis was indebted to the German I know not; but there is great merit in the description of the escape of Raymond and the Baroness of Lindenberg from the robbers' hut in the forest, and in the extravagant incident of Raymond's carrying off the real Bleeding Nun instead of Agnes disguised to represent her. Very picturesque, too, is the account of a procession of nuns on the Festival of St. Clare, during which the Domina is violently put to death by the enraged populace, who are led to believe that she had murdered Agnes.

In a very small volume, little known, entitled *Poems by M. G. Lewis, Esq.*, 1812, is an Italian version of one of them by no less a personage than C. J. Fox. I give here both the original and the translation. . . . [50]

I conclude this article with some pretty and ingenious lines by Lewis, which are printed in the *Journal* mentioned above. . . . [51]

MARY RUSSELL MITFORD [*ff. 125–37ʳ*]

The earlier literary attempts of this lady gave no indication of her ever being able to compose such a drama as *Rienzi*, which certainly ranks with the best tragedies of the time,—with those of Sheridan Knowles and Lord Lytton. The great curse of her life was her father, a swaggering extravagant dissolute old man, who seduced her maids, squandered her money, and kept her in a constant state of poverty and agitation. (He had been remarkably handsome in his youth; nor did he scruple to confess to some of his friends that [. . .].) Her health was very indifferent; and her habit of taking opium rendered it still worse. She would pass the whole night in reading. She seemed almost a cham[. . .]; for she lived on the smallest possible quantity of food: during the last visit I ever paid her at Three-Mile-Cross cottage, near Reading, she did not taste dinner; and on my asking why, she replied, that she was not hungry, having had "a substantial breakfast, a cup of *pease-soup.*"

When *Rienzi* was first running its very successful course at Drury-Lane Theatre, she came up to town to see it, accompanied by her father; and, in her primitive simplicity, she brought with her on the top of the stage-coach an old lame faithful female servant to witness her triumph. I joined her in her private box: and, on the fall of the curtain, she went round to the Green-Room, where she was complimented to her heart's content by the various performers in her tragedy. Nay, even Harley, who had no part in the piece, offered her his congratulations, and entreated her to write a farce containing a character that would suit him; which she promised to do.

Miss Mitford's plays have been collected into two volumes; wherein, besides *Rienzi,* are several striking things,—particularly in *Otto of W*[*ittelsbach*], a tragedy which has never been acted. . . . [52]

> "Three Mile Cross
> Wednesday
> I beg your pardon my dear friend from the bottom of my heart. I should have asked & waited for your answer—but I had enquired about you amongst the Walters & Dowsons, & one had heard of you at your Chapel & another at your school, so that I fully believed you to be well & in full activity—& this suspense & anxiety which I have been enduring for the last six months has had an effect on my nerves & health & temper which sometimes frightens me—& I have been so out of spirits that I have felt as if the whole world (except for Talfourd) was forsaking me—& your friendship is one of the things which I could least afford to lose—& so I wrote that foolish letter—for which once again I sincerely ask your pardon. The dividends I was sure had

escaped your memory.— Mr. Kemble has certainly behaved very un-
kindly—very. Although Mr. Talfourd saw him immediately on his
return from the circuit before he came here for the Sessions, yet we
(that is Mr. Talfourd) never got his final answer till about ten days
ago—& even if he could not have induced Mr. Young to take the part
(which I firmly believe that he could have done) yet surely the point
might have been earlier ascertained & the suspense & expectation removed.— But he never answered my letters—his first conversation
with Mr. Talfourd was a long tirade against my father for showing the
play to Miss Kelly—& his answer when given at last was in one word
No—an incivility which to such a person as Mr. Talfourd is quite un-
justifiable—he did not add one single word but hurried [?] off as
soon as he had announced [?] his determination. Now the great evil
of all this is that I might certainly have brought Rienzi out at Drury
Lane this season (as Kemble well knew) if I had not considered myself as pledged to him & him as pledged to Inez—and now the season
is over, lost—a great loss to people so poor—& God knows whether the
opportunity may recur [?]. However I have not quarrelled with him
& do not mean to do so—I never cared enough for him to be tempted
into that folly—I never do quarrel except with those whom I like very
much indeed.— Can you tell whether Kemble is likely to be Manager
next season? or whether the newspaper report is true that he is going
to America? And if Manager do you think from the tenor of his conversation that he is likely to bring Inez out then?

Have you seen Mrs. St. Quentin & Emily? They were three or four
days last week at Dr. Valpy's & I saw a good deal of them. Mrs. St.
Quentin is a very amiable Methodist—& Emily a charming girl—not
perhaps pretty except from expression—but very delightful in manners & mind. Mary would like her exceedingly—Mrs. St. Quentin
spoke of course of your dear sister with the affection which all who
know her must feel for that sweetest person—our kindest love to her—
& once again pray forgive me. I might have waited till I had to acknowledge [?] the money—& ought perhaps rather to have done so
than have troubled you with this—but I got your note this evening &
really could not sleep untill I had written an ample apology & sent it
forth on its way— It is right to state that the injustice [?] was all my

own—my father & mother were kinder & wiser. I earnestly hope that you are quite recovered—God bless you— Ever yours M R M
To
    The Rev⁴ William Harness
        17 Heathcote Street
            Mecklenburgh Square
[Postmark: 9 May?]"

> "Three Mile Cross
> July 2ⁿᵈ, 1828

I am quite sorry my dear friend to find from the tone of your last letter that you are a good deal worried & harrassed & tired of Town. How I wish you had a good living hereabouts!—for selfish as the wish seems, it is not purely selfish— The country is just of the character you describe, pretty & pastoral— The country ladies are really of a good class in mind & manner although one cannot say quite so much for the gentlemen, & you would have your friend Mr. Milman & your other friend Mr. Hitchins [?] to make up for the deficiency of literary inter-course. You know I suppose that Mr. Hitchins has a living about ten miles off—hardly perhaps so much—& is exceedingly popular in all ways. I met him at a friend's house in the winter & liked him much—he happened to mention your name, & that was Open Sesame to both our feelings. I have never heard one man speak of another with more de-lightful warmth than he did of you—for generally speaking I observe that you lords of the creation seem ashamed of letting out the strength of your friendships, & talk of the man you would go to Cairo [?] to serve just as if he were a common acquaintance.— Mrs. St. Quentin speaks of dear Mary just in the same way—but she's a woman—so the wonder is less—besides which nobody could talk coldly of Mary Harness.— Now to the drama— Many thanks for your kind attempts to find out Mr. Kemble's intentions—I believe the theatre is in so un-settled a state that he hardly knows them himself— I believe moreover that Miss Kemble is writing or has written a play which will prove to [?] be his first object— Under these circumstances I have thought it best (without making any quarrel & still leaving Inez in his hands) to withdraw Rienzi from Covent Garden & transfer it to Drury Lane, where it is to be the first new Tragedy produced with Mr. Young next season— You & I both know that Mr. Young is not exactl[y the] actor we should have chosen—& had [it] pleased Mr. Kemble to let me know at the proper time that Inez would not be done last season, we should have brought out Rienzi with Macready & made an immense hit—but as matters stand I think that I have done right in giving the play to Mr. Price—Macready is not likely to be in London— Kean is quite out of the question—Young is very popular—is enamoured of the part, in which Mr. Price says he becomes more & more interested every day, & means to take the play with him to study during the vacation & to spare no pains to make himself perfect— Price is also full of hope respecting the Play, has engaged a new actress, who if she succeeds in Juliet & Belvidera is to play Claudia, & means to produce it with every advantage that the Theatre can furnish. Tell me if I have done right? At all events the thing will be off my mind—& if the tragedy were to be acted at all it seemed the only chance—to say nothing of Price's terms being much better than Kemble's. Do tell me if you think me right? Adieu my very dear friend—kindest love from all to all—

Ever most faithfully yours

M. R. Mitford

To
   The Rev⁴ Wᵐ Harness
     17 Heathcote Street
      Mecklenburgh Square
[Postmark: 3 July 1828]"

"Three Mile Cross⁵³

Saturday

My dear friend— You will be glad to hear that my Play *[Rienzi] is now to come out certainly on Saturday week—i.e. Saturday the 11ᵗʰ of October *[18[28]]—& I think under very favourable auspices— Mr. Young has been studying the part for the last three months—Stanfield is painting the scenery, & amongst the new scenes is an exact representation of Rienzi's house which is still standing at Rome & is shewn as a curious specimen of the domestic architecture of the middle ages— They have procured the sketch on purpose— The songs are setting in the best manner—the costume is to be in highest degree splendid & exact—& the new actress *[Miss Phil[lips]] makes her first appearance in the heroine. This looks like a very bold as well as novel experiment—but the truth is that Mr. Talfourd has heard her rehearse the principal scenes *out* on the stage of Drury Lane & he is *sure* of her— Mr. Price *[the manager] & Mr. Cooper are most sanguine respecting her success—so is Mr. Young who writes me word that she never omits working hard with him every day, & that he shall continue to instruct her in the character to the very hour of representation— This is very kind. She has great sensibility, a very pretty figure, an attractive countenance—no affectation—a delightful voice, & a most pure & perfect intonation. In short nobody fears or doubts my young actress. We may fail—for in the drama there is always danger—but it will not be the fault of the manager or his actors—for never were a set of people so sanguine & zealous & hearty in the cause. They really astonish me.— The only danger is in the earliness [of] the season & the emptiness of [London]. Do get every body to go that you can.—

I think to be in Town somewhere about Thursday week—or perhaps before & will let you know where we pitch our tent. I quite long to see Mary whom it is so very long since we have seen.

Pray excuse the wafer—I am sending a frankfull of notes to Mr. Talfourd & am afraid of over weight.

Adieu my dear friend. Kindest regards from all to all—

Ever very faithfully yours

M. R. Mitford

Will Henry be with you still? It would be a great pleasure to see him before his departure. Mr. Young read the play in the Greenroom yesterday.

To

The Rev⁴ Wᵐ Harness

17 Heathcote Street

Mecklenburgh Square

[Postmark: 29 Sept. 1828]"

"Three Mile Cross

Friday Night.

A thousand thanks my dear friend for Otto— It will be of the greatest use—especially as regards the character of the hero, which is not only well adapted to the age & country—quite what one fancies of an old German Knight, but dramatically effective, & what is still better *within my actor's compass*. As soon as I have arranged my whole scheme old & new together I'll send it you—I should like your opinion & Mr. Dyce's—(make my best comp^{ts} to him & tell him that I have now read Peele through & am charmed with the David Play!)— You got my packet I hope— I was much disappointed—but I am convinced that the lesson is want of space. Nothing can be more unaccountable than Mr. Walter's shyness about that paper—but so it is— If it were a pawnbroker's shop that supplied his income he could not be more ashamed of the source—more desirous to get quit of it (for a proper consideration understand) or more anxious that people should believe he had got quit of it. It is the only subject on which he tells fibs.— I think you did qu[ite] right about the chaplaincy—*you* are not by any means a fit subject for martial law with your fine spirit of independence —your habit of thinking for yourself & of saying what you think. Besides I don't at all think it the road to preferment— You would be less known, less talked of there than in Town—& some day or other your celebrity must bear its proper & natural finit—a stoll or a great living —or both—for when Fortune does come she will come with both hands full.— God grant it may happen soon!— Adieu my very dear friend— Once more a thousand thanks. Love to dear Mary Everyone's

M. R. Mitford

Reading November twenty nine 1828
    Revd Wm Harness
        17 Heathcote St.
            Mecklenburgh Sq:
J. B. Monck London
[Postmark: 1 Dec. 1828]"[54]

THOMAS MOORE [f. 138^r]

Moore not merely disliked people to talk while he was singing, but felt unable to go on if they did so. One night, at Bowood, as he was

about to sit down to the piano, Lord Lansdowne went round the drawing-room, and requested his other guests, among whom was Senior,
to be silent; which, of course, they promised to be; and Moore began
his song. At the same time Senior moved to a table not far from the
piano, and proceeded to write letters with great vigour, the scratching
of his pen on the paper forming a sort of accompaniment to the poet's
song. This completely upset Moore, and he suddenly ceased singing.
Upon which Senior exclaimed, "O, pray, Mr. Moore, don't stop on my
account; I assure you, you don't annoy me in the least." *On the authority of a person present.*

Sad, sad was the gradual darkening of Moore's brilliant intellect.
During his last visit to Bowood he forgot in what part of the house his
room was; and asked Lutt[. . .] to find it for him. And I remember
that, while he was staying a day or two in St. James's Place, Rogers
gave strict orders to his servants not to go to bed till they had ascertained that "Mr. Moore's candle was extinguished."

PART 3: THE ROGERS CIRCLE[55]

SAMUEL ROGERS [*ff. 159–76, 181ʳ*]

My acquaintance, or rather, my intimacy with Rogers extended
over a period of many years, during which, in "the London season," I
was in the habit not only of occasionally dining, but of breakfasting
two or three times a week, at his house in St. James's Place;[56] till at
last the treasures of art and the numberless curiosities which it contained, became as familiar to me as to their owner himself: nor is
there any affectation in my saying that I never catch even a distant
view of that "[. . .] suburban dwelling," without such feelings of
regret as are awakened by no other locality associated with recollections of the past.

During his later years, when the friends of his youth, with one or
two exceptions, had all passed away, and when many of the friends of
his middle age had also gone down to the grave,—Rogers confined his
hospitalities chiefly to breakfast-parties, which he had always pre-

ferred to dinner-parties, because at the former there was comparatively
an absence of restraint and ceremony, and because the guests arrived
with their spirits fresh and unimpaired by the business of the day. Ten
was the nominal hour of those morning-meetings, which seldom broke
up till two in the afternoon; for the conversation turning chiefly on
literature and art was so interesting to the venerable host that he always showed an unwillingness to let his visitors depart. Indeed, no
man in the prime of life could have felt more enthusiastic admiration
for whatever was beautiful in writing, in painting, and in sculpture
than Rogers did when an octogenarian: nor, I must add, was he less
sensible to the καλόν in human conduct; for his eye would glisten, and
his voice falter, if he mentioned any instance of true heroism or
generosity. The charm of those breakfasts was enhanced by the adorn-
ments and accompaniments of the room where they were held,—a room
which had its walls entirely covered by pictures of the highest class,
and which, looking out on the Green-Park, through a small garden[57]
full of shrubs and flowers, gave one the idea of being in the country
rather than in London. It was pleasing, too, to recollect how many
distinguished characters had at various times been assembled in that
room,—writers, statesmen, dignitaries of the church, warriors, and
even royalty itself,—from the year 18[03], when Rogers celebrated
his removal to St. James's Place, by a dinner-party, at which Fox so
simple and so wise, and Sheridan so artificial and so witty, were, at
their own instance, "the chief-invited guests."

The oldest and most confidential friend of Rogers was William
Maltby (a cousin of the Bishop of Durham's). Their friendship commenced while they were little boys at the same school, and was only
terminated by the death of Maltby, which preceded that of Rogers by
[nearly two years]: together, in the bloom of youth, they walked up
Bolt Court with a determination to introduce themselves to Johnson,
but wanted courage to knock at his door;[58] and together, in the extremity of age, they dined at Miss Burdett-Coutts's, when that lady,
to gratify a wish of Maltby, had kindly invited him to meet the Duke
of Wellington and Lord Brougham. Though Maltby had been entered
as a student at Cambridge, and had resided there for some time, he
quitted the university without taking a degree. He afterwards prac-

tised as a solicitor in London; but his love of literature, both ancient and modern, was so engrossing as to be almost incompatible with success in his profession; and, on the decease of Porson (with whom for years he had been very intimate), he obtained an employment in perfect accordance with his tastes and habits, being appointed in 1809 to succeed that illustrious scholar as Principal Librarian to the London Institution.[59] During the long period of his holding that office, he materially improved the library by the addition of many volumes which were purchased at his recommendation. In 1834 he was superannuated from all duty: he, however, continued to occupy handsome apartments in the Institution, which were crammed with books that it had been the great pleasure of his life to collect; and there, poring over some favourite volume to the very last, though blind of one eye, he died towards the close of his ninetieth year, January 5th, 1854. In Greek and Latin Maltby might be termed a fair scholar; he was well read in Italian; his acquaintance with French and English literature was most extensive and accurate; in a knowledge of bibliography he could hardly have been surpassed: and the wonder of every body was, that, with all his devotion to study and with all his admiration of the makers of books, he should never have come before the public in the character of an author.— On more than one occasion Rogers profited by the extensive reading of Maltby; who, for instance, assisted him in consulting various works which served to furnish materials for the poem of *Columbus*.

Accompanied by the old friend whom I have just described, Rogers, for a series of years, went to Broadstairs, and established himself at the chief inn, where his coming was looked forward to as an important event, and where he usually spent several weeks. Indeed, he greatly enjoyed the quiet of Broadstairs, which he always spoke of as "the beau ideal of a watering-place": but I suspect that, if he had lived to see it as it now is when the rail-way brings to it so many visitors, he would have been inclined to retract that encomium.

As I frequently was staying at Margate during Rogers's periodical sojourns at Broadstairs, he kindly insisted that I should breakfast with him nearly every other day,—Margate being only about two miles from Broadstairs. Thither, accordingly, in the bright summer mornings I walked across the fields, and through the beautiful church-yard of St. Peter's, where Rogers by appointment used to meet me, and where I generally found him sitting on a tomb-stone in deep meditation: sometimes, if I happened to be a little past my hour, I would find the tomb-stone deserted; and, on coming out into the high-road, would see Rogers at a considerable distance trudging back to Broadstairs with his peculiar shambling gait. When in all haste I had overtaken him, I was sure to be scolded for my want of punctuality; but, before we reached Broadstairs, his ill-humour had evaporated.

I was not always the only guest at Rogers's Broadstairs breakfasts: for he occasionally invited to them such acquaintances as he chanced to fall in with among the sojourners at Ramsgate, to which place he drove over nearly every day. Most of these, however well born and well bred, were persons of no mark; but among them I particularly remember Mr. John Hardwick the London police-magistrate, and Poole the successful dramatist, who owed much to the patronage of Mr. Hardwick and was then residing with him at Ramsgate. A more polished gentleman or a more lively and intelligent companion than Mr. Hardwick is not often to be met with; and the author of *Paul Pry* overflowed, of course, with amusing reminiscences of players and play-wrights.

Whatever guests there might be at those breakfasts, I remained till they had all taken leave, in order that I might accompany Rogers in his daily drive, and walk about with him during certain intervals of the excursion. Maltby, who had neither the bodily vigour nor the animal spirits which his friend so wonderfully retained, seldom went with us: he preferred strolling on the heights of Broadstairs, or poring with his single eye on some favourite volume.— About two o'clock Rogers's carriage was ready at the inn-door. We generally proceeded first to Ramsgate; where we sauntered repeatedly up and down the very long and noble pier, my companion showing no symptoms of fatigue, and, with equal activity of mind, taking an interest in all the objects that met his view,—the rosy-cheeked children that were sporting past us, the steamers that were smoking in the far distance, and the vessels that were leaving or entering the harbour. Sometimes we drove to Pegwell

Bay; a scene now familiar to many who have never been there by the exquisite picture of my relative William Dyce, in which, however, he has rather embellished its features, and rather misrepresented the colour of its cliffs. One afternoon at Ramsgate we unexpectedly encountered the Duke of Wellington, who forthwith carried Rogers off to Wolmer. The furthest limit of our drive was Margate, where I was then lodging; and where a very tolerable band, which played every afternoon on the pier, had great attractions for Rogers, who was so passionately fond of music that he could relish a performance even of an inferior kind: indeed, with that true wisdom which essentially contributes to the happiness of life, he was always "easily pleased." When the band had ceased playing, he dropt me at my lodgings, and returned to Broadstairs.— I may notice here what Rogers often dwelt on with surprise, —the difference as a place of resort between the Margate of his youth and the Margate of his old age. "I remember," he would say, "when the Duke of York and his party were staying at the York Hotel, and when the town was so crammed with company of the very highest rank, that it was scarcely possible to procure a lodging."

But to resume the account of Rogers's London life. He had long been accustomed to walk to public places and to evening-parties, and also to walk home from them, however late the hour; and when he had reached the age of eighty-six, his faithful servants, fearing that an accident might befall him in consequence of his deafness, urged him, but in vain, to make use of his carriage on those occasions. Even in the day-time he walked about at a considerable risk; for one forenoon, just as he stepped upon the pavement after crossing Regent Street, he was startled by the scream of a woman close beside him; and to his inquiry "what was the matter?" she replied, "I screamed because you were on the point of being run over." . . ."[60] At last the dreaded event took place. He was returning on foot and alone from an evening assembly at Lady Londonderry's, when, attempting to avoid the cabriolet of a gentleman, whose first warning to stand aside he had not heard, he fell with great violence, [. . .] As soon as this catastrophe was known, it caused no ordinary sensation in the London world, and drew to his door such a host of inquirers of various ranks that his servants were under the necessity of placarding a daily bulletin for their information: among those who sent to make particular inquiries concerning him were her Majesty and Prince Albert.

Though his general health was not materially injured by the shock he had received, Rogers was never again able to set foot on the ground: he was carried, like a child, from room to room and to and from his carriage when he took an airing. But yet under these melancholy circumstances he showed the most perfect resignation and even cheerfulness; and, now that he could no longer mix in society at others' houses, he enjoyed more than ever his almost daily breakfast-parties, at which sometimes two, sometimes three or four, and sometimes as many as six of his friends were present. His most frequent guests were his nephew Mr. Samuel Sharpe, the Reverend John Mitford, Dr. Alexander Henderson, and myself: next to these in frequency were his niece Miss Martha Rogers, Luttrell, Lord Glenelg, Crabb Robinson, Dr. Beattie, and Moxon the protégé of Rogers and the publisher of the latest editions of his works; while occasionally the requisite number for the breakfast table was made up from a very ample list of persons male and female, some of them of high rank and fashion, some of them of distinguished talents, and all of them equally ready to testify their respect for the aged poet and to contribute to his amusement.

His lady friends and lady visitors were nearly, if not quite, as numerous as his friends and visitors of the other sex.

Among the former, whether titled or untitled, two were pre-eminently his favourites,—Mrs. Carrick-Moore and Mrs. Forster. He had known them long, and almost always spoke of them familiarly by their maiden names, as "Harriet Henderson" and "Lavinia Banks,"—Mrs. Moore being the posthumous child of the celebrated actor Henderson, and Mrs. Forster the daughter of the sculptor Banks, whose fine genius was not sufficiently appreciated by the public during his life-time.[61] Both ladies were not merely accomplished; they were highly intellectual: and Mrs. Moore in her youth must have possessed extraordinary personal charms; for even in her old age, when I used to meet her in St. James's Place, she might still have been called beautiful. The last years of both were saddened by the same calamity,—the loss of sight.

As Lady Holland was the wife of one of Rogers's most valued

friends, he could not fail to be intimate with her also; and to the world in general their intimacy wore the semblance of friendship: but I believe that there never was much cordiality between them; and it was no secret to their mutual confidants that latterly they felt for each other what was nearly akin to strong dislike.— "Suppose," said Rogers to Lady H. when she was once complaining of want of amusement and ennui, "suppose you were to try, just by way of variety and as a new means of excitement, the doing [of] some kind and generous action."— She had on more occasions than one fallen so violently in love with pictures of moderate value in Rogers's possession that he thought himself obliged to make her a present of them. At last she took a prodigious fancy to a beautiful little piece by Stothard from a story in *The Spectator:* knowing, however, that it was a favourite with Rogers, she told him that she should be quite content if he would lend it to her for a time, that she might have the pleasure of looking at it as it hung in her dressing-room. Her wish was granted. Weeks, months, and years crept on: Rogers threw out sundry hints that he should like to have the picture back again; but all in vain: nor even after her ladyship's death was it returned to him; for she had bequeathed it, as a token of her regard, to the Duke of Sutherland.— One forenoon in St. James's Place a visitor mentioned his having read a paragraph in some newspaper where by mistake Lady Holland was spoken of as being still in existence. "Perhaps," said Mitford laughing, "she is come back from the grave." "O, God forbid!" cried Rogers.

Of the acting of Mrs. Siddons, who was among the earliest of his friends, Rogers always spoke with admiration; and he fully appreciated the talent of her not-unworthy successor Miss O'Neill, who, when Lady Becher and a widow, was, during the last years of his life, an occasional guest at his breakfast-table, and sometimes also passed an evening at his house. She generally concluded her evening-visits by reading a scene of Shakespeare or a chapter of the Bible. Her serious turn of mind led her to propose readings from the latter book; and Rogers always assented to the proposal with the utmost willingness: but he was not always equally willing to listen to her, when, with more zeal than discretion, she ventured to lecture him on points of faith.— A rather ludicrous scene occurred, when, abou[. . .] after Rogers had met with his accident, I first became aware that Lady Becher was in the habit of reading the Bible in company. She, two other ladies, Rogers, and myself, formed the whole party. It was a winter-evening, and we were gathered round the table at which, not long before, Rogers had dined (for being then a complete cripple, he used to remain in the dining-room till his servants carried him upstairs to bed). I supposed that she was about to give us something from Shakespeare, as on the former occasions when I had been present at her readings; and she not a little puzzled me by saying, "But I fear, Mr. Dyce, that I am intruding on your province." I could only answer that "Mr. Rogers would certainly prefer her reading to mine." She then, addressing our host, said, "Should you like to hear me read the fortieth chapter of the prophet Isaiah?" "I should like it of all things" was his reply. Accordingly, after altering the position of the table-lamp, and clearing her throat by some preliminary hems, she proceeded with "Comfort ye, [comfort ye my people"] in a deep full voice, distinctly articulating every word, without any approach to a theatrical tone or manner. Rogers, seated in his arm-chair, listened at first very attentively; but the rather monotonous reading, combined with the drowsiness incident to old people after dinner, gradually overpowered him: his head sunk lower and lower on his breast, till at last nothing of it, except the bald crown, was visible above the high standing-collar of his large loose coat; and, before her ladyship had reached the end of the chapter, he was in the land of dreams. On finishing her performance, the only notice she took of the sleeper was by a side-long glance with a countenance "more in sorrow than in anger." Presently, he awoke with a great start; and perceiving how he had committed himself, he, without losing a moment, made an ingenious attempt to get out of the scrape: clasping his hands together, he exclaimed in an affected rapture, "O, I could listen forever to those divine words and that enchanting voice!" Lady B., taking the compliment at what it was worth, acknowledged it by the slightest possible bow.

With the exception of Maltby, his friend from boyhood to extreme old age, there was, I believe, no one with whom Rogers was so intimate, or for whom he entertained so sincere a regard, as Lord Holland; and after the death of that benevolent and accomplished nobleman he loved to dwell on the recollection of the many happy days he had passed at Holland-House, where genius and learning won for their possessors as much respect and attention as were elsewhere paid to rank and wealth. One circumstance connected with that mansion he would frequently relate as an instance of the astonishing powers of Lord (then Mr.) Brougham. They both slept at Holland-House the night previous to the day when Brougham made his celebrated speech in Westminster Hall during the trial of Queen Caroline: on that night they both, as well as Lord Holland, sat up rather late, discussing various literary subjects, particularly the merits of Boswell's *Life of Johnson:* next morning after breakfast Rogers and Brougham walked together in the garden, and renewed the subject of Boswell's book, about which Brougham —apparently quite regardless of the task which he had to perform so soon—continued talking with great earnestness, till it was time to start for Westminster Hall, to which Lord Holland conveyed him in his carriage.

In consequence of some perhaps groundless report that Rogers had spoken of him in unfriendly terms, Byron wrote that venomous satire, of which John Murray told me he possessed a manuscript copy long before it was printed in *Fraser's Magazine* [VII (1833), 81–84]; and in allusion to which, one morning in St. James's Place when Rogers happened to be out of the room, Beckford remarked, "I have just been reading some verses so damnably ill-natured that one would almost think they must have been the devil's own composition: I should like to know if Rogers has seen them."— Rogers doubtless had seen them.

On one occasion, by an ill-timed jest, Rogers unintentionally gave great offense to the person for whom, of all others, he entertained the most unfeigned admiration and respect. He told me the circumstance in the following words. "I was on a visit to the Duke of Wellington, at Strathfieldsaye. A small party consisting chiefly of ladies, the Duke, and myself, were in the drawing-room: it was an intensely cold forenoon; and the Duke having seated himself close to the fire, seemingly without any regard to the comfort of his guests, I unfortunately remarked that 'gentlemen sometimes showed great consideration in screening ladies from the fire.' No sooner had I spoken than up started the Duke in a violent passion: 'O, pray, sir, come as near the fire as you please,—pray, sir, sit *in* the fire, if you prefer it.' My visit expired next morning; and I left Strath[fieldsaye] under the idea that I should never be there again, and that my intercourse with its master was at an end. But not so: some time after this, the Duke, who perhaps thought he had been rather hasty, sent Lord Douro to invite me to his house: I went; and we were as good friends as ever."— Not only was Rogers a frequent guest of the Duke, but the Duke frequently dined with Rogers in St. James's Place.

Rogers used to say, "Kings and queens are personages of a rank so exalted, so utterly above their subjects even of the highest degree, that I should never dream of being offended however insolently *they* might treat me; but in my intercourse with dukes and lords I expect that they are to behave to me as one gentleman does to another, without any assumption of superiority": and I have heard him mention that he broke with the Duke of Gordon, because his grace was not content to be his acquaintance on terms of equality.

While Earl (then Lord John) Russell was preparing for the press [*Memoirs, Journal, and Correspondence*] of Thomas Moore, he sent to St. James's Place a packet of letters which Rogers at various periods had written to Moore, in order that the writer might look them over, and select such as he thought the most fit for publication. Rogers had not yet examined the letters, when one evening, after I had dined with him *tête-à-tête,* he desired his faithful attendant Edmund Payne to bring them to him, and requested me to read some of them aloud. I proceeded to do so; and Rogers listened for some time without interrupting me by any remarks: but, on my reading a letter which contained an account of Sheridan's funeral, he suddenly stopped me, exclaiming, "I will not allow *that* letter to be printed." The truth was, his pride was hurt by its containing some mention of his having been rather slighted by certain great people during the funeral. "I will not allow *that* letter to be printed," he repeated; "I will tear it in pieces at once": and he was on the point of making good his words, when Edmund Payne, who was standing a little way off at the side-board, instantly came forward with a melodramatic rush, and seized the offensive letter. "Sir," he cried; "you really must not destroy it; it is not your property; you are answerable to Lord John Russell for all these letters." So saying, he swept up the whole series, and forthwith carried them away: nor did I ever hear Rogers speak of them again.

On the death of his father in 17[93], Rogers became possessed of so ample an income that he was enabled not only to indulge his taste by purchasing works of art, but to gratify the natural generosity of his disposition, during the remainder of his very long life. Of the assistance he lent to Sheridan and to one or two other men of genius there is a permanent record, because they happened to be individuals in whom the public took an interest: but his many unostentatious charities,—his readiness to hold out a helping hand to misfortune in all its forms,— were known only to his own family and to his more intimate friends,— and, indeed, not always even to them. His bounty could hardly fail to be sometimes wasted on undeserving objects; and it would seem that he had not always resolution enough to break off at once all connection with those whose worthlessness he had discovered: at least, I well re- member that he continued patiently to endure the visits of a certain gentleman who, under various pretenses, had borrowed from him sums which he knew would never be repaid; and that one morning before breakfast when he saw him about to enter the dining-room by the glass- door which opened into the garden, he whispered to me, in a tone of resignation, "Here comes the enemy."

The face and figure of Rogers were very peculiar. Though he had a fine ample forehead, his eyes were heavy and lustreless, his under-jaw was too prominent, his chin of more than ordinary length, and his complexion deadly pale. He was of the middle size, and strongly-built; but ill-made in the lower limbs, and so awkward and shambling in his gait, that he sometimes attracted the notice of strangers in the street: yet in his youth he had been fond of dancing, and talked with pleasure of having had Miss De Camp (Mrs. Charles Kemble) for his partner at dancing parties given by Mrs. Siddons when she lived in Gt. Marl- bro' Street; nay, at a much later period, as I have elsewhere recorded,[62] he danced with Queen Caroline at Kensington Palace, and did not foot it with sufficient quickness to satisfy that undignified piece of royalty.— The portrait engraved from a picture by Hoppner, representing Rogers in his forty-sixth year, is not an agreeable one, though the painter has endeavoured to soften whatever was faulty in his features, and concealed the prominence of his chin by leaning it on his hand, a device on which Hoppner prided himself, as his daughter Mrs. Galway told me. Sir Thomas Lawrence has had recourse to the same artifice in what may be called the popular portrait of Rogers, which is prefixed to his works and which exhibits him as a comely middle-aged gentleman, the flattery of the pencil being carried to the utmost. But whoever is curious to know how the poet looked while seated, a cripple, in his chair a year or two before his death, ought to procure the perfectly faithful likeness of him lithographed from a photograph taken by his attendant Mr. Edmund Payne.— Not only had the personal appearance of Rogers been wantonly and unfeelingly ridiculed, at various times, by writers in newspapers, &c, but even Byron stooped to make it a subject of reproach in a copy of verses which will be given presently : and probably some of my readers have not forgotten the copper-plate caricature of the old poet in *Fraser's Magazine* (of which he once complained to Southey),[63] and the lithograph by H. B. which represents him defending himself with his umbrella against the "ladies" who mobbed him in the Green Park. All this considered, Rogers may perhaps be excused for showing a rather unphilosophic anxiety about the treatment of his features by those artists to whom he latterly sat. I once mentioned to him that I just saw his portrait (painfully like) in the studio of Linnell, who was only waiting for another sitting to finish it. "I wish I could *finish it*," replied Rogers; who really did perform that operation on a picture of himself by Jackson, indignantly thrusting his foot through the canvas, and leaving it to lie, torn and unframed, on the floor of a lumber-room,—a catastrophe the less to be regretted, because, as a work of art, it was quite unworthy of that eminent painter. Even not very long before his death, he was equally offended by a portrait for which he had sat at the request of a youthful artist. He desired his servant to set it on a chair opposite to him; and after examining it very attentively, he said, "If I look like *that thing,* I am enough to frighten women and children : take it away, and never let me see it again." On such occasions he invariably turned for consolation to his portrait after Lawrence. . . .[64]

Though nature had endowed Rogers with a very feeling heart and a very generous disposition, she had not bestowed on him the best of tempers. At times he would show a touchiness which, as his old friend Maltby assured me, had involved him in sundry quarrels during his youth, and which the associates of his later days, with all their respect for his age and position, sometimes found it not always easy to endure.— While travelling on the continent with his sister and Sir James Mackintosh,[65] he had such a quarrel with the knight, that, for a considerable part of the tour, they ceased speaking to each other: which was, no doubt, a great vexation to Rogers, who decidedly thought that Mackintosh's conversational powers were unequalled by those of any of his contemporaries. When Rogers gave an account of this quarrel, it assumed the form of a pleasant fiction (for he was fond of indulging in caricature) : "Sir James and my sister," he said, "rode in the dickey of the carriage and talked incessantly, while I was left inside, solus. On arriving at any town, Sir James—without making the slightest mention of me—booked himself and my sister as 'Sir James Mackintosh, knight, membre du Parlement Britannique, &c, et Miss Rogers, *sa femme,'* —thus taking away my sister's character over a quarter of Europe."

So prevalent was the notion of Rogers' being in the habit of satirizing his friends, that I know Sir Walter Scott remarked on one occasion, "It matters not what ill we say of Rogers behind his back, since we may be pretty certain that he has said as much of us behind our backs." And, no doubt, Rogers had great quickness in discovering the faults and weaknesses of those with whom he associated; nor was he slow in proclaiming his discoveries: but I believe that, being aware of the opinion which had gone abroad of his *maledicentia,* he at last would frequently amuse himself by supporting the character of a back-biter, and would utter, in pure jest, things which were afterwards repeated as proofs of his ill-nature.— One forenoon, at the Deepdene, the conversation turned on Lady Lansd[owne]. Rogers bestowed the highest encomium on her, and then quitted the drawing-room. "Well," said Mrs. Hope as he went out, "I am not sure that I ever before heard Rogers allow so much merit to any human being." She had scarcely spoken when the door opened, and Rogers, putting in his head, added, "But there are spots in the sun."

I have heard it asserted that Rogers had little sense of religion; a misconception which perhaps originated in the vulgar idea that a man who passes for a wit is not unfrequently a free-thinker. The truth is, he never alluded to the Deity or to the Saviour without reverential awe; and, I am sure, that at his own house he would have checked any tendency in others to treat religious subjects with levity: he prized his English Bible for much more than its felicities of language; and towards the close of life, when he was no longer able to read it for himself, I have seen him listening with deep attention to its words of consolation from the lips of an affectionate niece. He was, indeed, brought up, and continued to be, a dissenter, like his father and most of his family: Dr. Price had been the object of his boyish admiration; and in his middle age he had greatly esteemed and honoured the amiable Priestley; nor need it be concealed that he was little affected by a message from the pew-opener of St. James's, informing him that his hassock from disuse was half eaten up by moths :—but he was so far from cherishing any feelings of dislike towards the established Church, that during his whole life he had cultivated the acquaintance of several of its chief ornaments; and till the very close of his career, the Bishops of London and Exeter (Blomfield and Phillpotts)—not to mention less dignified ecclesiastics—were among his occasional visitors.

Tied down to the desk as a banker's clerk in his youth, Rogers had comparatively little leisure for literary pursuits; yet even then he contrived during the evenings spent under his father's roof at [Stoke] Newington to read the best authors not only in English but in French and Italian. He once showed me a manuscript-book filled with choice passages from Beaumont and Fletcher's plays which he had extracted at that period; and I possess a copy of [B. Varchi's *Storia Fiorentina* (1721)] which, about the same time, he annotated on the margins from beginning to end. Of Greek he knew nothing; and so little of Latin, that his knowledge of Horace was chiefly obtained through the medium of Smart's prose version: but he had a profound respect for learning; and felt a sort of pride in having been intimate with the greatest scholar of his day, Porson, to say nothing of Dr. Parr and Gilbert Wakefield.

In conversation, Rogers had not those powers which produce an effect in large parties: he could talk with fluency to his next neighbours at table, and every now and then amuse them by pointed and sly remarks (though he never made one quarter of the bon-mots which were fathered upon him) ; but he could not command the attention of a whole company, like Hallam or Macaulay, by whose monopolising eloquence he sometimes felt himself unpleasantly thrown into the shade.

The person so unmercifully (and unjustly) assailed in these lines was Mrs. Clermont,[66] a respectable upper-servant in the Milbanke family, who passed into the service of her young mistress on her marriage with Byron.

Rogers died a bachelor. But there is no doubt that, at an early period of his life he made an offer of his hand to the youngest Miss Thrale (afterwards Lady Keith) :[67] and in his extreme old age besides earnestly advising all the young men of his acquaintance not to let the proper time for marriage pass by, he composed a short exhortation to the same effect, "Haste to the altar" &c,—the very last copy of verses he ever attempted. . . .[68]

I now proceed to give more particular notices of five persons who have been already mentioned as the most constant frequenters of Rogers's breakfast-table,—viz. Luttrell, Mitford, Crabb Robinson, Dr. Henderson, and Lord Glenelg.

I. *HENRY LUTTRELL* [*ff. 177–80*]
[. . .][69]

Soon after returning home, he became so noted in the fashionable world as to excite the jealousy of his father, who aimed at a similar distinction; and this unfortunately led them to regard each other with an unnatural animosity. Luttrell was the welcome guest of the celebrated Georgiana Duchess of Devonshire, and, in short, of all who then led the ton; and when these had successively passed away, he, like Rogers, formed an intimacy with new generations of the beau monde, and, even towards the very close of his life, continued to figure as one of the lions of society. And no wonder; for without usurping an undue share of the conversation, he never failed to produce an effect by the refined witticisms which he contrived to introduce in the happiest manner, and which assuredly, unlike the "clever things" of some professed talkers, were quite unpremeditated.

But, in addition to his notoriety as a brilliant [raconteur], he achieved considerable reputation as a poet, or, to speak more properly, as a writer of neat, graceful, pointed, and frequently brilliant, verses; for such are the characteristics of his *Letters to Julia* and his *Crockford-House,*—volumes which are so little known at the present day, that the subjoined extracts from them will probably be acceptable to most of my readers:—like his friend the Honourable William Spencer, he sang of fashionable life; the Muse of both was a Grosvenor-Square belle. . . .[70] Such were the easy-flowing verses which—more than half a century ago—Luttrell poured forth, and not without applause,—for the *Letters to Julia* reached a third edition: he sang of fashionable life to a fashionable audience, and his Muse was a Grosvenor-Square belle.

It was generally believed that, in spite of his highly-cultivated intellect and his love of books, Luttrell took little pleasure in the society of literary men, unless they belonged to the "certain set," among whom he himself had been so long accustomed to move; and there were perhaps some grounds for such an impression: hence the satirical exaggeration of Rogers that "if Luttrell, when walking with a man of first-rate genius, should happen to see a booby lord at a little distance, he would instantly quit the man of first-rate genius for the booby lord." Nor was Luttrell behind hand in exaggerating the foibles of his friend: "Rogers," he declared, "has such an inordinate craving for the excitement of crowded assemblies, that he would go to an evening-party even if the death-rattles were in his throat."

Luttrell had a very hasty temper; nor, as I have already noticed, was Rogers's temper of the best: the consequence was, that every now and then they would quarrel about the merest trifles. Suppose them setting out together on a journey in a post-chaise, and the following dialogue taking place (as it really did);

"R. Pray, put up the glass: I can't endure a draft.

L. I prefer its being down: there's no fear of catching cold.

R. But there *is* great fear; and I don't choose to travel with an open window.

L. (*much excited*) You're, without exception, the most disagreeable man I know."

On one occasion I was the innocent cause of strife between them. During a breakfast at Rogers's house in St. James's Place, Luttrell was addressing some remark to me, who happened to be sitting opposite to him: Rogers, being very deaf, was trying, with his hand behind his ear, to catch Luttrell's words; and, not succeeding, he rather peevishly exclaimed, "If you keep talking in a whisper to Mr. Dyce, over the table, do you imagine that I can hear you?" This was enough to put Luttrell out of humour; he frowned, and said in a half-soliloquy, "I will *not* repeat it." Rogers, fancying that he had said, "I will not return here," immediately rejoined, "O, very well: if you don't choose to come back, you can stay at home." Luttrell, looking "fierce as ten Furies," spoke no more till the party was over; and then as I walked with him up St. James's Street, on his way to Brookes's (while he leant heavily on my arm, for he was weak and paralytic), he inveighed against Rogers as "a person who had quite forgotten how to behave himself in society, from which it was more than time for him to withdraw entirely." I felt almost hopeless of their being ever again reconciled: but only a few days had elapsed, when, to my great satisfaction, I saw Luttrell enter Rogers's drawing-room with a countenance all smiles, and shake him by the hand as usual.

Once when the conversation turned on charity, Luttrell said, "The English are the subscribing*est* people on the face of the earth. If a man were to cut a slit in his street-door, and write above it "Subscriptions received here,"—without specifying for whom or for what,—by heaven, I believe, he would have his till quite full in a single day."

He was not partial to the society of dignitaries of the church: "I effervesce," he said, "when in company with a dean; and a bishop makes me explode." No explosion, however, ensued when he met the Bishop of Exeter (Phil[lpotts]) in St. James's Place. "My lord," said Rogers, "let me introduce to you Mr. Luttrell."— "Sir," said the Bishop to Luttrell, "I am truly glad to form your acquaintance," and then, with an aside to Rogers, "Who *is* Mr. Luttrell?"

There was something very sad in the last meeting of Rogers and

Luttrell,—a meeting by chance, not by appointment. It occurred at the Hyde Park Exhibition of 18[51], to which they were wheeled, each in a Bath chair,—Rogers being then quite helpless from the effects of his accident, and Luttrell nearly worn out by age and complicated disease. All around them was glitter and joyous bustle: and one could not help reflecting under what different circumstances, and with what different feelings, they had often met in the gay crowds of other years. They conversed together for some minutes; when, at parting, Rogers said, "I am going very soon to your favourite Brighton,[71] where I hope you will be able to join me." Luttrell shook his head, without making any reply. He died, not long after, [19] Dec.ʳ 1851.

2. THE REVEREND JOHN MITFORD [ff. 184-85ʳ]

There were few persons whom Rogers used to welcome more heartily to St. James's Place than John Mitford; and, for my own part, I must always remember him as the familiar friend, whose intimacy with me (which commenced when I might still be reckoned young) materially gladdened my life during many a year, our tastes and pursuits being exactly similar.

It may be said[72] that he made a near approach to his favourite Gray in the variety of his learning and acquirements. He was a constant student of the Greek and Roman classics, and familiar with the works of the scholars who have illustrated them from the Scaligers and Casaubon down to Porson, Hermann, and still later critics. With whatever was most excellent in Italian, French, and German he had made himself acquainted. In divinity (especially as expounded by our old divines), in history, and in biography he was deeply read; and he took great interest in the narratives of voyagers and travellers. His knowledge of English poetry was not confined to the standard authors: it embraced a whole host of minor writers both for the stage and the closet, whose very names are scarcely known except to "poetical antiquaries"; and he was among the first to hail the appearance of a new work of genius by any of his contemporaries. Passionately fond of painting (particularly of the Italian school), and an enthusiastic admirer of external nature in all its features, he would spare no trouble or expense to see a beautiful picture or to visit an interesting scene; and of his taste in landscape-gardening he gave a striking proof in the grounds attached to his vicarage-house at Benhall, which, in spite of their comparatively small extent, he so embellished as to render them an attractive show-place.[73] But one gift nature had denied him—an ear for music; a deficiency, however, which is not uncommon even in persons who, like Mitford, are keenly alive to the subtlest harmonies of poetry: I will not say, as Rogers somewhat satirically said of his friend Lord Holland, that "music gave him absolute pain"; but I am sure that it never afforded him the slightest pleasure.— Allan Cunningham, I remember, more than once declared, and perhaps rightly, that Mitford's Memoir of Dryden contained some of the best criticism which had appeared since the publication of Johnson's *Lives of the Poets;* and I have heard Leigh Hunt bestow high encomiums on the reviews & essays which he contributed to *The Gentleman's Magazine.*— Of his numerous poetical compositions, which are of very unequal merit, the following specimens will most probably be new to the reader, & can hardly fail to be considered as far superior to the generality of occasional [verses.][74]

3. HENRY CRABB ROBINSON [*ff. 157-58ʳ*]

The parents of Henry Crabb Robinson were non-conformists. After serving an apprenticeship to an attorney at Colchester, he succeeded to a little property; and having a decided literary turn, he studied for some time at the University of Jena; formed an acquaintance with several illustrious Germans,—particularly with the greatest of them all, Goethe; attended the funeral of Schiller; and became the special correspondent of *The Times,* in which capacity he was at Corunna in 1809. On his return to England, he entered himself a member of the Middle Temple; was called to the bar in 1813; went the Norfolk circuit (including Bury St. Edmunds and Cambridge), and eventually became its leader. Being, however, comparatively indifferent about money, he determined to give up the law as soon as his exertions had gained him an independence. He accordingly retired from the bar in 1828, and devoted the remainder of his long life (towards the close of which his income was much increased by the death of a near relative) to the pleasures of reading and of cultivated society.— Besides his contributions to *The Times* (both while he was its foreign correspondent and afterwards) and to other periodicals, he printed a paper on the etymology of the word Mass,[75] and a defense of his friend Clarkson in connection with the slave-trade;[76] nor must it be forgotten that he communicated "recollections" of several distinguished persons to various publications: but such a scanty list of compositions by one who was so ardent a lover of literature in all its departments is a sufficient proof that he was far from anxious to acquire notoriety as a writer.— Of Goethe, whose correspondent he had been, he never failed to speak with the enthusiasm of a disciple for an idolized master. Next to the author of *Faust,* the object of his admiration was his intimate friend Wordsworth, to whom he used to pay an annual visit at Rydal Mount; and of a tour which they made together in Italy in 1837 the poet has left an imperishable record in a dedication to his companion.[77] Among others with whom he kept up an intimacy may be mentioned Mrs. Barbauld, Coleridge, Southey, Lamb and Miss Lamb, Flaxman, Rogers, and Kenyon.— A more generous or a kinder-hearted man than Robinson never existed; it is, indeed, no exaggeration to say that he overflowed with the milk of human kindness. In politics he was a liberal; in religion a dissenter, but entirely free from sectarian bitterness and prejudice.— His great peculiarity was his unceasing flow of talk. He was, I believe, more powerful at "monologue" than any of his contemporaries with the sole exception of Coleridge, over whom he had at least the advantage of being on all occasions intelligible: he would pour out a stream of words which defied interruption, and which, however interesting or even instructive it might prove at first (for in the language of Johnson, it was always impregnated with thought), became at last not a little wearisome to the passive listeners. He had another peculiarity; he could fall asleep whenever he chose. I have heard Kenyon frequently mention that while Southey and Robinson were travelling with him in France, they went all three to see some cathedral; that Robinson, not wishing to wander through the interior of the building, preferred remaining alone in the porch till the others should rejoin

him; and that, when they did so, they found him comfortably asleep.—
Rogers had a great liking for "the Crabb," as he used to call him, and
a high respect for his character; but at times he writhed under his over-
powering talk: "I try in vain," he would say, "to interpose a syllable;
and when at last the Crabb is silent, and I turn round eagerly to answer
him—lo, he is asleep!"— Robinson died Feb. 5, 1867, aged 91.

4. DR. ALEXANDER HENDERSON [AND LORD GLEN-ELG] [*ff. 182–83ʳ*]

Dr. Alexander Henderson, in his younger days, practised as a physician in London; but having succeeded to a handsome family estate in
Scotland (Caskieben, near Aberdeen, at which city he was born) he
relinquished the medical profession, and occupied his leisure with
science,[78] literature, and art. He attended the lectures at the Royal
Institution; he dipped into the ancient classics, and became tolerably
familiar with the best French, Italian, and German writers; and he took
every opportunity of seeing the finest pictures, and hearing the finest
music. In short, he possessed a much greater store of information on
various subjects than those who met him only in general society would
have supposed; for, being extremely shy, he then spoke little, and,
moreover, being fastidious in his choice of words, he expressed himself
with a painful hesitation.

To the earlier works which he published[79] no interest attaches now:
but he must always be honourably remembered by his valuable *History
of Ancient and Modern Wines,* an elegant quarto volume which appeared in 1824. When I urged him, some years before his death, to
publish a new edition of that standard book, he replied; "I should
like much to do so: but to render it as perfect as I could wish requires
a greater knowledge of chemistry than I can boast; for since the first
edition was printed, chemistry has made great advances; and, alas!
I have no Doctor Prout to assist me as on the former occasion." This
difficulty, however, he got over by engaging a gentleman, who was a
competent chemist, to make certain alterations in the work on condition
of receiving (what the author himself disregarded) the entire profits

of the publication. But, most unfortunately, soon after commencing his task, the gentleman died; and Henderson had neither health nor spirits remaining to take further trouble in the matter.

Henderson regularly spent several months of every year at his country seat in Scotland; and there he was carried off by a sudden attack of illness in [16 September] 18[63], at the age of [83].

I had known him from my boyhood, and was frequently invited to join the agreeable select dinner-parties which he gave at his house in Curzon Street, where the cookery was first-rate, and where he set before us wines with which princes might have been proud to regale their guests.

Lord Glenelg was not so shy or so silent as Dr. Henderson; but assuredly his manner and conversation conveyed to strangers no idea of his having been the Charles Grant once so distinguished for his eloquence in the House of Commons. He was a most amiable unassuming man, with a deep sense of religion, which led [him] to compose several hymns of more than ordinary beauty.

On his first being raised to the peerage, Lady Holland, in her provoking way, would pretend to forget his exact title: when he came up to her, she would say, "O, how do you do, Lord Glen*leg?*"

Sometimes, while he was in office, he found it necessary to give dinners to persons of very high rank; and if he had any doubts about which of them ought to take precedence of the others, he used to settle that important point by referring it to Rogers.

He died at Cannes, 23ᵈ April, 1866.

PART 4: MISCELLANY

HENRY MACKENZIE [*ff. 7–8*]

The Nestor of the Edinburgh literati, during my boyhood, was Henry Mackenzie; whom his townsmen generally spoke of, and pointed out to strangers, as "The Man of Feeling,"—the title of the earliest of those works which had procured for him a reputation more than proportionate to their merits. I by no means deny that there is considerable pathos in some portions of his *Man of Feeling* (particularly in the story of Edwards, over which I shed so many tears when a boy), or that his tale of *La Roche* in *The Mirror* is an affecting one, or that his sketch of Colonel Caustic, who figures throughout *The Lounger,* shows a masterly hand: but surely his *Man of the World* and his *Julia de Roubigné* would try the patience of the habitual novel-readers of the present day, even of those who do not require the excitement of "sensational" fictions. What mainly contributed to keep his reputation alive was, I believe, the praise so liberally bestowed on his writings by his much younger and kind-hearted friend Sir Walter Scott, both in print and in conversation.

The preceding remarks apply, of course, exclusively to the prose-productions of Mackenzie. But he also attempted poetry and the drama, —the former more successfully than the latter. Among his poems is one entitled *The Old Bachelor,* which has been stamped with the approbation of two men of genius, both of whom were ignorant of its author's name. It was inserted by Southey in the second volume [pp. 176–83] of *The Annual Anthology,* [Bristol,] 1800, with a notice that he had "reprinted it from *The Town and Country Magazine* for 1777," and that he had "never seen it elsewhere, though its excellence ought to have rescued it from obscurity." It was again reprinted, from Southey's collection, by Campbell in his *Specimens of English Poets* as an anonymous composition; and even Mr. Peter Cunningham, who carefully revised the second edition of Campbell's *Specimens,* and who can boast a very extensive acquaintance with the poetry of the last century, has failed to discover that it was written by Mackenzie.[80]

Perhaps not the least valuable effort of Mackenzie's pen is a biographical essay which he wrote at a period when it was supposed that he had withdrawn for ever from the field of literature. I allude to the *Life of John Home* the dramatist, which, having been originally read before the Royal Society of Edinburgh in 1812, was prefixed to the *Works* of Home in 1822; a memoir wherein are preserved many anecdotes of the friends and contemporaries of the author of *Douglas,* much curious matter about David Hume, some interesting letters of Lord Bute, &c.

Mackenzie, though an old man when I used to see him, was apparently exempt from the infirmities of age. Wearing a rather scanty brown wig, dressed in a plain suit of black (with long gaiters), and carrying a gold-headed cane, he walked about the streets of his native city at a rapid pace and with the elastic step of youth. His figure was very slender, not to say emaciated: but his cheeks had that ruddy hue which betokens health, and which he partly owed perhaps to his love of rural sports; for he still continued to shoot and fish with unabated ardour. As he had always lived in the very best society, his manners were those of a perfect gentleman.

I retain a pleasing recollection of a summer's day which, when a mere stripling, I passed with Mackenzie and some of his family in a lodging at Portobello, whither they had removed from their house in Edinburgh for change of air and sea-bathing. On that visit I accompanied Mr. John Hay Forbes (the second son of Beattie's biographer, who was afterwards raised to the Scottish bench with the title of Lord Medwyn) and his wife, a sister of Sir William Gordon Cumming. In his domestic circle Mackenzie appeared to great advantage; by which expression I do not mean that he made a display of his talents, but that he showed much amiability: he was cheerful, and chatty, joining occasionally in the gossip of the ladies about their friends and neighbours,—e.g. "he thought it very likely that the Reverend Mr. S—— would marry the pretty widow A——, for she was exactly the person to fascinate a young man": in short, nobody would have taken him for the author of pathetic and sentimental tales. The two first Cantos of *Childe Harold* had not been long published; and Mr. Forbes having started the question whether the poet's name was to be pronounced "Bȳron" or "Bўron"; Mackenzie remarked (not much to the purpose, it must be confessed) that Mrs. Siddons, when playing Isabella in Southern's tragedy [*The Fatal Marriage*], "always said 'Bïron.' " The only books on the table of the little drawing-room were a well-thumbed copy of Bell's edition of Shakespeare, copies of early editions of *The Mirror* and *The Lounger,* in which, at the end of each paper, Mackenzie had written the author's name, and a new novel, attributed to Lady Charlotte Campbell, which he had just been reading, and which he described as "not so bad." When, in the evening, I returned on foot to Edinburgh, along with Mr. and Mrs. Forbes, we were escorted part of the way by Mackenzie, who walked and talked with equal briskness.

Many years afterwards, while preparing my edition of the Poems of Collins, I wrote a letter to Mackenzie, inquiring if he had ever heard any anecdotes of that poet from the mouth of John Home, to whom Collins inscribed the well-known *Ode on the Popular Superstitions of the Highlands of Scotland,* &c. I received the following answer:

"Heriot Row, Edin^r, 4 January 1826.

Sir,

In the present state of my health, writing is not an easy matter to me; but I am anxious not to delay acknowledging your letter on the subject of your proposed edition of Collins. It would gratify me if I could contribute to it; but I do not recollect hearing any anecdotes from Mr. Home, or having any communication with him or any one else, regarding Collins, the close of whose life made the subject rather a distressing one.[81]

I am, Sir, Your most obed^t and
very humble servant,
H. Mackenzie.

The Revd A. Dyce, }
Rosebank, Aberdeen." }

Mackenzie died, Jany 14, 1831, in his 86th year: very shortly before which date, Thomas Campbell, on returning to London from a visit to Scotland, told me that he had seen him in Edinburgh; and that "he was so attenuated, he could compare him to nothing but a spelding."[82]

MRS. [ANNA] BARBAULD [*ff. 15–18^r*]

Though Mrs. Barbauld published several works at various times and with success, she certainly was far from showing any eagerness to obtain celebrity as an authoress (some of her writings, indeed, being intended solely for the benefit of children and young persons): but even if her craving for literary reputation had been ever so great, the praise bestowed on her prose by such a philosopher as Dugald Stewart, and on her verse by such a poet as Wordsworth, would have been enough to satisfy it amply. Stewart quotes largely from the earlier portion of her essay *Against Inconsistency in Our Expectations,* prefacing his quotations thus; "Upon the foregoing passage *[of Epictetus] a very ingenious and elegant writer, Mrs. Barbauld, has written a commentary so full of good sense and of important practical morality, that I am sure I run no hazard of trespassing on the patience of the reader by the length of the following extracts."[83] And Wordsworth, on hearing Crabb Robinson repeat her lines *On Life,* exclaimed, "Well, I am not given to envy other people their good things; but I *do* wish I had written *that*".[84]

> "Life, we've been long together,
> Through pleasant and through cloudy weather:
> 'Tis hard to part when friends are dear;
> Perhaps 'twill cost a sigh, a tear;
> Then steal away, give little warning,
> Choose thine own time,
> Say not Good-night, but in some brighter clime
> Bid me Good-morning."

The volume of *Poems* which Mrs. Barbauld gave to the public in 1773, while she was Miss Aikin, and which, though now nearly forgotten, was several times reprinted and greatly admired, contains much that may still be read with pleasure. I add a few extracts from it. . . .[85]

In 1774 Miss Aikin married the Rev. Rochemont Barbauld, a dissenter and an Arian. He was a man of considerable talents; and their union was a happy one, till Mr. Barbauld was seized with a morbid affection of his spirits, which, gradually increasing, ended in insanity; and on one occasion he attempted to kill his wife. This kept her, of course, in a state of constant agitation; but she persevered in watching over him with the utmost tenderness, never leaving his side, whether he was within doors, or whether he was wandering about the streets in the restlessness of his incurable malady. At last he contrived to elude her vigilance, and drowned himself in 1808.[86] "Rather early in the morning a gentleman of his acquaintance met him running along the

City Road; and when he asked him 'where he was going?,' the answer was, 'To throw myself into the New River,'—which he did, though the gentleman supposed that he had spoken in jest. He had been such a torment to the whole family, that his brother-in-law Aikin said to me, 'When the body was taken out of the water, *we were half-afraid that it might be restored to life.*'" *William Maltby.*

Mrs. Barbauld belonged to the sect of English Presbyterians, whose opinions at that time were Arian, but are now Unitarian. "One day, not long before she died, I called upon her, and found her reading with great attention Hooker's *Ecclesiastical Polity.* 'I am not sure,' she said, 'but that, if I had read this book when I was a much younger woman, my opinions on sundry important points might have been very different from what they now are.'" *Crabb Robinson.*

Mrs. Barbauld died March 9, 1825.

[THOMAS HOPE ON] PATRONAGE OF PAINTING IN ENGLAND; BRIT[TON] [f. 48ʳ][87]

"We are constantly hearing people say that the British public is very remiss in patronizing young painters. Now, for my own part, I think that too much encouragement is given them: the consequence is, that youths, who mistake in themselves a love of art for genius, produce a number of very bad pictures, and spend their whole lives in comparative poverty; who, had they been content to become merchants' clerks or lawyers' clerks, might gradually have acquired a comfortable independence."

"Brit[ton] is an architect who can't draw, and an author who can't write."

T. Hope, the author of Anastasius, &c.

MRS. JOHN HUNTER[88] [ff. 49–54ʳ]

This lady—one of the latest survivors of the literary circle of which Soame Jenyns, Horace Walpole, Mrs. Montagu, Mrs. Carter, Mrs.

Delany, Mrs. Vesey, and Hannah More, were the chief promoters and ornaments—was the wife of the celebrated physiologist John Hunter, and the sister of Sir Everard Home, who lies under (and, it would seem, deservedly) the heavy imputation of having published as his own what he found among the papers of the deceased John Hunter, whose pupil he had been.

For some time after her husband's death, Mrs. Hunter, I believe, had to struggle with pecuniary difficulties; but when I used to see her at her house in Lower Grosvenor Street, there was nothing in her menage which indicated straitened circumstances. Though she was then at an advanced age, her appearance was wonderfully juvenile,— the more so because her hair, which was of the lightest flaxen colour, had undergone little or no change from years; she still retained much of the good looks of her youth; and though unusually tall, she was perfectly graceful and lady-like in all her movements.

Forgotten as she now is, Mrs. Hunter once enjoyed considerable notoriety as a writer of elegant verses; and to her many persons attributed the first volume of Joanna Baillie's plays, which originally came out anonymously. Passionately fond of music, she wrote several songs which were set by Haydn; among others, "My mother bids me bind my hair," which may be still occasionally heard at London concerts, the audience having no idea to whom Haydn was indebted for the words.

In 1802 Mrs. Hunter published her collected *Poems* in a small octavo (which were disparagingly noticed in *The Edinburgh Review*); and in 1804 a 4to pamphlet entitled *The Sports of the Genii,* consisting of verses to illustrate groupes of winged boys sketched by Miss Susan Macdonald, eldest daughter of the Right Honourable Sir Archibald Macdonald,—a young lady who died at Lisbon in her 22^{d} year.

That Mrs. Hunter may claim a respectable place among English poetesses (whose number at the present day amounts to legion!) is proved by the subjoined specimens, which will probably be new to most of my readers. . . .[89] Mrs. Hunter died Jany 7, 1821.

Her beautiful and highly-educated daughter, who married, first, General Sir J[ames] Campbell, and secondly Colonel Charlewood (brother to the Duchess of Roxburgh), was an intimate friend of mine.

And it is worth while noticing that when she was quite an elderly woman, no one could talk to her without wondering at the perfect regularity and the dazzling whiteness of her teeth; for which she accounted thus. "During my girlhood my father, John Hunter, was constantly examining them, cleaning them, filing them, &c,—I might say that his fingers were never out of my mouth: I thought this a great annoyance at the time; but I am now reaping the benefit of it."

[ROBERT] OWEN OF LANARK [f. 123]

When Owen was first making a sensation in London, I used to meet him often at the house of the old friend of my family, Lieutenant General Brown: and in Owen's *Life . . . Written by Himself* [London, 1857] I find what follows. "I was intimate with General Brown, who returned from India after being forty years there, and I was a frequent visitor and guest at his table. Of our party was Mrs. Dyce, the wife of General Dyce, and sister to Sir Neil Campbell. Both this lady and General Brown took a warm interest in my 'New Views'; and when Sir Neil returned from Elba after Napoleon's escape, Mrs. Dyce was desirous that I should meet her brother Sir Neil. For this purpose a dinner was given, at No. 8 Curzon Street, by General Brown, that we might be introduced, and Mrs. Dyce requested that I would bring a copy of my Essays for her brother, which I did, and presented the volume to him after dinner. He looked at it with some surprise, and said, 'I have certainly seen a copy of this before. Oh, I recollect! While I was at Elba, General Bertram *[Bertrand] came to me with a book in his hand, a copy of this work, and said he had been sent by Buonaparte to ask me whether I knew the author, for he was much interested with its contents.' (There was much said about Napoleon in it). 'I looked at the title-page, and said I did not know the work or the author, and Bertram *[Bertrand] appeared disappointed.' I was subsequently informed that Buonaparte had read and studied this work with great attention," &c. [I, p]p. 111[–12]. In those days Owen was unwilling to declare openly his disbelief in Christianity; but on one occasion being urged to speak plainly by General Brown and my uncle

Sir Neil Campbell, he no longer concealed his opinion, and talked at great length and in a rambling way of the high improbability of its truth: "If I were to put my hat down upon the table," he said, "it is just possible, but extremely unlikely, that, on lifting it up again, I might find a fly under it," &c, &c.

My last meeting with Owen was at a crowded evening-party given by Thomas Campbell (in White-hall Place) to Fanny Kemble, who was then a newly-risen "star." He had very lately returned from America; and, notwithstanding the repeated failures of his plans, he was still confident that he should eventually be able to bring about a complete reform in our social system. After conversing with him for some time, he said to me, "I see you are acquainted with this celebrated actress: I am told she is a young woman of great abilities, and I should like to know her: will you introduce me to her?" I replied that I would present him to Mrs. Charles Kemble, who, I had no doubt, would introduce him to her daughter. On my mentioning his wish to Mrs. C. K., she said, "Of course, I can have no objections to introduce [sic] him to Fanny; but I suspect they have few ideas in common." Accordingly, he was introduced first to the mother—who reminded him that she had formerly met him at the house of Basil Montagu—and next to the daughter.

[CHARLES R.] MATURIN [f. 124ʳ]

Though there are passages in his novels which it seems odd that one of his cloth should have ventured to write, Maturin was always diligent and exemplary in the discharge of his clerical duties.

But his affectation was boundless. "As a sign that he was buried in thought and not to be disturbed, he used to stick a red wafer on his forehead: to a friend who visited him one day while he was thus abstracted from all worldly things, Mrs. Maturin said in a low voice and with great earnestness, 'Pray, don't speak to him,—he has his wafer on,—he's thinking.' This is fact.— Soon after the success of his tragedy of *Bertram,* which had been brought out at Drurylane Theatre by the influence of Lord Byron, and which I published, Maturin called on me, who had never before seen him. Immediately on entering the room, he fixed his eyes on a portrait of Byron, and the first words he spoke were, 'Good God, I had no idea he was half so ugly.' " *John Murray the elder.*[90]

The late Mr. W. J. Fox, M. P.—who was no incompetent judge of such productions—thought very highly of Maturin's novel, *Fatal Revenge, or The Family of Montorio.*

[JAMES] NORTHCOTE [*f. 140*]

"Northcote told me that when he first came to London, an adventurer, and dependant on his own exertions for his daily bread, he used to make drawings of birds and sell them in the streets" (*Mr. Adair Hawkins,* who for years was Northcote's next-door neighbour and very intimate with him).

Accompanied by Dr. Bisset Hawkins, I have visited Northcote in his painting-room; and there he was, a little slim old man, with eyes gleaming like a falcon's, in a dressing-gown and a velvet cap,—working away at some picture with all the assiduity of youth. Sometimes he chose to be rather silent; sometimes he would talk incessantly, without, however, laying aside his brush. In whatever he said the acuteness of his understanding was manifest. But he had received very little education and had read very little; and hence he was not aware that many of the remarks he made and which he considered as original, were to be found in books written centuries before he was born.

He professed himself angry—occasionally very angry—with Hazlitt for having printed his *Conversations:* but, I believe, that in his heart he was gratified by the notoriety which that entertaining miscellany had given him.

He said that at a certain period fashionable sitters flocked to Romney in preference to Sir Joshua.

Northcote never married; and his house was kept for him by his sister, a vulgar uneducated old maid. Her opinions were entirely

formed on his; and one Sunday she accounted to a lady-friend of mine
for not having been at church by saying with great simplicity, "You
know, *we be'nt religious.*"

Northcote's *Life of Reynolds* was chiefly compiled and written by
Laird,[91]—Northcote supplying some of the facts and the criticism; and,
as he had been the pupil of Sir Joshua, there is good reason to regard
it as an authentic record. But his *Life of Titian* is a mere abortion. It
was put together by Hazlitt and his son from scraps which they received every now and then from Northcote. "These scraps," as the
younger of the compilers informed me, "consisted of wretched manuscript, interspersed with printed words cut out of newspapers and
pasted down in spaces left for them,—yes, incredible as it may seem,
sometimes with such words as 'had' and 'was'! so that when my father
and I looked over these scraps of an evening, we absolutely used to
roar with laughter. My father at last grew tired of the job; and I by
means of an Italian Life of Titian contrived to complete the book."[92]

SHERIDAN'S "PIZARRO"; HIS EPIGRAM; HIS
DINNER [*f. 187*]

During the first performance of *Pizarro,* Sheridan's agitation was
extreme; for there were several things in it which the audience did not
quite relish: such was his excitement, that when a speech of Alonzo
was vehemently applauded, he threw his arms round the neck of
Morton the dramatist (as Morton himself told me), and wept like a
child.— Alonzo was played by my dear old friend Charles Kemble, to
whom Sheridan always professed himself grateful for his exertions in
the part,—calling him, to the last day of his life, "*my* Alonzo."[93]

Pizarro, being supported by the excellent acting of John Kemble, his
brother, Mrs. Siddons, and Mrs. Jordan, and being also plentifully
sprinkled with political sentiments which pleased the million, achieved
a popularity altogether disproportioned to its merits; for, from beginning to end, it is a wretched piece of bombast.— When Mr. Macready was manager of Covent-Garden Theatre, I remember his saying
that "he had ordered the scenery for *Pizarro* to be destroyed, because

it never would be acted again." Yet it *was* acted, a good many years after, at the Princess's Theatre, where Charles Kean revived it with great splendour.

Sheridan was married to Miss Linley at Calais. When they returned from the continent to England, he thought that the captain of the vessel had driven a very hard bargain with him; and took his revenge in a rather profane epigram, which I have heard Rogers frequently repeat;

"When Jesus hir'd a ship to cross the sea,
If, Williams, he had then applied to thee,
And Satan's self offer'd a penny more,
By G——, our Saviour had been left on shore."

I certainly do not vouch for the truth of the following story; but it was told to me by the late Dr. Croly, who insisted that it was a positive fact.

Sheridan, during the latter part of his life, was, it is well known, in a state of constant embarrassment, and sometimes even destitute of money to provide a dinner. Bushe, the chief-justice of Ireland, having come over to this country, was extremely desirous of becoming acquainted with the far-famed orator and dramatist, and solicited Croker (of the Admiralty) to bring about an interview between them. Croker, accordingly, wrote to Sheridan on the subject, and received in return a note requesting that he and Bushe would favour him with their company at dinner on a certain day. They, of course, accepted the invitation: Sheridan welcomed them to his house in the most hospitable manner, and was in a high flow of spirits. Dinner being served up, great was their astonishment to find that it consisted of two shoulders of mutton and two fruit pies. However, the strangeness of the repast was soon forgotten in the brilliant wit of their host, who put forth all his powers of conversation; and as they returned home at a very late hour, they agreed that they had never spent so delightful an evening. Croker accounted thus for the singularity of the fare:—Sheridan's finances were so low that he was unable to provide a regular dinner; and as it was "shoulder of mutton time" at the taverns, he had procured a supply from two different houses, the keepers of which were doubtless unwilling to disoblige "kind old Mr. Sheridan" by refusing to serve him with provisions on tick.

[C H A R L E S   C .]   C O L T O N ,   A U T H O R   O F   ' ' L A C O N ' '
[*f. 236*]

Dr. —— became acquainted with this gifted and dissolute man at Paris, where his later years were chiefly spent, and where he devoted his days and nights to gaming. At the commencement of their acquaintance, Colton was in flourishing circumstances; residing in elegantly-furnished apartments, hung round with valuable pictures in handsome frames; and boasting that he had found out a method of playing, by which, on the long run, "he could beat the tables." A year, however, changed the scene. The last time Dr. —— saw him, he was living in a mean unfurnished room, up several pairs of stairs, in the Palais Royal: in one corner of it, was his bed, without sheets, and apparently never made; on the hearth was the apparatus with which he cooked his dinner; and in a broken earthen-ware bowl was deposited his whole fortune,—a handful of Napoleons.

1. In the fairy-tale of *Phantasmion* by his accomplished—and I may add—learned daughter, the late Mrs. Nelson Coleridge, are several similar touches of intensely vivid description.

2. [Dyce quotes *Christabel* II, 572–96, then *The Ancient Mariner* IV, 272–81.]

3. See more concerning that poem under the article WILLIAM WORDSWORTH in the present work.

4. And see the article WILLIAM WORDSWORTH in the present work.

5. [Cf. *Henry Crabb Robinson on Books and Their Writers*, ed. Edith J. Morley (London, 1938), I, 29. For the next anecdote, cf. A. G. L'Estrange, *The Literary Life of the Rev. William Harness* (London, 1871), p. 144.]

6. [Dyce has copied out "To Fortune, On Buying a Ticket in the Irish Lottery."]

7. ["A Stranger Minstrel." I omit as well two notes by Dyce.]

8. In vol. i. p[p]. 221[–25] of Mrs. Robinson's *Poetical Works* [London, 1806], is an (by no means contemptible) *Ode Inscribed to the Infant Son* *[i.e., Hartley] [i.e., Derwent] of S. T. Coleridge, Esq., Born Sept. 14, 1800, at Keswick in Cumberland.*

9. [Cf. Dyce's *Recollections of the Table-Talk of Samuel Rogers. To Which is Added Porsoniana*, 3d ed. (London, 1856), p. 145 n.]

10. [*Gentleman's Magazine* LXX (Supplement, 1800), 1300; *The General Biographical Dictionary . . . A New Edition*, rev. Alexander Chalmers, XXVI (London,

1816); *Biographie Universelle* (*Michaud*), *Ancienne et Moderne,* nouv. éd., XXXVI (Paris and Leipzig, n.d.).]

11. ["The Mad Monk."]

12. But the fact is noticed in the *Memoirs* of Wordsworth by his nephew [I, 183–84, 188].

13. Vide *Poems by Edward Quillinan. With a Memoir by William Johnston.* I knew Quillinan well; and it was at his house in Bryanston Street that I first saw Wordsworth,—a memorable day.

14. In 2 vols., 1847. It is published anonymously, I know not if in deference to the prejudices of her father, who disapproved of women becoming authoresses, which, in most cases, he thought, prevented them from attending to household affairs, their proper province. Among his female acquaintance Mrs. Hemans stood high in his esteem, though he had not an opportunity of seeing much of her; but I remember he was extremely surprised and vexed at finding that she was totally ignorant of housewifery.

15. Few readers perhaps need be told that this was the late Edward Moxon of Dover-street, the publisher of Wordsworth's *Works,* and a person for whom he, as well as myself, had a great regard.

16. [I shall omit most anecdotes which are repeated from *Table-Talk* or duplicated by other works that Whitwell Elwin, perhaps with a view toward editing the MS, cited in marginal notes; hence the unexplained ellipses in the remainder of this article. Elwin may also have touched up the Rogers article in a few places.]

17. It should be remembered that, of the Sixteen Satires of Juvenal, Dryden translated only the First, the Third, the Sixth, the Tenth, and the Sixteenth.

18. [Cf. C. Wordsworth, *Memoirs,* II, 477.] Compare Wordsworth's Sonnet *To the Poet, John Dyer.*

> "Bard of the Fleece, whose skilful genius made
> That work a living landscape fair and bright;
> * * * * * * * * * * * * *
> A grateful few shall love thy modest lay,
> Long as the shepherd's bleating flock shall stray
> O'er naked Snowdon's wide aërial waste;
> Long as the thrush shall pipe on Grongar Hill!"—

But the Rev. Mr. [J. C. M.] Bellew is not one of the "grateful few" just mentioned; for he differs *toto cælo* from Wordsworth in his estimate of Dyer, and (poor gentleman) records the sort of martyrdom he endured while reading that poet: "It is," he says, "questionable whether many, except those whose literary occupations lead them to the study, know even by name, in the present age, such writers as *Dyer,* Cawthorne, Granger, Lloyd, Smart, Bond *[who is *he?*], Hart. It can only be the bookworm who grubs among these and many other such like authors. Having toiled through them all, *I can bear testimony to the torture* and fatigue of the undertaking." Preface to *Poet's Corner*[: *A Manual for Students in English Poetry* (London, 1868), p. v].

19. For some minute criticism by Wordsworth on Lady Winchelsea's poetry see his letters to me in his *Memoirs* by his nephew, vol. ii. p.p. 220–1, and p.p. 228–9.

20. There is now not the slightest doubt that the *Ode to the Cuckoo* was composed by Michael Bruce; that his manuscript poems, after his early death, having been consigned for publication to Logan, the latter most dishonestly and basely claimed and printed as his own the Ode in question. See [Alexander B.] Grosart's interesting *Memoir* of Michael Bruce prefixed to his *Works,* 1865 [pp. 51 ff.].

21. [This much of the paragraph is in *Table-Talk,* p. 207 n.]

22. In [James] Gillman's *Life of . . . Coleridge* [London, 1838], vol. i. p[p]. 301[-2] (no second volume has been published), is a curious statement of what was to have formed the subject of the Third and Fourth Cantos of *Christabel,* and to have closed the tale. [The information that follows is duplicated in a letter from Dyce to

H. N. Coleridge, printed in *The Poems of Samuel Taylor Coleridge,* ed. Derwent and Sara Coleridge (London, 1852), pp. 383–84.]

23. [I have omitted an anecdote on Bowles found also in *Table-Talk,* p. 262 n. Dyce adds this note:] That Bowles's poetry should have been so much read and praised has always surprised me. The admiration which Coleridge expressed for his Sonnets is well known; and I possess a copy of Bowles's *Sonnets and Other Poems,* 1796 (a single thin volume), on the fly-leaf of which Coleridge has written,—"Dear Mrs. Thelwall, I entreat your acceptance of this volume, which has given me more pleasure, and done my heart more good, than all the other books I ever read, excepting my Bible. Whether you approve or condemn my poetical taste, the book will at least serve to remind you of your unseen, yet not the less sincere, friend, Samuel Taylor Coleridge. Sunday Morning, December the eighteenth, 1796."

24. Printed by [William] Gifford in a note on his *Mæviad* [6th ed. (London, 1800), pp. 108–10]. Surely, the diction of the opening stanza is vile—

> "I wish I was where Anna lies;
> For I am *sick of lingering here,*
> And every hour *Affection cries,*
> Go, and *partake her humble bier."*

25. [To a remark on Campbell found also in *Table-Talk,* pp. 255–56 n., Dyce notes:] When I quoted to Wordsworth, from Campbell's *Gertrude of Wyoming,* the line,

> "A [stoic] of the woods, a man without a tear" [I, xxiii],

he said he thought it would be better thus,

> "A [stoic] of the woods, a man without a *tail"*

(alluding to Lord Monboddo's theory). But *that* he said in jest.

I agree with Wordsworth as to *The Pleasures of Hope,* which throughout is written in a rather tawdry style. *Gertrude of Wyoming* is much better: but surely there can be no dispute that Campbell's impetuous lyrics [. . .] are excellent.

26. Much too severe a criticism in my opinion. I have heard Campbell praise portions of it: and the present poet-laureate [Tennyson] once spoke of it to me in terms very far from those of contempt, though he thought it "somewhat deficient in colour." [There follows in the text an explanation of why Byron hated Wordsworth, originally in *Table-Talk,* p. 239 n. Of the woman who was the cause of the break, Dyce notes, "Wordsworth did not mention her name."]

27. I am much mistaken if Wordsworth's anger at De Quincey was not so much in consequence of what he had written about Coleridge, as occasioned by something he had published about a child of our poet who died very young. [See Mary Moorman, *William Wordsworth, A Biography: The Later Years, 1803–1850* (Oxford, 1965), pp. 212, 213 n., 236–37.]— For this attack on the Ettrick Shepherd I cannot account: but in a prefatory note to his *Extemporary Effusion Upon the Death of James Hogg,* Wordsworth remarks, "He was undoubtedly a man of original genius, but *of coarse manners and low and offensive opinions."* [Having been told by De Quincey that Wordsworth had insulted him, Hogg wrote parodies of Wordsworth. See Moorman, *Later Years,* pp. 275–76.]

28. At his *History of Ireland.*

29. The scene of this strange but clever poem is laid in heaven *at a period long after the Last Judgment!*

30. [There is an illegible note to this name, as also to "uncle" Southey below.]

31. [Cf. Leslie A. Marchand, *Byron: A Biography* (New York, 1957), II, 555; and Malcolm Elwin, *Lord Byron's Wife* (London, 1962), p. 332.]

32. [Cf. Marchand, *Byron,* II, 742.]

33. [*Conversations of Lord Byron with the Countess of Blessington,* 2d ed. (London, 1850), pp. 9–11.]

34. Afterwards Colonel Sherer, author [. . .] *Recollections of the Peninsula, Story of a Life,* [. . .] [The leaf is torn in this note and in the sentence in the text.]

35. [. . .] John Campbell, author of *Travels in [South] Africa, Undertaken at [the Request] of the Missionary Society.* [The leaf is torn.]

36. [The leaf is torn.]

37. [Cf. Edmund Blunden, *Leigh Hunt: A Biography* (London, 1930), p. 109.]

38. This novel originally appeared in two volumes; which were succeeded, first, by *Familiar Letters Between the Principal Characters in David Simple,* &c, and, secondly, by *The Adventures of David Simple, Volume the Last,* &c. It is a novel of some merit, though it is far from coming up to the praises bestowed on it by the authoress's brother in the clever Preface which he prefixed to the second edition.

39. "That feeble entertainment of which the Miss Porters, the Anne of Swanseas, and worthy Mrs. Radcliffe herself with her dreary castles and exploded old ghosts, had had pretty much the monopoly." Thackeray's *English Humourists of the Eighteenth Century,* p. 122, ed. 1858.
Anne of Swansea was Anne Kemble, a sister of Mrs. Siddons, and the only disreputable member of the family. She lived at Swansea, being allowed an annual sum by Mrs. Siddons and John Kemble, on the condition that she always kept at a certain distance from them and London.

40. ["Prologue Spoken at the Opening of the Theatre in Drury-Lane 1747," l. 6. Cf. E. V. Lucas, *The Life of Charles Lamb,* 5th ed. (London, 1921), I, 376.]

41. [Lamb made an analogous remark at Haydon's "immortal dinner." See Lucas, *Lamb,* I, 483.]

42. I have heard Sir T. N. Talfourd, whose word was not to be doubted, state this several times.— Barry Cornwall (Procter) says; "He *[Lamb on his death-bed] suffered no pain (I believe) ; and when the presence of a clergyman was suggested to him, he made no remark, but understood that his life was in danger; he was quite calm and collected, quite resigned. At last, his voice began to fail," &c. *Charles Lamb, a Memoir* [London, 1866], p[p]. 226[–27].

43. [I omit a long note documenting Quin's "particular veneration for John Dory."]

44. [I omit this letter to Mrs. John D. Collier (2 Nov. 1824) because it has been printed subsequently.]

45. Moxon, no doubt, was speaking of her in her old age.— According to Barry Cornwall (Procter) ; "After the fatal deed, Mary Lamb was deeply afflicted. Her act was in the first instance totally unknown to her. Afterwards, when her consciousness returned, and she was informed of it, she suffered great grief." *Charles Lamb, a Memoir,* p. 30.

46. [Dyce transcribes *Satan in Search of a Wife* (ff. 109ᵛ–13ᵛ).]

47. Lowndes mentions, in separate articles [s.v. "Tales," "Lewis, Matthew Gregory"], both *The Tales of Terror* and *The Tales of Wonder* as by Lewis; and, to make the matter more ridiculous, he informs us that Scott's ballads of *Glenfinlas* and *The Eve of St. John,* which really are printed in *The Tales of Wonder,* form part of *The Tales of Terror.* [See Louis F. Peck, *A Life of Matthew G. Lewis* (Cambridge, Mass., 1961), pp. 132–33. Peck is in agreement with Dyce.]

48. [See Peck, *Lewis,* p. 30, and the list of "Spurious Works" on p. 276.]

49. [See Peck, *Lewis,* p. 26.]

50. [I omit "Pleasure and Desire" and Fox's version, after which Dyce notes:] Here, in the vol. just cited, follows an original Canzonetto in Italian by Fox.

51. ["The Hours."]

52. [The following are holograph letters included as part of the MS. I have omitted the first (ff. 126–28), from "A O" (Amelia Opie) to William Harness on 6

April 1821, because it is very long and often illegible; also, it seems unrelated to the Mitford letters. Mary Mitford's hand is very difficult, and the bracketed question marks indicate only the *most* difficult readings. The few hiatuses, from tears and the like, are always filled in (bracketed) by a logical guess or, in the case of f. 134, by Dyce's reading.]

53. [This letter (ff. 133–34) is transcribed down to "pitch our tent" on f. 137^r, with ellipsis indicated. It may be compared to a letter in Vera Watson, *Mary Russell Mitford* (London, n.d.), pp. 180–81, which shows that in her voluminous correspondence she sometimes wrote the same thing to different people. I follow the original but insert Dyce's additions.]

54. [The date and address are in another hand. She has herself addressed it in another part of the leaf (f. 136^v), where the postmark dates it 21 (?) Nov.]

55. [The articles in this Part were clearly intended to be a unit, though they are shuffled and the foliation is odd.]

56. No. 3.

57. One season when its roses (flowers which generally do not thrive in London) were so fine that Rogers was quite proud of them, Lady Cork (of eccentric memory) called on him, and, not finding him at home, requested to be shown into the garden; where she remained some ten minutes or so. When Rogers returned to St. James's Place, he looked in vain for his roses,—they had all disappeared. He was destined, however, to see them once more; for on going that evening (or the next) to a party at Lady Cork's, he recognized them among the decorations of her supper-table.

58. See [*Table-Talk*, pp. 9–10. Much of this paragraph is duplicated by *Table-Talk*, pp. 297–98.]

59. In Finsbury Square.

60. [Dyce next makes two false starts in describing Rogers's accident (f. 162^r). The third version (f. 163^r), which follows, is the closest to P. W. Clayden, *Rogers and His Contemporaries* (London, 1889), II, 355.]

61. In the entrance-hall of the National Gallery is a fine marble bas-relief by Banks, presented to the nation by Mrs. Forster; the subject Thetis rising from the sea to console Achilles for the death of Patroclus. But a still finer specimen of that sculptor's powers may be seen in Lewisham Church [. . .] which Flaxman [. . .]

62. [*Table-Talk*, pp. 266–67.]

63. [II (1830), following p. 236. I do not understand the allusion in the rest of the sentence.]

64. [Dyce transcribes "Lord Byron's Verses on Sam Rogers, In Question and Answer" on ff. 171–72.]

65. [See *Table-Talk*, p. 199.]

66. [Something is obviously missing between ff. 174^v, 175^r. Byron wrote "A Sketch from Private Life" against Mrs. Clermont, thinking her "the dominating influence" over his wife during their separation (Marchand, *Byron*, II, 595–96). She left the service of the Milbanke family some time before Annabella's marriage.]

67. A report [was] printed when he was far advanced in years that he was about to be married to a niece of Lady Morgan, who was manœuvering with all her might to bring about the match. What truth there was in this I know not: but it gave considerable uneasiness to the poet's relatives. Moreover, it called forth one of Sydney Smith's jokes: "The nuptials," he said, "are to be celebrated at St. Sepulchre's; the bride's-maids are to be the two Miss Berrys; and it is a pity that the young lady's name is not Sexton, instead of Clark."

68. [On f. 176^r are scribbled extracts from Young's *Memoirs of Mrs. Crouch* concerning theatrical compositions by Rogers. On the verso, mostly illegible, is some scrawling about illness, perhaps a rough draft of a letter. What follows is from f. 181^r.]

69. [Luttrell was sent to the West Indies in 1802.]

70. [There follow lines from *Letters to Julia,* 3d ed. (London, 1822), pp. 8–12, and from *Crockford-House* (London, 1827), pp. 30–34, 77–81.]

71. Luttrell always spoke of Brighton as "that delightful place."

72. I here quote a few of my own words from a sketch of Mitford's life in *The Gentleman's Magazine* for July 1859 [Ser. 3, 7], p. 85. [Dyce paraphrases freely.]

73. Finding that the English potteries could not supply him with garden seats of a peculiar green colour, he commissioned them [. . .]

74. [This word is supplied from f. 181ʳ, which contains a cancelled draft of the article. Neither leaf gives an example of Mitford's verse.]

75. *On the Etymology of Mass, &c. in a Letter from H. C. Robinson, Esq., Addressed to John Gage, Esq., F. R. S., Director. Read 7ᵗʰ March, 1833,*—in the *Archæologia,* vol. xxvi. p. 242.

76. *Strictures on a Life of William Wilberforce . . . with a Correspondence Between Lord Brougham and Mr. Clarkson* [ed. H. C. Robinson], 8ᵛᵒ, 1838.

77. Prefixed to *Memorials of a Tour in Italy,* 1842.— The writer of a biographical sketch of Robinson in *The Gentleman's Magazine* for April 1867 [Ser. 4, 3], p. 533, states by mistake that Wordsworth "in 1842 dedicated the 'Excursion' to him *[Robinson]" :—*that* great poem was dedicated in 1814 to the Earl of Lonsdale.

78. Early in life he became acquainted at Edinburgh with Lord Langdale (then Mr. Bickersteth) ; and they kept up a correspondence for many years on physiological and other subjects : see [Thomas D.] Hardy's *Life of Lord L.* [*Memoirs of . . . Henry Lord Langdale* (London, 1852)], vol. i. p. 96.

79. [Dyce notes three titles.]

80. It may be found (slightly altered) with his other poems and his plays in the eighth volume of his *Works* [Edinburgh, 1808].

81. There had been madness in Mackenzie's family.

82. Or *spelden,* or *speldin,*—the Scotch term for a small fish split and dried in the sun.

83. Stewart's [*Collected*] *Works* [ed. Sir William Hamilton], vol. vii [Edinburgh and London, 1855]. p. 331.

84. Wordsworth's *Memoirs* by his nephew, vol. ii. p. 222.

85. [Dyce transcribes "Song" ("Come here, fond youth, whoe'er thou be"), "Ode to Spring," and "A Summer Evening's Meditation," ll. 1–17, 35–52.]

86. Our authoress's niece and biographer, Miss Lucy Aikin, slightly passes over, or rather wholly conceals, the nature of this catastrophe. She tells us that Mrs. Barbauld's "anxieties and apprehensions of a peculiar and most distressing nature, found their final completion on the 11ᵗʰ of November 1808, in the event by which she became a widow." *Memoir* [in Mrs. Barbauld's *Works* (London, 1825), I], p.p. xliii–iv.

87. [There is a version of this article on f. 47ʳ, without the presumed allusion to John Britton.]

88. In [Robert] Watt's *Biblioth[eca]. Brit[annica].* [(Edinburgh, 1824), I, entry 527u] she is stupidly confounded with Mrs. Rachel Hunter of Norwich, a third-rate novelist.

89. [Dyce transcribes "Ode to the Old Year, 1787," ll. 19–30 ; "A Vow to Fortune" ; "The Lamentation of Mary Stuart" ; "The Death Song" ; "Song" ("O tuneful voice, I still deplore") ; and "Song" ("My mother bids me bind my hair").]

90. [This much of the article is in a canceled draft on f. 236ʳ.]

91. "Northcote assured the writer of these pages that Laird, not himself, procured the greater part of the materials for the Life of Sir Joshua, and put them together ; his own part was small, and confined chiefly to criticism on art and artists." [Sir James] Prior's *Life of [Oliver] Goldsmith* [London, 1837], vol. ii. p. 572. [Cf. *Table-Talk,* p. 23.]

92. The youngest of the Hazlitts writes thus, "It may be here just mentioned that

my grandfather helped Northcote with what is called 'The Life of Titian,' a strange jumble, which was printed in 1830, in two volumes octavo, and of which N. did some, my grandfather some, and my father the rest! The total result is not, it must be confessed, highly satisfactory," &c. *Memoirs of William Hazlitt* by W. C. Hazlitt [London, 1867], vol. ii. p[p]. 212[–13 n.].

93. [Cf. James Boaden, *Memoirs of the Life of John Philip Kemble* (London, 1825), II, 237 n.]

APPENDIX

LEAVES AND PORTIONS OF LEAVES OMITTED FROM THIS EDITION

This list does not include omissions mentioned in the text.

6^r: "A Cure for Sore Eyes": on a fishing trip near Balmoral, Dyce is advised by a native that "plenty o' whiskey" is the best cure for that affliction.

11–12^r: "Mary Lady Clerk," the eccentric widow of Sir John Clerk, passed on to George IV tableware that she untruthfully claimed were "relics of Prince Charles."

14^r: "A Strange Story" about the senile widow of Sir Robert Strange the engraver. By a footman's happy choice of words, she was enabled to recall her own surname.

28: "Mrs. Bligh (Countess of Mornington)," a childhood companion of Dyce; a brief comment on her unfortunate marriages. See the *DNB,* s.v. "Wellesley-Pole, William, third Earl of Mornington."

29–30:   no leaves with these numbers. This section of the MS is in alphabetical order, and if leaves are missing between "Mrs. Bligh" and "Lord and Lady Byron" they may have pertained to Sir Samuel Egerton Brydges.

32ʳ: "The Prince Regent and Sir Neil Campbell": a compliment by the Prince Regent to Sir Neil, Dyce's uncle, who had been British Commissioner at Elba: "Sir Neil, I was just telling Lady Hertford that you did not receive these orders [decorations] for letting Buonaparte escape."

42–43:   "Fielding": a dubious account of Fielding's calling Warburton "a sycophantic son of a b——." (Cf. John Forster, *Walter Savage Landor* [London, 1869], I, 33–34. I am indebted to Professor Henry K. Miller for this reference.) Also the glosses by Horace Walpole in Dyce's copy of Fielding's *Dramatic Works* (Dyce Collection, item 3713).

114–15:   "William Nanson Lettsom, Esqre.": canceled; first appeared in the *Gentleman's Magazine,* CCXIX (1865), 790–91.

116A: unnumbered portrait of Mrs. Siddons following f. 116.

226ʳ: "Simile by Swift": Dyce claims that Swift's *On Poetry: A Rapsody,* ll. 177–80, is from Defoe's *"Tour through Great Britain, vol. iii. Sec. Part, Account of Scotland, p. 200, ed. 1727."* The resemblance is close.

228ʳ: "Unpublished Verses by Dryden": two poems drawn from a MS in Dyce's possession (item MS 43): "On the Dutchesse of Portsmouth's Picture" and "An Epitaph on Lamentable Lory." Neither are now ascribed to Dryden. Both may be found in the *Poems on Affairs of State.*

230:    "The Song Entitled Pompey's Ghost, Attributed to John Lowe": contradicting Burns and Cunningham, Dyce finds it originally a song introduced by Mrs. Katherine Philips in her translation of Corneille's *Pompée*.

232:    "Unpublished Verses by Gray": the two poems, "Satire Upon the Heads" ("O Cambridge, attend") and "Epitaph on a Child" ("Here, freed from pain"), have subsequently been published.

233:    five poems from a MS in Dyce's Collection (item MS 44).

236^v, following the Colton anecdote: "Dr. Charles Burney, Madam D'Arblay, and her Son": fragmentary and canceled. "D'Arblay" is also mentioned in a deleted portion of f. 28^v.

237^r: a deleted rough draft of a portion of f. 28^v.

237^v–38^r: "Mrs. Coutts (the Duchess of St. Albans)": her habits, along with a mention of Fuseli the painter.

238^v: "Sir Neil Campbell": fragmentary and canceled. End of MS.

INDEX

INDEX